AN OFFICER, NOT A GENTLEMAN

Dream big dreams!

Mandy Hickson

AN OFFICER, NOT A GENTLEMAN

THE INSPIRATIONAL JOURNEY OF A PIONEERING FEMALE FIGHTER PILOT

MANDY HICKSON

First published in UK in 2020
Text © Mandy Hickson 2020
Design: Burge Agency
Cover photograph: Dan Tidswell,
Photo Engineers

All photos are from the author's
collection, RAF photographers or
Crown copyright. The publishers
will be glad to rectify in future
editions any errors or omissions
brought to their attention.

A CIP catalogue record for this
title is available from the British
Library.

ISBN 979-8-6492-9782-0

www.hicksonltd.com
FB @MandyHicksonSpeaker
Twitter @MandyHickson
Insta @mandyhicksonspeaker

ABOUT THE AUTHOR

Mandy Hickson (née Wells) was born in Cheshire in 1973. She gained a BSc Joint Honours Degree in Geography and Sports Science from the University of Birmingham. Mandy has over twenty five years experience within aviation. She joined the Royal Air Force in 1994 and was only the second woman to fly the Tornado GR4 operationally; she operated in hostile environments, including patrolling the 'No Fly' zone over Iraq; completed three tours of duty and flew fifty missions over Iraq with No. II (AC) Squadron.

Since leaving the RAF she retrained as a facilitator in human performance factors. Her company, 'Experience From The Front Line', draws on her experience of calculated risk-taking, decision-making under pressure and the critical role of the human in the system, where she transfers vivid lessons from the cockpit to other management and leadership contexts.

Mandy is now in high demand as a keynote speaker across a range of business and education sectors, where she talks with humour and great passion to inspire those around her. She has been invited to share her insights with some of the most successful organisations across the world, where she describes the strategies and behaviours that can be adopted when the stakes are at their highest.

Her latest challenge was to climb Kilimanjaro in October 2019 on a fundraising expedition with 20 women from all walks of life. Mandy is married to Craig and has two children, Jack and Jamie.

DEDICATED TO ALL THOSE
WHO HAVE GIVEN THE
ULTIMATE SACRIFICE WHILE
SERVING THEIR COUNTRY.
THE HEROES THAT WILL
NEVER GROW OLD.

ACKNOWLEDGEMENTS

First and foremost, I would like to thank Rob Hodgetts. Without his unbelievable talent, help and excellent skills this book would never have become a reality. He really pulled it all together. I can't thank you enough. Thanks to Steve Cox and Ali Georgiou for your guidance.

This book covers over three decades of my life and sadly I cannot express my gratitude to everyone that has guided, encouraged and lifted me along my way. From my teachers at school, instructors in the RAF and friends old and new, you've all had such a huge impact on me at every turn.

My wonderful family, my Mum and Stanners, Dad and Sue, Sarah and Frances who believed in me and always encouraged me to be the very best version of myself. You truly were my foundations when you listened and smoothed away my worries whenever I needed it. Mum you've been such a fantastic role model and for that I will be eternally grateful. Sarah, I feel truly blessed to have you as my sister and my best friend. Thank you for your unconditional love.

Craig, you have been my wingman for over half my life. You are quite literally the wind beneath my wings and I can't tell you how much I appreciate your constant support, your humour and your love. To Elliot, Chessie, Jack and Jamie, you've completed my life and made sure that life will never be dull. I couldn't be prouder of you all. I love you.

CONTENTS

IRAQ
OPERATION SOUTHERN WATCH
MAY 2002

It's as black as space outside the cockpit as the Iraqi desert flashes by underneath us. I keep half an eye on the green numbers ticking over on the canopy in front of me, occasionally scanning the glowing flight instruments, but really, my mind is thousands of miles away.

I turn my head to look for my wingman somewhere out there to the right, remembering first to pull my night-vision goggles down from the top of my helmet so they don't bang on the glass. I'm always doing that. The background static of the jet engines thrums in my helmet, not loud, just a constant high-pitched chhhhhrrrrr, like the noise children make waving around toy planes.

I'm relaxed in my little greenhouse-hot cocoon of glass, metal, switches, levers and dials, the straps of my ejector seat holding me snug. The g-suit, an aggressive constrictor when we're pulling a tight turn, is quiet and resting as we cruise straight and level at 20,000 feet.

But even though I'm screaming along close to Mach One in my thirty-five-million-pound government-issue RAF Tornado, bristling with bombs and laser-guided missiles, I'm dreaming of going home.

Back to the Real World. My own bed in my own house, not a camp cot in a prefab hut in a boiling, dusty airbase in the Kuwaiti desert. Back to the boyfriend I haven't seen in eight weeks. Back to the girlfriends who can talk about real feelings and emotions instead of banter, boobs and football.

I've got a great suntan and I'm feeling fit. There's little else to do away from flying but go to the gym and I'm absolutely determined to trouser the £100 jackpot for the winner of the weight-loss challenge.

I treat myself to a little smile. Well, it's not like anyone can see me. We're patrolling the no-fly zone over southern Iraq, just to remind them that we are an ever-present force in the skies above. The main routes between Baghdad and Al Basra have been fairly hectic with a lot of traffic, but down here near the border with Saudi Arabia it is quiet. It has been for our entire tour. Tumbleweed-tastic.

I'm quite keen it stays that way for another hour or so.

The radio offers sporadic bursts, my Spartan formation team-mates updating me on fuel status every ten minutes or my navigator Jacko in the backseat quietly talking me around various Iraqi radar stations, which we can tell are looking at us by the signals they emit.

'SA6, right three o'clock, come left four zero degrees, roll out two four zero,' whispers Jacko, sounding like a librarian directing me to the fiction aisle.

It's all spoken in a low, clipped professional hush. No extra chatter needed. Stinger, my wingman in Spartan Two, with the squadron boss as navigator, is a mile-and-a-half to my right. Fred and Block as number three and Bob and Tom in number four are behind us, in a square four-ship formation. I can't see any of them but I have that soothing, reassuring feeling they're sticking to me like glue.

I like flying at night. It's very calming, in a relative sort of way given I'm in a supersonic weapon capable of causing misery and destruction at the flick of a switch. Tonight, of all nights, I can feel the tension of the tour ebbing away from my shoulders.

And that's when the missile streaks up towards us.

'MANDY, BREAK RIGHT...' Jacko's urgent scream shatters my bubble of bliss like a balloon exploding. Before my brain has got past the 'W' of 'What the...' my right hand slams the stick across and we tip over sideways, like a hard right turn on a roller coaster. I tense my stomach muscles to accept the punch in the guts from the g-suit, which clamps my legs tight to force the blood to my brain and stop me from blacking out.

'Missile launch, five o'clock...' says the strained voice of my nav into my headset.

I yank back the stick and force the twin throttles forward with my left hand and we roar away into the blackness. My heart thumps through the various layers of my flight suit as I work the Tornado through the manoeuvre. Now we are upside down and my shoulders strain on the straps as gravity thrusts my helmet towards the canopy. I try to turn my head to look around the sky but because of the centrifugal force it is now unnaturally heavy and a real effort to move. I am not daydreaming anymore.

Where's the bloody missile?
Are we going to get hit?
I wonder what it will feel like?
This isn't actually a drill.
This manoeuvre better bloody work.
They said it would in training.
Someone down there is taking pot shots at us.
Someone down there wants us dead.

With missile lock on, they're doing a pretty good job of it so far, too. And the day before I'm due to go home.

Bugger. It is still locked on. I can't pull the stick back anymore but try anyway. Urgggh. Come on...come on....

'Where is it? I can't see it...' I'm panting now, as my surging heart pumps electricity around my body and I try to keep up the short exhalations needed to counter the g-force.

The seat straps are biting into my shoulders as I look straight down through the canopy into the dark abyss below. Time and my sense of reality have become suspended. Then I'm blinded by an intense white light in my rear-view mirror. 'What... is... that?' I slur into my radio.

'Flares,' answers Jacko, who is glued to his screen watching the missile as I rock the jet through the evasive manoeuvre. To confuse it, he's fired off the mini pyrotechnics, which burn at a super-high intensity in the hope the missile mistakes them for our engines and explodes with us long gone.

Seconds later a second white starburst fills my mirror, another sky-filler which cascades down like a giant firework. Looks like the flares have fooled the missile into thinking it has found its target and it explodes behind us.

My reality roars back to the present from the blur of hyper space. 'Bloody hell, I can't believe we've been shot at...' I manage. As we race away from the danger zone I pull some semblance of thought back together.

I remember I'm leading this mission – even though my boss is up here too – and I muster my calmest pilot's voice to radio the Commander in Chief (CinC) flying in the AWACS command and control aircraft over the Persian Gulf.

'Warrior, this is Spartan One. We've been locked-on by a SAM (surface to air missile). We've evaded it. Are you happy for us to engage targets?'

'Roger that, Spartan One. Stand by.'

We fly on, working out a route to re-join our Spartan team-mates, while the CinC comes up with a plan. If you have been subjected to an aggressive act – being shot at definitely counts – you are allowed to prosecute an attack on a specified target that you have been pre-assigned.

The radio crackles to life again.

'Spartan One, you are free to engage targets.'

I look at my fuel gauge. Bingo, plus not much. Bingo is a pre-agreed fuel state used as a check-in with the rest of the formation. Chicken fuel is just enough gas to get you home and land.

Bugger.

I've got a decision to make. Either we fly to our designated target and attack it – hoping we find it the first time, get clearance straight away from higher up, execute the mission with no other issues because by then we'll be on fumes and we've still got to get home, and it is pitch black and there's a sandstorm brewing up, and... oh, my gosh, this is hard. Or we head to Saudi to hook up with an air-to-air tanker first... but there are thirty-odd aircraft from four different countries up here somewhere, all running out of fuel and it could be a high-level international bunfight.

My brain is whirring so fast it feels like it might spin off its axis. I'm worried I'm reaching max capacity. I remember the feeling well from training in the Hawk at RAF Valley when I struggled to absorb the constantly changing parameters of that navigation mission and felt like I was drowning as I screamed through a deep valley below Cadair Idris in Wales. 'Keep calm, Wellsey,' I mutter to myself. Saying it out loud helps me to focus and stay in the moment.

I get on the radio and allocate jobs to the team. Jacko in my boot will find the target, the boss is to track down the tanker, number three is to work out the exact route from the tanker back to the target, how long it will take, how long we'll have on target and how much fuel we'll need. Number four's job is to check the weather at base because it is deteriorating and we don't want to shoot ourselves in the foot trying to do the mission but not being able to land because of the weather.

There is a pause while everyone is engaged in their mental gymnastics. I fly on, my whole system fizzing as my entire career is distilled down to now. All that training, all the heartache of not quite making the grade, the battles to prove myself, the sheer bloody hard work and mind-twisting learning curve and the struggles to find my way in the squadron. It was all building up to this moment. And it was worth every single second.

I love the three-dimensional aspect of flying.
I love the freedom of being up there in that vast, limitless sky.
I love breaking through thick cloud into a world of deep blue, far from the humdrum of everyday life.
I love that every flight is different, every aircraft is different.
I love the risk involved.
I love that it challenges me.
And I love the fact it makes anything seem possible.

What had drawn me to the RAF was that it seemed I could be myself. Being gregarious and loud never seemed to be a problem. In fact, it appeared to help. I didn't have to pretend to be something I wasn't. I didn't have to be a pretty girl wearing high heels and make up. I could be true to myself. I fitted in and I relished the camaraderie.

But as I set out on my career there were times when I felt that being a quiet, 'grey man' might have been a lot easier. Of course, I was never going to be a man of any description, so I stuck out like a sore thumb from the start.

Sometimes that was a bonus. Sometimes doing exactly what the boys did got me in trouble. I was just trying to fit the mould of a junior fast jet pilot. Some people didn't like that.

During the first term of officer training at RAF Cranwell I was standing in my full NBC suit, including boots but minus the mask, which I was carrying under my arm, as I waited in the corridor like a naughty schoolgirl outside the boss's office.

It was 'Grey Tuesday', the name given to the first assessment day when verdicts on our worth as potential officers and even human beings were delivered by our flight commanders. These exchanges were known to be frank and brutal at times.

'Come in, Wells.'

Formal marching in all this gear was not easy, especially holding the mask with one hand. I stamped into the room and snapped to attention with my crispest salute, or the best I could muster given the circumstances. Lucky I was carrying the mask under my left arm or it would have been awkward.

'Ah, yes, Wells. At ease.'

'Now Wells, it has been brought to my attention that although you are very Amazonian in nature, you are not particularly feminine.'

My eyebrows and mouth twitched, both straining to explode with fury as I recoiled at his statement. Excuse me? I was fighting hard to remain impassive as the inside of my head swirled in anger and confusion. My future as an RAF officer and potential fast-jet pilot lay in this man's hands.

He was right, to the extent that I was six feet tall and fairly boisterous, with a laugh that has variously been described as 'like a sea lion enjoying themselves' or 'a foghorn after sucking on a helium balloon', but what on earth was all this?

I mustered my best stab at diplomacy, which, to be fair, was still not great. 'With all due respect, Sir, when would you like me to be more feminine? Is it when I'm wearing my NBC kit? Or when I'm crawling through mud and hiding in bushes in my combat trousers and jacket?'

'Or is it in the bar when I'm wearing a skirt and drinking half pints?'

'Yes, but you do insist on buying two half pints, Wells.' We had been advised early on that female candidates on officer training at RAF Cranwell were not to drink pints.

But I'd just spent three years at university doing exactly that. I was fairly proficient at it. Now I was supposed to return to my 'proper' role as a demure member of the fairer sex and buy nine pints and a half when I was getting a round in for my flight, which was encouraged by the way because it's all part of being in a team. That's what they'd been banging on about twenty four hours a day since I'd been here, helping my flight mates clean toilets with toothbrushes and picking up fluff with Sellotape and arranging our pants and socks in neat RAF-prescribed piles and marching and drilling and lifting a rifle up and down together in time for hours on end on a freezing parade square at unfeasibly early hours of the day, and a million other minor gestures towards team work, leadership and conduct becoming of an officer in preparation to pilot a sophisticated warplane into battle, drop millions of pounds worth of weaponry on an unseen enemy, and maybe, one day, kill people.

'But Sir, I'd feel like the odd one out and I'd be sitting there for ages without a drink and then I wouldn't be part of the team. And as we know, the RAF is...'

'Sort it out, Wells. Be more feminine. That is all.'

Often, I couldn't work out what approach to take. Fit in but get accused of trying to be one of the boys or be treated differently because I stand out and then be berated for not being part of the team. Either way, I had to learn to live with it. You are who you are.

I spent nearly seventeen years in the RAF, then seven years as a volunteer reservist, logged almost 2000 flying hours, flew fifty combat missions across three tours in the Gulf in the Tornado and was only the UK's second female Tornado pilot, out of only five in total. I must have got something right.

CHAPTER 1

FIGHTING THE SYSTEM

I blame Tom Selleck. The moustachioed star of hit TV programme Magnum PI was my first crush. I loved that show. Tom's twinkle, the Hawaiian shirts, the Ferrari... the slug balancing. There were not many guys like that in Sale. Well, actually there were plenty with dodgy 'taches, but none of them as cool as Magnum's.

So, every Tuesday night I'd come home from school, wolf down my tea and settle down in front of the TV, ready for Magnum. One night, my mum was reading the local newspaper and saw an advert for the Air Training Corps.

'Hey Manda, it says they're taking girls for the first time. Apparently, they do stuff like canoeing. Every Tuesday, it is.'

I was very outdoorsy and a bit of a tomboy, but not on Tuesdays. 'Not interested.'

'There might be some boys there.' I did a quick mental reappraisal. Mr. Selleck had stirred something inside me. It was worth a try, so I went. If I hadn't been unfaithful to Tom that night, I may never have become a pilot and may never have got shot at over Iraq.

I wasn't particularly interested in flying, nor did I have much of a military background, despite Grandpa's tales of being a fighter pilot in World War Two.

My mum was a home economics teacher and Dad ran his own carpet business. They had divorced when I was two and I lived with mum, a role model for strong, capable women, and my older sister Sarah.

But as a sports-mad thirteen year old who went to an all-girls' school, the idea of running around outdoors, shooting, canoeing and going on camps with the boys did appeal and very quickly 318 Squadron Air Training Corps in Sale became a twice-weekly fixture. There was a fair bit of marching and polishing shoes, but it seemed like a fair swap for all that adventure and learning about flying.

My first flight was in a Chipmunk at RAF Woodvale near Liverpool. I loved it, but we only got the chance to fly about once a year. Dad fuelled my growing fascination and treated me to a short flight from Barton airfield for my fourteenth birthday.

I was really into it, but after my GCSEs I told the commanding officer at the squadron I was thinking of leaving. I just had too much going on with school, sport and Rangers, which is the next stage on from Girl Guides. He offered me a promotion to sergeant and suggested I apply to the RAF for a flying scholarship, a no-strings-attached chance to log thirty hours flying at the RAF's expense. You only need forty for a private pilot's licence. OK, I'll stay then.

I went down to RAF Biggin Hill south-east of London for a day of tests and an interview for the scholarship. There was also a medical. A nurse asked me to get on the weighing scales. 'Ooh,' she said. I wasn't quite sure what 'ooh' meant but it didn't sound good. I was taken to see the chief examiner, a Wing Commander Diaper. 'I have good news and bad news,' he said. 'You'll fit in the aircraft, but you have an obesity problem.'

'I beg your pardon?' I was six feet tall and weighed twelve stone and played sport at every opportunity. Apparently, his dated old height chart only went up to five feet eight inches for women, so he'd added on some pounds for the extra height. Which technically made me obese. He said I had to get down to just under ten stone.

'We can't offer you a scholarship until you remedy your weight problem,' he said.

I HAVEN'T GOT A BLOODY PROBLEM! I was mortified and cried the whole way home in Dad's car.

I duly received a letter offering me a scholarship, deferred until I had resolved my 'medical issue.' I could have said, 'sod it' and walked away, but I had been bitten by the flying bug, and anyway, I wasn't going to let these buggers win. I'd show them. I had five months.

So, at the age of sixteen I went on the world's biggest diet. Every day I went to the gym for an hour before school, writing down the calories I had burned. Lunch was a Slim-a-soup with two Ryvita and cottage cheese. I'd add the calories consumed onto my chart. For dinner I had chicken and broccoli. Every night. At Christmas I had no sweets, no chocolate or mince pies or puddings. Life was pretty bloody miserable. I was doing so much sport anyway, then the gym before and after school.

In April, just before the deadline to send back the form, I went to the family doctor to get her to sign it. She walked straight past me in the corridor and then did a double take. 'Gosh, sorry, I didn't recognise you. You're looking very skinny. What's happened?'

I told her the story.

'Obese? That's absolute rubbish. A fit young girl like you doing loads of sport.'

She dug out her height-weight chart. 'Mine only goes up to five feet ten inches but even allowing for the extra inches you're nowhere near obese.'

I was still a little over the RAF's 'target.'

'Give me that form, I'll sign it, stupid people,' she said.

I gorged on cakes and Cadbury's cream eggs that night and then had diarrhoea for two days as the sugar shocked my system. If I'd known that I could have saved myself three weeks of dieting.

The scholarship came through with no further queries. In the summer of 1991, just after my A levels, I spent a month living in a B&B in Blackpool, learning to fly in a Piper PA-28 Cherokee. I used the money I had saved up from my paper round to pay for the additional ten hours that I needed to gain my Private Pilots License (PPL).

I was eighteen years old. I had exactly forty hours flying, my brand-new PPL in my pocket and I walked out to the aircraft under a crystal clear blue sky. It was the day I was taking my family flying for the first time, with me as the captain. I'd planned a flight to take in the stunning Lake District after flying up the coast, over the cresting waves of Morecambe Bay. After executing a perfect landing, I looked at my mum and had never felt so proud of myself. I saw that same pride reflected straight back at me. My dream had begun to become a reality.

Although I wanted to fly, I still had no real ambition to join the RAF. As far as I was concerned, the only point in joining would be to fly fast jets and women weren't allowed to fly fast jets, so there was no point. I wasn't interested in flying multi-engines or helicopters.

I couldn't get my head around why women couldn't fly jets. There was nothing that any boys I'd met so far could do that I couldn't. I was fit, strong, I had a brain. Why could they go on to become fast-jet pilots and not me? It didn't make any sense, but what could I do about it?

Obviously, at my scholarship interview I played the game and reeled off a host of reasons why I thought a career in the RAF was for me. But I still had my misgivings about the military. At the Air Training Corps, I was put off by a couple of senior cadets, who wielded power in a moronic way.

If you were late or made a mistake during drill they would ridicule you in front of the rest, making you recount nursery rhymes or sing silly songs with your hands on your hips or skip everywhere for the rest of the evening. For all my confidence and sociability – I was head girl in the sixth form – I was still mortally embarrassed by it. I knew that if I were ever in that position I would be a much better leader, but I'd made the assumption the real RAF would be like that. Nope, not for me. I'm going to be a policewoman.

I wonder how many other people have been put off their dreams by jumped-up little clowns?

I was desperate to keep up my flying after the scholarship and picked Birmingham University partly because of its student air squadron.

I got a place to do sports science and geography, but the studies quickly took a back seat to sport, parties and flying.

The University of Birmingham Air Squadron (UBAS) only accepted thirty new students a year, spread across eight universities in central England. Some of those places were already taken by people who had been offered RAF sponsorship through university. Competition was fierce, but I must have done enough at interview because I was soon being measured for uniforms, a helmet and a flying suit. We were also given a replica cardboard cockpit of a Bulldog, the two-seater trainer we'd be flying, with all the gauges, knobs and dials, plus full manuals and checklists to study at home.

It was all completely free, and we got paid thirty-two pounds a day when we flew for our efforts.

'Town Night', as the UBAS evenings were called, was on a Thursday at the redbrick squadron headquarters on

Birmingham's leafy campus. They consisted of lectures on all aspects of flying and sometimes a guest speaker, followed quickly by beers and then a curry at the Sundarbon on the Bristol Road.

There didn't seem to be any marching or the military rubbish I had associated with the RAF through the demeaning sergeants' behaviour at ATC. One early icebreaker ended up with us all partially clad on the squadron bar singing 'I'm climbing up sunshine mountain...' I was already starting to see a very different picture of military life... and I was loving it.

Flying took place at RAF Cosford to the northwest of Birmingham. You could sign up for as much you could squeeze in around lectures and sport.

Wednesdays were out for me because that was netball followed by a monster party at the Old Varsity Tavern in Selly Oak, so Tuesday afternoon became my regular flying slot. Given I already had my PPL – I went solo after seven hours twenty-five minutes.

The big difference was learning the checks that are essential for any type of flying, from pre-start checks to taxi, take-off and landing checks. During my Blackpool days I was allowed to read the checks off a notebook on my knee. In the military they all had to be done from memory. I really struggled with the compass checks. The correct 'mouth music' when moving the rudder pedals left and right while taxiing was: 'To the left, needle left, ball right, numbers decreasing, numbers decreasing. To the right, needle right, ball left, numbers increasing and increasing. Horizons erect and synchronised.'

I just couldn't get it right. It just came out as a jumble of nonsensical words. One of the instructors had even been known to stab people in the leg with his aircrew knife if they couldn't do it. Fortunately, I was spared this punishment, but he still got exasperated with me: 'For God's sake Mandy, it's not that hard.'

I knew I had to sharpen up. You could get booted out if you didn't put the work in. I would make studious notes after each flight and sit in my room in Mason Hall going through the checks on my cardboard cockpit while my friend Zoe followed the list. 'Nope, try again,' she would sigh, checking her watch to see if it was time to go to the bar.

There was a progress chart in the ops room, which was the first thing you checked when you arrived at Cosford. 'Who's been up? What stage are they at?'

I was in fierce competition with fellow Brummie boys Matt Lindley (Mattly) and Paul Carvosso, known presumably since he was a baby as 'Vossers'. There were a few other girls too, Vanessa Haven (Ness) and Nicola Hoskins and we all became incredibly close friends.

We were getting into this life, and began to think we were the dog's nuts, strutting around the base in our baggy green flying suits. The RAF regulars must have been laughing their heads off.

As well as flying we went on an adventure training exercise in Wales and that summer there was a week's sailing course out of Hamble on the south coast, and then a two-week camp at RAF Laarbruch in Germany, where Jaguars and Tornados were based.

We did lots of flying, plenty of sport and had tours of the base to meet the fast jet crews.

I was happier than Little Miss Happy. I still wasn't really thinking about careers, but already I couldn't imagine myself doing anything else. I definitely knew I didn't want an office job. I loved the camaraderie and all the new experiences on offer. We were sharing such intense moments all the time.

Just before Christmas in the second year – December 1992 – I was in the Cosford bar with Ness when the boss, Sqn Ldr Karl Bufton, walked in with a grin on his face.

'Good news, girls. The RAF has just announced it is taking on female fast jet pilots for the first time,' he said.

Ness and I stared at each other open mouthed.

I'd been at a bit of a crossroads because to stay in the air squadron in the third year you had to show some sort of commitment to the RAF. Even though I loved the flying and the opportunities, I wasn't sure yet I wanted to join another branch of the service.

This was the green light I had been waiting for and faster than Usain Bolt off the starting blocks, I put in my application and was called to the Officer Aircrew Selection Centre at RAF Cranwell.

Ness and I were on the same selection dates and travelled over together. We were billeted in stark barrack blocks and spent three days going through the rigours of selection.

In my dodgy fawn jacket and matching skirt with cream frilly shirt I went through the rounds of medicals, aptitude tests, group exercises and interviews. After what happened at my scholarship medical, I was petrified as I waited outside the doctor's room.

With almost two years of good university living under my belt, which had to be loosened a few notches because of all those curries and beer, I was way heavier than at that initial scholarship interview. I hadn't had any breakfast that morning, as if that would have made all the difference.

The doctor opened my medical file, which was quite big by then because of all the correspondence concerning my weight. 'Blimey, what's been going on here,' he said. I began the tale but he cut me off. 'What size were you at the start of all this?'

'I was a stone lighter than I am now.'

'Stand up. Turn around. You look fine to me.'

In the interview in front of a three-man board I was quizzed on why I wanted to join, my opinion of defence matters, my knowledge of the RAF and current affairs, and my quickfire mental ability such as coming up with my age in years, months and days. I hadn't read a newspaper in months. If it wasn't to do with uni or flying I wasn't interested. A quick crammer on the train and some decent acting and serious facial expressions seemed to go down well.

The aptitude tests were a marathon session in front of the rudimentary computers. There were tests with a box on the screen with a dot in it which kept trying to escape. You had to use the control column and pedals to keep it centred. Halfway through the controls would reverse, so it was testing how quickly you could adapt.

Another made you navigate a blob through a wiggly course, a bit like Sonic the Hedgehog, to test your hand-eye coordination.

Then there were maths questions to test your mental arithmetic, such as basic speed-distance-time equations. If a car is travelling at sixty miles an hour and it needs to travel seven miles, how long will it take? They got progressively harder. There were memory tests to see how many numbers in a random pattern you could recall after they flashed up on the screen.

At the end of day one they read out a list of people they would like to stay to continue selection.

My name was on it, but I was called in for a chat.

I hadn't passed my aptitude tests for pilot selection. I felt tears welling up before he had finished speaking. Would I consider continuing as a navigator? I just about held myself together. Of course I would. In fact, I'd be thrilled. Not.

You had to put down two preferences for your prospective branch, so I put down navigator and air traffic controller.

I managed to leave the room with my dignity intact but spent the rest of the night in tears. All I wanted to do was fly and it looked like I had failed at the first hurdle. I still dreamed of joining the RAF, but as what now?

The following morning we pitched up at a vast, domed hangar for the practical exercises. In green overalls with a blue bib with a number on it we were divided into teams of five. We were briefed on the scenario, such as a river to be crossed, and then had to work as a team to get across the span, using just the planks, barrels and ropes in front of us. There were five different scenarios giving each of us the chance to lead. Luckily for us, Ness and I were in the same team, which meant we could appear breezy and relaxed as we discussed our options. Everything you do and say is scrutinised. Not only were they looking for leadership potential but also whether you could form part of an effective team. Were you aggressive as a team member, always trying to force your point or were you supportive? You were well aware you were being watched and it was easy to be self-conscious every time you opened your mouth. Or didn't. Was I contributing enough? Should I shut up? Was I being encouraging? How should I get my point across? It was a game within a game.

Some of the scenarios were actually impossible to complete but they wanted to see how you worked towards the goal anyway.

When it was my turn as leader the task had become more difficult. We had to straddle a large gap with a selection of ropes that were temptingly hanging down from the roof. But like a computer game with hidden cheats, there was a secret technique, which luckily, I'd picked up from friends who had been through section before me. The key apparently was to get someone across the high part first and then swing back across. Armed with this knowledge we succeeded as a team, which was very handy for me.

At lunchtime a few more people were sent home for lacking leadership potential or officer qualities.

In the afternoon we had more group exercises. Sitting on a row of chairs in front of the selection board we would have to work out solutions to issues. One had us tasked with organising a huge party but as we solved one piece of the puzzle they would throw in another curve ball. I was at the end of the line so it was hard to know how forceful to make my points without sounding like I was shouting but at the same time I didn't want to be ignored.

Several weeks later I was called into the boss's office at Cosford. He handed me a letter. My heart thumped as I opened it and read it, to myself at first. 'They've offered me a bursary as an air-traffic controller. It's a twelve-year short-service commission to start after I graduate.' It also meant I got sponsorship for my final year of university.

I could feel my eyes filling up again. I'd been trying to get to terms with being a navigator, where at least I would have been flying, but now I would be firmly rooted to the ground.

'Well, what do you think?' he said. My immediate panic was that if I took a bursary for a ground branch they would stop me from flying on the air squadron.

I voiced my fears through the tears.

'Don't worry, we'll let you carry on flying,' he said. 'That's my decision.'

I asked him to guarantee it in writing.

'My advice would be to take it,' he said. 'You've still got one more chance to do the aptitude tests to pass as a pilot. I'll push for you.'

My commitment to the squadron couldn't be questioned. I'd flown more than 100 hours, been awarded every piece of silverware on offer and had taken on several secondary duties. I think the boss saw I had potential.

Reluctantly I accepted, but I was truly gutted.

Ness had been offered a full cadetship to become an acting pilot officer. She was really sweet and didn't rub my nose in it.

At the end of April I was selected to represent UBAS in the De Havilland Trophy, an aerobatics competition against Oxford, Cambridge and East Midlands air squadrons.

My finals started three weeks after the competition. I had to make a call. If I committed to this aerobatics flying I wasn't going to do very well in my degree because I wouldn't have the time to put in the work. But at the same time, this was a chance to show the air force what I could do.

I threw myself unconditionally into aerobatics training.

While this was going on the boss had been fighting my corner with the RAF. He invited two examiners from the RAF Central Flying School (CFS) to come and fly with me. Both graded me as an above average pilot.

I was too busy flying and learning my routine to give it much more thought. I had three minutes to show off my skills so myself and my instructor Flt Lt Phil T sketched out the routine on paper and then practised each individual element before stringing them all together.

There was everything from loops to Canadian breaks to half Cubans, to outside loops where I rolled the aircraft inverted and pushed it over the top. The negative g-force was right on the limits both for the Bulldog and for me.

The competition was held on a clear, crisp day at RAF Cosford and all the UBAS gang plus carloads of other uni mates and my family piled down to watch. As I taxied back in, everyone held up score cards and placards with my name on them. I knew it had gone well by the smiles on their faces.

I won, beating three RAF-sponsored pilots in the process. That meant far more to me than any piece of paper with a degree on it.

So, I can't pass the RAF's aptitude test, but two independent instructors have vouched for my ability and I've won a prestigious aerobatics contest.

The boss asked the authorities if I could do my aptitude tests again. I flew from Cosford to Cranwell. I failed again. They told me straight afterwards. I just couldn't believe it. I almost wasn't upset because something felt wrong. In fact, I felt quite angry at the injustice of it.

'Don't worry, Mandy, it's just more fuel for your case,' the boss consoled me on the phone. 'The tests are clearly not right. You have the ability, it's the tests that are wrong. I've a feeling it's because they're not designed for women.'

I'm all for equality but it appeared a one-size-fits-all test was needlessly weeding out very capable women. The boss vowed to fight on. It looked like I would have to go to officer training and take my chances as an air traffic controller.

CHAPTER 2

CHASING
THE DREAM

R AF College Cranwell is the RAF's historic officer training centre, akin to the Army's Sandhurst or the Navy's Dartmouth. It's in the middle of nowhere in the flat Lincolnshire countryside between Newark-on-Trent and Boston.

Turning off the A17 I crawled down Cranwell Avenue and pulled up outside the huge wrought-iron railings of the gates bearing twin crests with a bird's wings, topped with a crown and the RAF's motto 'Per ardua ad astra', which means 'Through adversity to the stars.' If it was a song title this would be the soundtrack of my life.

Through the railings across a vast lawn stood a huge, wide imposing two-storey brick building with neo-classical columns on the front and a rotunda topped by a lighthouse in the centre.

I got out my car and stood, gripped by the enormity of the moment, as I'm sure many others had before me. I felt overwhelmed with emotion; proud, excited and nervous that I was about to be part of all this. What a magnificent setting to begin my RAF adventure.

Or at least it would have been, but the directions in my joining letter told me to head for the nasty bare block on the other side of the road. This was Number One Officers' Mess, a very drab, very basic, two-storey, does-what-it-says-on-the-tin barracks surrounding a parade square. Nice. Not.

I reported to the guardroom and was escorted to the first floor corridor I would be sharing with the eight others on my 'flight'. Normally you shared a bedroom with one other person but as the only girl on my flight I got a room to myself, which suited me perfectly.

The stark room had a thin brown carpet, two single beds (sprung, and therefore uncomfortable), with white sheets, grey blankets, and hideous yellow, brown and green striped bed covers.

There were two wardrobes, two desks and chairs and a sink. And it was spotless, which immediately rang alarm bells. The next four weeks of my life would revolve around keeping that room as immaculate as it was now, as if no-one was actually living in it.

There were about 100 people on this October intake, many of them students who had graduated that June and asked for the summer off.

In our flight, Mark, an ex-airman who had been in the RAF already, and John, an ex-sergeant, were very much the daddies. They sat us down in a circle very early on and gave us a chat to drum home that our best route through this was to work together, to help each other out, to do things for others before they even ask, to act selflessly and to not let the rest of the team down. It was inspiring stuff and quite often I had to go back to that talk and remind myself of it when I was dog-tired and fed up.

The only instructions we received on that first day were to report to the parade square at seven a.m. the following morning, so we had plenty of time to settle in.

It felt like the first day of university all over again, although a lot more serious. I had butterflies in my stomach, a definite 'start of the rest of your life' feeling. I gave myself a talking to in my room, about how it was up to me now, how I was going to have to put in some effort here.

At dinner in the Number One Officers' mess that evening I bumped into a few faces I knew from the air squadron circuit.

Banter flew, mainly about my strangely dark hands which stood out against the rest of my pale Mancunian skin, the result of a slight mix up in the dark between massage oil and self-tanning cream at the weekend.

There was lots of chat about how fit we were. Or weren't. We were meant to turn up in peak physical condition but I'd been a bit busy since graduation. I had travelled to Thailand with a couple of my uni house mates Liz and Paul and was then invited to represent UBAS at a big shindig at RAF Akrotiri in Cyprus, essentially two weeks of flying and partaking in the local hospitality every night.

I knew I would be OK, but I could see that some of the guys were real racing snakes, they were incredibly fit.

My great friend from Birmingham, Nicola Hoskins, popped over later that evening. She was on the intake before me and had plenty of soothing advice. She said it will probably feel bloody awful to begin with, and that the early days are tough, but if I kept my head down and cracked on, I would enjoy it. It was lovely to hear all this from a good friend who was two months down the track and still smiling.

The next morning, I joined the early birds for breakfast at six a.m. to give myself time to get ready, and then got into my suit (skirt and jacket) for our first parade.

We were all out there early in the damp October dawn, mooching around and looking very unmilitary.

'WHAT. THE. BLOODY. HELL. IS. THIS? '

A barrel of a man with a neck as thick as a Goodyear tyre was screaming at us.

'THIS ISN'T A PARTY. THIS IS THE R... A... BLEEDING ... F.'

He was carrying a shiny stick, wearing a shiny hat and had very shiny shoes and was shouting in military fashion. A lot. I could see the breath billowing out of his mouth like steam from an old train as he yelled in the cold morning air.

Everyone immediately clamped on their serious faces and pretended to be in the military, which from the outside must have looked like total comedy. Even though a lot of us had been in university air squadrons, we hadn't really done much 'soldiering'.

We formed up as best we could as the station warrant officer paced menacingly between us, like a lion waiting to pounce on a weak member of the herd.

He organised us in strict rows, shoulders back, chests out, thumbs pointing down the seam of your trousers or skirt, chin up, facing the front.

Puffing himself up, he launched into the full repertoire, like a pantomime villain on opening night. 'Don't you look at me, keep your eyes forward,' or 'Don't call me Sir, I'm not an officer, I've worked for this rank' and other equally pithy lines saved for occasions such as this. To be fair, he played the part very well. I was trying my hardest to look earnest and serious and not stand out.

He had a taller but equally immaculate sidekick in the College Warrant Officer, another man not to be messed with. Once we were in some sort of order on the parade square, he delivered a shouty speech about how we were theirs to do with as they pleased, so toe the line or we'd be out.

I got the impression he expected 100 per cent from us, mainly because he must have said it about half a dozen times.

If we didn't give it, we'd be out. You need to prove to us you're good enough to be here. Or you're out. It went on. It was his moment of glory, shouting at potential new officers, and he was loving it. He was definitely doing his best to scare us and he was succeeding.

'BY THE LEFT, QUUUIIIIIIICK... MARCH.' We attempted to march off the parade square in pristine military order but we just looked like a right gaggle.

We were headed for the college to commit to a life in the RAF, to serve Queen and country, an important step which includes making a pledge. I stood there holding up my brown hands as I promised to serve the RAF for the next twelve years.

As I stood, about to sign my life away, the enormity hit me like a steam train. I was still employed as an air traffic controller and was making a huge leap of faith that it would all work out in the end and I would get to be a pilot somehow. That's all I ever wanted to be and I still had this absolute belief it would happen, but as my pen hovered above the paper those stomach-churning doubts washed over me...what happens if they don't make me a pilot? My future was in someone else's hands.

It didn't help when people would constantly ask me what branch I was in. I would say, 'Well, I'm an air trafficker now but I'm waiting for a branch change to pilot.' To which the usual response was, 'Mmm', or 'Well, good luck with that', or 'You've got no hope.' It was a real test, but I've always been a believer in visualisation. I pictured myself as a pilot in the RAF and I truly believed I would make it.

That afternoon back in the mess a member of the training staff, who were all tough-as-old-boots RAF Regiment corporals and sergeants, showed each flight how to set up a room to the exact required standards.

That meant everything immaculately ironed and folded, shoes on the left, boots on the right, shirts to the left, jumpers to the right, underwear rolled up. We were each handed diagrams with how the clothes in your cupboard should look. Inspections would come thick and fast, they said, some scheduled, some when you weren't expecting them. And the room had to be beyond spotless.

We were also shown how to bull a pair of shoes. I knew a bit about it from the Air Training Corps but it was clear now that was amateur stuff. This was the pro league of polishing. A proper deep shine to the front of the shoe could take two to three hours. If you scuffed them, you had to go back to the start and build up the whole thing from scratch.

The first room inspection came on day two. We stood to attention outside our rooms, and as mine was first on the left as you entered the corridor through the fire doors, I was first up for the treatment.

The sergeant breezed past me and I could hear pacing and tutting from inside the room. I was standing there on tenterhooks, my mind racing and flicking around a mental map trying to check if everything was in order.

'Wells, get in here...NOW'

Oh my gosh. It must be something terrible.

'Why is this tap dripping, Wells?'

'I don't know Sir, I mean sergeant.'

'One of these tiles is cracked, Wells. This wardrobe looks crap. And as for this bed...'

He yanked off the cover and blanket and threw them back in a crumpled heap. 'Not good enough.' He stormed out and into the next room.

'What the bloody hell...? Get in here you miserable worm. Have you even heard of a hoover?' And so it went on, up the corridor.

The sergeant was working himself up into more and more of a fury, but the angrier he got, the funnier it seemed, at least to those of us who had been dealt with.

Standing back to attention outside my room I didn't dare laugh or even try to catch anyone's eye. This was not the time for corpsing. And you certainly can't argue. It's just a rite of passage you have to go through. As time went on, I found myself swinging internally from 'This is bollocks,' to 'It's all part of the game, just roll with it.'

The first week was a blur of marching, ironing, pressing, bulling. Haunted by my first inspection I would get up extra early to make time to iron my sheets and pillowcase before putting them back on the bed so it looked like it hadn't been slept in.

I'd hoover and then work around the floor on hands and knees with a roll of Sellotape, picking up dust and dirt. The taps, mirror and sink would be gleaming.

Occasionally, I'd wander next door to see how they were getting on, only to realise my pants were in the wrong order, or my shirt needed to be moved slightly to the left and rush back to make the changes before the staff came.

Mark and John had done all the shouty stuff themselves but were now being treated like something you had stepped in. It must have been weird for them as they knew some of the sergeants but they were brilliant with us. They knew the system and pulled us together as a flight.

We had bulling nights when we had to clean the block from top to bottom. The overall course leader, an ex-warrant officer on one of the other flights, was brilliant. He was serious and didn't mess about. He knew where he wanted to go in life and didn't want to have lots of annoying students ruining it. He would dish out the jobs, so one flight would be on toilets, another on showers, another on the central areas. We polished them to perfection, using nailbrushes and toothbrushes to get in close so the place was absolutely glowing. We would shut all the toilet doors and tape them like a crime scene, keeping one for use overnight so we only had to give it a quick blitz first thing in the morning ready for inspection.

This was life in the 'BIM', the four-week Basic Induction Module where you are on the receiving end of a short, sharp shock into how to be military.

You got up before the crows had even stirred, made sure your room was as pristine as it was when you'd snuck into your pit a few short hours earlier, before you shovelled in a monster breakfast, lined up outside your room for an early inspection, practised marching, rifle drills and saluting ('up two three, down') for two or three hours, took a break by doing some intense physical training (PT) such as running, swimming or the assault course, did some academic study such as English or learning about the Royal Air Force, stuffed limitless calorific stodge down your neck in about ten minutes for lunch, went to more lessons, did some more marching and PT, scoffed even more for dinner, especially sticky toffee pudding, cleaned your room and block until it was as spangly as it was the last time you did it about twelve hours ago, ironed your kit, bulled your boots, crashed out completely knackered....and did it all over again from five thirty a.m. Happy days.

Spot inspections could be called at any time. One day, Paul was still hoovering as the staff approached our corridor. Panicking, or using his initiative depending on how you look at it, he opened his window and lowered the Hoover down on its lead.

It would have been a great ruse, except his room happened to be above one where another Sergeant was inspecting a lower floor room, from where great shouts of 'What the effing heck is going on?' ushered forth as the Hoover hove into view.

Any time you walked from one activity to another, you had to march. You couldn't just walk from the classroom to the PT hall, you had to march. Even if you were carrying a heavy bag full of books and gym kit. I quickly found I had to hold the bag out from my body as it was snagging my tights every time. It killed my wrists, but I was going through so many pairs of tights it was ridiculous.

Slowly, your mindset adjusted to life as a soldier. On a rare occasion I spoke to a friend outside of this little bubble I mentioned how marching everywhere just looks a lot smarter than walking. 'Oh my gosh, Mandy, you've become brainwashed, what happened to the Wellsey we know and love!' guffawed the voice from the other end of the phone.

There were about twenty women in the whole of my intake, in a variety of branches, from pilots to suppliers. I made a great ally early on with Hels Fletcher. We were all trying to fit in but Hels had gone the extra mile. She had a mound of untameable curly hair which had attracted her a torrent of abuse from the staff. To control it she had a brutal haircut, which made her feel bad enough, but worse was that the curls just kept on escaping from under the beret, attracting even more abuse.

It really helped to get together with the girls for chats. All the aches, pains and gripes were dissected and we realised we were all in the same boat. We all had hopes and dreams for our careers in the RAF which we mulled over. I still had not heard anything back from the RAF about my branch change to pilot, even though I'd now written dozens of letters. The reality was starting to dawn that my future might end up being firmly grounded before it had even taken off.

As part of our introduction to general soldiering we were taken to the range to fire our weapons. We were each issued an SA80, the infantry's general assault rifle and shown how to take it apart, clean it, put it back together, change a magazine and clear blockages. Once we'd got the basics we were timed so it became a slick operation. I'd done a bit of shooting with a .22 rifle on ranges with the Air Training Corps and thought I'd be OK at the firing bit.

Lying in the prone position I let off my ten shots at the target at the end of the range. Yep, nailed that, aren't I the girl? When we looked at the big round targets, mine was pristine, absolutely untouched. I couldn't understand it. Looking around, I caught the person next to me appearing equally confused with the twelve holes in theirs.

Like a prize chump I had been aiming at the wrong target.

One of the more unpleasant sessions was learning to use our nuclear, biological and chemical (NBC) suits and gas masks – essential in the event of an attack. This involved a trip to the gas chambers, which were actually just concrete sheds on the perimeter, like the sort of places derelicts might hang out in.

Outside we would all stand in a circle and put on our NBC suits, which were made of a specialist rubber with chemical retardants and went over the top of whatever we were wearing, including boots, like a protective condom with arms and legs.

Inside the shed, the instructor popped a CS gas canister and we would all shout 'Gas, gas, gas' before wrestling on our gas masks within ten seconds. You had to make sure they were fitting snuggly and were sealed because breathing in the gas was like inhaling pure fire.

We then had to practice unscrewing the filter on the front and swapping it for a new one while holding your breath, followed by taking the masks off to dab yourself down with decontamination paper, again holding your breath. When you put the mask back on you were supposed to blow out first, like when you surface from snorkelling, before you could breathe clean air again. This was where some people panicked because they had been faffing and had run out of breath and didn't have enough left for the blow, so they sucked in a lung full of pain and misery. I, along with most people, have run from the shed retching and spluttering at some stage. The last drill was to try and take a drink using the straw that was tucked into the bottom of the mask. You had to curl it out with your tongue to plug it into the top of the water bottle. Watching your mates stand around in a circle trying to do this was comedy gold, but this wasn't the time for japes, especially with my great big inhale of a laugh.

That first month was full-on squaddie training, knocking off all our rough edges as the military likes to describe it, and beginning the process of polishing us up into officers, a bit like bulling a pair of boots. That's easy to write, so much harder to go through in person. I didn't think it was possible to be so tired and still function enough to polish, clean, tidy, iron, march, learn, run, shoot, eat, shine, bull, mop, march and polish for eighteen hours a day, in cold, wind, rain and sometimes shine. On top of that we had to deal with the petty crap dished out by the sadistic staff who took gleeful delight in pushing us to the limits. I'd have to give myself a talking to now and again to suck it up, play the game and put my all into it. But flipping heck it was tough.

On the final Friday of basic training we went to the bar to celebrate. There was no leave, the course carried on the next day but we were determined to mark the occasion.

Late on, I made the stupid comment that I had a bottle of wine hidden in my room. I had stashed it like some contraband from the Great Escape in the bottom of my kitbag. 'Wayhay, Mandy's for a party,' went up the cry.

We had the stereo on full blast and were jumping on beds, dancing away. Someone was lying on top of the cupboards moonwalking on the ceiling. I woke up in the morning with my feet lower than my head. The bed had collapsed and the mattress was touching the floor.

Looking around the room I spotted cracked ceiling tiles from the moonwalker and streams of condensation from the heat of our bodies flowing down the walls like the Mississippi delta.

The room was trashed. Bloody hell, this is serious. I stumbled out to find help and came back with Paul, Giles and Batters. We went at it like a human tidying tornado and wrapped up as the staff were approaching.

I stood with fingers figuratively crossed outside the room. I didn't dare actually cross them in case some eagle-eyed corporal trying to impress by showing how anal he was spotted me.

'Wells, IN,' roared the sergeant from inside.

Is it the tiles? Or the propped-up bed? Or the water-stained walls? Probably all three and then some.

'Wells, WHAT...is this hair doing on your sink?'

I had never been more relieved to see a stray hair.

One morning after drill and before getting changed for PT, I diverted to the `pigeonholes on the ground floor of our block to get my mail.

Sitting there in my slot, all unassuming, was a slim brown envelope with an RAF crest bearing my name in type.

I didn't have much time and wasn't really expecting anything so I ripped it open and scanned the first few lines.

'Dear Pilot Officer Wells...' Yes, yes, come on. I'm going to be late. '... bla, bla, bla... following your request to switch branches the RAF would like to confirm your appointment as a pilot...'

A charge of electricity surged through my body. I read it again. Yes, that's what it says. GET IN, YOU BEAUTY! My grin stretched from ear to ear. I kissed the letter. Well, well, I've bloody done it. After all those knock backs and then joining the RAF for a career I didn't really want. It was almost like jumping off a cliff hoping the parachute would open. Well now it had. I floated off to PT feeling like I had come home, that I was back among my brethren and no longer a wannabe on the outside looking in. I had only been at Cranwell for a few weeks but now I felt like I could fully commit to this path I was on, no matter how hard it might get.

Strangely, even though I wasn't expecting it, I didn't feel surprised or shocked. Somehow, I just knew, it would happen. Much later, I discovered I had been taken on as a test case to see how far I would get before I failed. Too many women had been failing the tests compared to the men. Not that I cared. They'd opened the door. I was ready to barge through it.

CHAPTER 3

STAYING OUT OF TROUBLE

We had proved we could polish, bull, scrub and clean. We had shown we could take all the banter and bullshit. We even got the hang of marching most of the time. Now we were entering a new phase of training.

We were introduced to our flight commander for the first time, an individual who would be taking a much more hands-on role in our progress, or lack of, and welfare. The second I met him my heart fell. He was the epitome of vanilla. When we first met, I searched his eyes for some kind of spark but there was nothing there. As time went on, I realised we couldn't have been more polar opposite. He didn't quite know what to make of me and I found it increasingly difficult to warm to him. He was low key and dour and I quickly nicknamed him Flt Lt Beige. Since then, I've met many officers just like him, ones that just didn't quite know how to cope with me and with my gregarious and buoyant energy, who tried to put me into the box of a sedate female officer. I knew then that I was going to have my work cut out for the next five months.

Leadership in the field was the main thrust of this section of training so we spent much of November, December and January in full combat gear or NBC suits taking it in turns to lead our flight on exercises in the countryside behind Cranwell.

We still had inspections, though not quite as regularly as before, which meant all our muddy kit from the field had to be cleaned and polished every night.

The leadership sessions would begin with lectures on the theory before static activities like building tripods took over.

Then we would progress to a situation in the field. Each of us in the flight took it in turns to be the leader. The brief would be something like a chemical attack and we had to retrieve pieces of equipment stashed around the training area while being evaluated on our leadership, decision making, problem solving, communication and general attitude. We were introduced to the SMEAC brief: 'S' Situation, 'M' Mission, 'E' Execution, 'A' Administration 'C' Command

The flight commander would brief the leader on the mission and they'd get a few minutes to jot it all down on a notepad before briefing the team and handing out tasks. Then you would all set off to find your equipment and build whatever it was. You could be covering a couple of miles each time and you'd pass other flights going in the opposite direction looking equally harassed.

The recent students among us were desperate to show our qualities, like young puppies yapping away and eager for attention, but the more experienced guys came at it with a more calming sense of perspective.

The best piece of advice I got at this stage was to lead as if you're a Sherpa. It's easy to rush in and assume you have to be leading from the front, but often when you think about a mountain climbing expedition, it's the Sherpas at the back who keep an eye on the conditions and monitor how the team are doing physically and mentally. By being at the back you can get a bigger picture of the whole operation and respond accordingly, help the slower ones and reign in the faster ones pushing the pace.

The big thing for me was always talking too much. I realised it was something I had to watch in my personality. I'm loud enough as it is and when I get nervous, I have a tendency to go into verbal diarrhoea mode.

Leadership is so much about listening, active listening, taking on another point of view and then making your decision.

Equally, I found it quite difficult to rein in my enthusiasm when someone else was leading. That was a big learning point for me, not to get over-excited and step on other people's toes.

We would be evaluated at the end of every exercise, not just the leader but the team as well. It was incredible how stressful a scenario could be when you knew every word was being analysed. I was probably a bit cocky and it was no bad thing to be knocked back down a bit and shown how important it was to listen to team members.

One of the big things they were looking for was strong decision makers and people happy to put themselves forward and be held accountable.

What they didn't want was the leader deferring to a dominant personality or a brilliant problem solver every time. They wanted to see your initiative and your ability to bring in other members of the team.

The cleaning-toilets-with-your-toothbrush squaddie stuff was receding and the course was becoming more sociable. We had weekends off and there was the occasional night in the bar or a fancy-dress party, which always ended up being a toga party as we only really had the sheets on our beds with which to make costumes.

'Grey Tuesday' was the name of the first assessment when verdicts on our worth as potential officers and even human beings were delivered by our flight commanders. They were known to be frank and brutal at times. This was when Flt Lt Beige gave me his infamous 'Amazonian' speech. Demanding that I 'be more feminine'.

I left his office fuming and bemused. Outraged that he could treat me like that, trying to pigeonhole me just for being a woman, but also confused and bewildered. What was I supposed to do? Who was I supposed to be?

I got on very well with some of the other flight commanders and I told a couple of them about my issues with him. They were all shocked and very much on my side. Keep your head down, keep plodding on, play the game, you'll be fine, was the message. This became more difficult to action as each day passed. The tension between the two of us became almost palpable. Although I did not realise this at the time, but this would be the first of many encounters with more senior officers who had a problem with women taking on new roles within the RAF.

The Field Leadership Training module ended with a big ten-day exercise at the Otterburn training area in the southern Cheviot Hills of Northumberland.

We were billeted in glorified Portacabins, ten on each side of a central planked walkway. They were as basic as they come with eight people to a hut sleeping in bunks. We lived largely on ration packs and spent days and nights conducting various missions and generally being soldiers in the woods.

Despite being on this desolate training base, we made a point of celebrating Burns Night and we all crammed into the central cabin, a bit bigger than the accommodation huts, to feast and make speeches.

I had the misfortune of finding myself sitting next to my best friend, Flt Lt Beige, and I had to give myself a quick lecture on keeping my head and behaving professionally, even though he rankled big time. At the back of my mind was the thought that people were now getting chopped and I didn't want to fail on account of a personal issue with this chap.

Back in the classroom we had to prepare and deliver presentations on various military aspects.

I did mine on the case of Private Lee Clegg, a British soldier who was convicted of the murder of two teenage joyriders in Northern Ireland. He fired at the car as it sped through a checkpoint, but the prosecution argued the fourth bullet, which killed the passenger, was a shot in the back after the threat had passed. Clegg eventually had his conviction overturned. I presented a case for both sides of the argument, and every single aspect of my delivery, from body language to inappropriate use of humour, was analysed.

Apparently, I made a clicking noise with my tongue every time I opened my mouth. In my ten minute presentation, I did it seventeen times, I was told. I lacked impact and apparently would never make much of a public speaker, they said.

'Black Thursday' was the name given to the second crucial assessment day, when we learned if we had passed the Field Leadership Training phase. It was a big culling stage. Some people had been failed already and a few hadn't got through BIM because of fitness or medical reasons.

Some were back coursed to the start of FLT or even to the beginning of BIM, which must be tough to take when you've already proved you can clean a toilet with a toothbrush.

So, not for the first time I found myself standing outside Beige's office like a naughty schoolgirl waiting for my name to be called.

I knew I had to wind my neck in. My life was in his hands. Did I really want to go through all that again just to score some points?

You can be cut for all sorts of things, from a lack of leadership skills to public speaking.

I marched into the office in my crisp No.2 uniform and saluted.

He ran over my performance so far, skirted the feminine stuff, and in a very perfunctory way said, 'Congratulations, you've passed.'

I fought back a huge grin as I saluted and wheeled out of the room. 'Yesssss,' I wanted to scream but I couldn't because the next in line might not be so fortunate. Instead, I bottled it up for use in the bar that night, when we properly uncorked.

For the next phase of training we moved across the road to a room in Cranwell's iconic College Hall. It was like entering a different world.

Instead of a spartan barrack block, this grand old building oozed history and presence as the home of RAF officer training since it was opened in 1934.

Inside the main entrance framed with colonnades was a square atrium with grand old oil paintings on the walls and twin staircases sweeping down. As students we were forbidden from setting foot on the carpet and had to edge around on the marble floor skirting the walls. If we came home a touch tipsy or feeling a bit brave, we'd stick our toes on it and laugh.

High above was the dome of the rotunda and above that was the soaring lighthouse, which just happens to be the furthest lighthouse from the sea in the UK. Cranwell is the only RAF station to have a lighthouse in its grounds.

Jutting out from either end of the main building were two u-shaped wings. We would be living in one of the wings, still in our flight and still in fairly basic rooms, but a step up from Number One Mess.

Instead of a canteen, dinner was now served by waiting staff at a table in a smart dining room. It was all very imposing and made you feel like you had to be on your best behaviour at all times.

But with that came the feeling that the whole mood of the course had changed. We were now treated less like new recruits and more like potential officers. The relationship with the staff had gone from being a first year at school to a sixth former.

We even got our sheets changed for us and we could leave the base whenever we wanted, within reason.

The next four weeks were spent on what is known as 'The carousel'.

It kicked off with a week up at Grantown-on-Spey on the northern edge of the Cairngorms in Scotland. We went hiking, mountaineering, kayaking and all sorts of other hearty outdoor pursuits.

Back at Cranwell we were being groomed in some of a RAF officer's hospitality duties.

There were a lot of events and drinks parties where we were scrutinised on our ability to socialise and host VIPs. One of my strengths had always been the ability to chat to people at any level and so I was always given high-calibre guests to look after.

My apparent 'lack' of femininity didn't seem to be a problem here.

One evening we had a practice dining-in night, a very formal dinner in College. Time to break out the interim mess dress – interim because we were still cadets – which consisted of our No.1 uniform with the blue shirt and tie replaced with a white shirt and black bow tie, otherwise known as No.4 dress.

It was a chance to learn a few more dos and don'ts of being an RAF officer, such as learning which cutlery to use, not to touch the mess silver in the middle of the table, and how to pass the port (to the left, without letting the bottle touch the table).

When we had attended dinners at the university air squadron the established practice was to down your wine whenever you saw the wine waiter approaching to ensure a top up.

Still in this mindset I was trying to lead Mark and John astray and urging them to 'neck it', but the moment I slammed my empty glass on the table, Flt Lt Beige turned to us and said, 'And of course, one thing you absolutely don't do is to gulp down your wine at the first sign of a wine waiter.'

The final stage of carousel was an exercise called Operation Peacekeeper.

It was a seven-day field exercise at RAF Barkston Heath in Lincolnshire, where everyone was assigned different roles in a massive operation.

The scenario was that an enemy force was trying to capture our airbase and we had to defend it, not just from conventional attacks but also NBC attacks.

We spent the week fully camouflaged up and sometimes had to rush into our NBC suits if the siren went up warning of a chemical attack.

We were expected to keep our weapons with us at all times, like proper soldiers. If you left it lying around and the directing staff found it, they would take it and then you would be hung, drawn and quartered.

There was a central command tent with some of the course high-flyers pushing for the Sword of Honour (the highest prize for outstanding leadership) getting the top jobs such as station commander or head of intelligence. I was doing well but I wasn't shining enough to be in the running for any end-of-course marbles.

My job was to lead my troop out on patrols and report back with what we had seen. The scenario would change constantly and it was all about pulling together those skills we had been developing in field leadership training, plus tactical patrolling, first aid and NBC responses. I relished the opportunity to prove how much I had learnt and really show Flt Lt Beige that I was worthy of graduating as an officer. I felt my confidence growing daily.

One night I had my patrol hide behind some hay bales for as long as we could get away with it, just to have a rest and avoid running around in our NBC kit, which was hideously restricting and hot and made the sweat run down into your boots. We lay there for a couple of hours until someone came on the radio demanding our whereabouts.

It turned out to be incredibly difficult to lead in NBC gear as you're trying to shout through a rubber mask while the whole thing is steamed up with condensation because you're running about carrying a heavy weapon.

You can't take the mask off because there is a chemical warfare threat and you can't even do it subtly because if they notice you'll fail the course. Notwithstanding the obvious dangers it makes you realise a chemical attack would be seriously challenging.

The more tired you get, the more realistic the exercise becomes. One time I charged out of some bushes to see a helicopter on fire, a burning mass belching smoke with injured people lying around. You know it's not real and the injured are just extras drafted in, from the directing staff to physical training staff to students, but you get to a point where you can't separate it from reality. Maybe that is the point, that this is your current reality. Tasking our medic to assess the wounded, we set up a defensive formation around the helicopter. We immediately began to receive incoming rounds of shots being fired and had to peer through the drifting smoke and the dark to spot the muzzle flashes.

'Anyone got eyes on?' I screamed. There was a pause. 'Yes, large tree.' 'Ok, visual large tree.' Our weapons training had taught us how to talk your team on to a target. 'Left large tree, gate post.' 'Visual gate post.' 'Behind gate post, enemy.' Right let's shoot the buggers then. 'Engage the target'

The scenario shifted constantly. On another occasion we had a radio call to say there was a crowd of people with placards staging a mass demonstration outside of the base. We had to calm down the situation and show a different side of leadership, using soft skills and diplomacy. One morning I was told I was to act as a press officer and give an interview to a gaggle of newspaper reporters. That was almost harder than running a mile in NBC kit.

The exercise ended in a right royal firefight in the full NBC works with an attacking force trying to breach our command centre. We were laying down fire and manoeuvring like proper soldiers. There was a lot of noise, smoke, shouting and testosterone flying around. Eventually the enemy retreated and a siren went to signal the threat was over and that was that.

The final practice for graduation was a full dress rehearsal but when I was getting dressed I had a bit of trouble getting into my No. 1 smart skirt. They can't have measured me properly, I thought, but as I strolled out onto the parade ground, I discovered all the guys had been struggling to get into their trousers. It seemed that when we had been fitted for this kit in our early weeks we were all lithe because of the amount of physical activity we were doing.

With that went appetites like rabid rhinoceroses, but since then we hadn't been burning off quite the same number of calories. The last few weeks had been quite a relaxed, sociable time. There were more than a few buttons straining under jackets on that parade ground.

On Graduation Day we got up for an early breakfast and squeezed into our very best passing out uniform, including sparkly sword and brown gloves.

I had my mum, dad and sister there as well as my granny and grandpa. It was his ninetieth birthday and as he was a former Wing Commander and Second World War pilot, he was invited as the guest of honour. It was a wonderful touch and made me realise that when you are in the RAF, you are part of a club that you belonged to for the rest of your life. Whether he was being mischievous or had simply forgotten I'll never know, but the first thing he did when we sat down to lunch was pick up the mess silver. And everyone knows you don't do that.

With the guests all seated and the top brass suitably coffee-ed and biscuited we wheeled out from behind College Hall to the thunder of the band.

I had a distinct lump in my throat. I had never felt prouder, not just for myself but for my family sitting in the big grandstand watching me.

To show off a bit to the guests we did slow marches, fast marches, with the Sword of Honour winner barking the orders as master of ceremonies.

We came to attention for the speeches and a fly-by from a Jaguar aircraft. All the pilots couldn't resist flicking their eyes up to catch a glimpse and I caught the warrant officer smiling, knowing we were all dreaming of the next stage of our careers.

The final part of the parade was marching up the steps of College Hall and in through the front door. When we were all on the sacred carpet, we received a salute from the College Warrant Officer, gave ourselves three cheers and then launched our hats into the air.

There were plenty of tears when I met up again with the family to walk to the service of dedication in the chapel.

All the corporals and sergeants who had beasted us and bellowed at us like we were the lowest life on God's earth were lined up. One by one they gave me their first salute and said things like, 'Hello ma'am, congratulations. It's been a pleasure.'

The one that meant the most though was when Flt Lt Beige came and shook my hand. 'Congratulations Mandy, you've worked so hard for this, you deserve it.' I had a lump in my throat as I smiled back. Sometimes you have to work at relationships, find the good in them and the common ground and although we would never be great friends, I had learnt about mutual respect, biting my tongue and just getting on with it. I had certainly learned to be more resilient which would hold me in good stead for the next few years.

It was a momentous, thrilling day. How I didn't sob uncontrollably, I don't know. Maybe it's because I was now an officer in Her Majesty's Royal Air Force.

CHAPTER 4

TAKING OFF

If turning up at Cranwell with strangely dark hands wasn't the best of looks, I took it a stage further with a swollen nose and scabby face when I arrived for my first posting at RAF Barkston Heath near Grantham in Lincolnshire.

I'd had a mishap with an icy pavement after misjudging a rugby tackle on a night out on a skiing trip in the French Alps. It would have really hurt if the cold mountain air and the gallons of gin hadn't numbed it, but here I was back in RAF work mode looking like the elephant woman. Not very professional.

Even though I was living back at Cranwell and getting a minibus to nearby Barkston Heath every day, it was a very different feeling to training. As a new officer, people were now saluting me and calling me 'ma'am', which took a bit of getting used to.

With me was Dave, known as 'DK', a friend from officer training who was originally a navigator, but, like me, had got a branch change to pilot. As it happened, he was one of those I beat in the aerobatics competition at university.

We were supposed to be on the Joint Elementary Flying Training (JEFTS) course, but because we both had loads of hours (I had about 200 hours by this point) the RAF, in its infinite wisdom, decided to save money. Instead, the plan for us was to skip this and work on the Barkston Heath operations desk while we 'held.'

I had misgivings because instead of a fast-jet station it

was a bit of a sleepy satellite airfield, used mainly for circuit practice. The holding role had the potential to be as dull as a new recruit's boots, but on our first day our immediate boss John Craven, not the Newsround legend but ex-military and a lovely guy, said he would get us up flying at any opportunity.

I was soon lined up for a flight in a Firefly, a propeller plane very similar to the Bulldog of my air squadron days.

It was my twenty second birthday and I was sitting around the crew room waiting for the instructor, when in walked a very good-looking Navy pilot with sandy hair and the bluest eyes I had ever seen in my life.

'Hi, Mandy is it? I'm Lt Hickson, I'll be your instructor. It will be an honour to fly your first official flight since you joined the RAF!' Oh great, and I'm scab face, nice to meet you. He was sparky, very relaxed and put me at ease.

When we were airborne he asked if I had done much aerobatic flying. I told him about my De Havilland Trophy and offered to show him my winning routine. When I had finished throwing the plane around the sky he said, 'Right, well, you're better at this than me.' I ended up demonstrating a couple of the moves. It was a fun flight and I thought nothing more of it.

While DK and I were there as staff, we had plenty of time to chew the fat with the guys actually on the JEFTS course, a mix of new Navy and RAF pilots, over endless brews of tea and games of Ludo, ukkers or cards in the crew room. They integrated us into their midst and invited us to all their social activities.

DK and I soon latched on to how the job would work and covered each other on the ops desk, packing our time with flying and signing up for as many courses as we could through the Joint Services Adventure Training Unit.

One time, I joined Lt Hickson and Lt Thomas in flying down to the Culdrose Air Day at Royal Naval Air Station Culdrose in Cornwall. I'd not worked with the Navy before, so it was great to see them in action, particularly as the weather was terrible so the flying was limited and the partying unlimited. Another bonus was getting to know Craig and Shakey a bit better, outside of the normal instructor/student relationship. Craig really made me laugh and I definitely felt some sparks between the two of us.

In August, after a couple of weeks of sun and laughs in Turkey with a group of girls from university, I was given a new holding post with 29(F) Squadron, a Tornado F3 outfit, at RAF Coningsby.

This is an historic base, which for a spell in 1943 hosted the 'Dambusters' of 617 Squadron before becoming the home of Vulcan bombers and then Phantoms. Since 1976 it's also been the home for the Battle of Britain Memorial Flight of the RAF's last remaining Spitfires, Hurricanes, a Lancaster Bomber and a Dakota.

Instead of being south of Cranwell like Barkston Heath, this was north east, but still in deepest, darkest rural Lincolnshire.

I drove up one filthy October night, stopping every few miles in the flat, winding country lanes to check the map. Can this be right? It felt like I was getting further and further into the countryside. This place made sleepy old Cranwell feel like the centre of the universe.

I found it eventually and pulled up in front of the mess to unload my car. I didn't know for how long I'd be here, so I had enough stuff to make my room feel like home – stereo, posters, and pictures – but not too much to keep carting around.

It was a bit daunting walking into this strange environment at night on my own, not knowing a soul. It was the first time I had pitched up anywhere without a wingman. I was busy propping open the fire door to ferry my stuff up when a guy appeared and asked if I needed a hand. He invited me to join him and some others in the bar once I had unpacked, which helped me settle but I still had to give myself a talking to on my bed before I went down. Come on, you've got to make an effort here, rouse yourself.

Unlike Barkston Heath, which had proved to be a great posting, it was made very clear there would be no flying. It was an operational squadron and as a junior officer my job was to be general skivvy on the ops desk, driving pilots around, taking them lunch and other highly skilled tasks.

I would be sharing the role with another new officer in a holding role, an eighteen-year-old called Bob, who had been there for a while and who showed me the ropes.

The squadron buildings were in hardened aircraft shelters, domed-shaped bunkers, which were very dark inside with no natural light. Other than Bob, I was the youngest by far, and because most people were married, they lived out of the mess, which made for a slightly strange existence. Being a fast-jet squadron, the atmosphere was very punchy with a lot of testosterone flying around. I reflected that this is what I had been aspiring to do with my life since my first flight at the age of fourteen and yet now I was here I wasn't so sure that I liked it.

Very soon I realised there were not many jobs for two of us to do so I got into my fitness and went circuit training every day just to fill my time.

After a few weeks it was announced most of the squadron were deploying to Gioia del Colle in southern Italy in support of Operation Allied Force, the policing of the no-fly zone over Bosnia.

I wasn't on the list, instead I would be part of a skeleton crew kept at Coningsby. With no chance of flying and very little to do it had all the signs of being a horrendous few months of boredom. Was this really what I had gone through all that effort and heartache for?

A few days after the squadron flew out, I went back to my mum's in Manchester for the weekend. On the Saturday evening the phone rang and mum passed it to me. 'Mandy, we need you out in Italy. Bob's too young to drive. You're booked on a transport plane leaving tomorrow.' Right. Crikey.

I felt a surge of adrenaline. Action stations. Someone wants me. I'm off to Italy for Queen and country. I stuffed my kit in my car and sped off back to Coningsby.

The next morning I flew out of Brize Norton on a VC10, bound for Gioia del Colle airbase, due south of Bari in Puglia province at the top of the heel of Italy's boot.

Bob was there to give me the lowdown. My role as ops clerk was to study the lengthy air tasking documents that came through on the printer from higher command and go through all the codes with a fine-tooth comb to work out when our crews would be needed for operations. Most of their duties were air combat patrols on the other side of the Adriatic Sea. I then had to work out what time the pilots needed to be in and help organise the logistics.

We were operating from the same buildings as No.3(F) Squadron, who flew Harriers. I won't beat around the bush; they were right up themselves. I found them to be so condescending to the Tornado pilots and navigators, just because they flew single-seat jets compared to the two-seat Tornado. They thought they were the bees' knees and made it pretty clear. There was a lot of very harsh banter and animosity between the squadrons started to build. It was the way they spoke, especially to the navigators, that I found really rude. They were so arrogant and it really put me off wanting to pursue Harriers, even if I was good enough. I didn't want to get into this mentality of 'we're the best, you're nothing because you fly with two seats.'

We were all staying together in a hotel in Gioia, a pretty medieval town on a plateau with a charming old quarter and more than a dozen churches.

It didn't take long for boredom to set in in the evenings. I had taken a dice game out with me and every now and again I'd suggest a game. 'No, shut up,' was the usual reply.

After a while as the novelty of being on a tour had worn off it was, 'Get your flipping dice game out.' And from then on it became an obsession with the entire detachment. I had to leave it in my key slot behind hotel reception so everyone could get at it when they were free. I'm not sure now why we didn't just buy more dice. Even going out for meal, we'd take our dice in our hands and the second we'd ordered we'd carry on playing. As a perk I was allowed home for a few days over Christmas. My dice were grounded in Gioia.

Late on New Year's Day I was due to fly back to Bari out of RAF Lyneham so I went out for dinner with some friends in London first and then pointed the car west.

I arrived in the little Oxfordshire village south of Chipping Norton but I couldn't see any sign of an airbase, only a golf course. There was a public phone box, so I called the operator and asked to be put through to the RAF station.

A woman's voice answered and I said, 'Hello, I'm just wondering where you are, where exactly is Lyneham?'

There was a pause, and then she said: 'Ah, are you at that telephone box near a golf course in that village in Oxfordshire? We have so many people ringing us from there.'

I'd driven to the wrong Lyneham on my map. I should have been at Lyneham in Wiltshire north east of Chippenham.

How long will it take to get there? An hour? Oh, bugger, my flight leaves in about an hour. I was panicking. I was a very junior officer and was going to miss my flight back to work. I dived into my shiny new Peugeot and floored it. There was a humpback bridge just outside the village and I may well have got all four wheels airborne (kids, don't try this at home, it is neither big nor clever). As I landed I spotted the bright blue light of a police car. One single flash was enough. I pulled over and the officer strolled up. I wound down my window. He poked in his head. 'Good evening, madam. Oh, are you a pilot?' I was wearing my flying suit. 'Yes I am,' I replied confidently, even though technically I wasn't. 'Where are you off to in such a hurry?'

'I'm sorry officer, I'm having a nightmare. I'm trying to join my squadron in Italy but I've come to the wrong Lyneham and now I'm going to miss my flight.'

'Well, let's sort you out. If you're flying for Queen and country, it's the least we can do.' He ran back to his car and with blue lights flashing escorted me as far as the border with Wiltshire. He alerted colleagues in the next county and another panda car picked me up to escort me to RAF Lyneham.

I skidded up at the real Lyneham by the seat of my pants and dashed through the terminal building. The world's favourite question that night seemed to be 'Did you go to the wrong Lyneham then?'

The moment I entered the operations building in Gioia I could feel a palpable tension in the air. You could literally have cut the atmosphere with a knife. I was immediately filled in on the whole situation. During the Christmas festivities, tempers had run a little high culminating in some sort of fisticuffs between the two squadrons. Some of the squadron had been moved into accommodation on the air base while the incident was investigated. The RAF would not tolerate this sort of behaviour and punishments were administered. Not the best way to start the new year.

I hadn't been in Gioia longer than a couple of days when I got a message to say I was being sent on a JEFTS course after all. Finally, someone with some nous had decided I had been holding too long without flying. I packed up all my stuff again and flew back to Blighty. It felt like quite a breathless, transitory period, but I knew the score and didn't have any dependants so it didn't bother me.

In fact, it was exciting, just what I had been after, albeit without the flying. That would come.

With my car looking like a gypsy encampment I drove back into Cranwell on a Sunday afternoon.

This time I would be billeted back in College Hall Officers' Mess, but in the right-hand wing, on the opposite end of the old building from where I had finished my officer training.

As I got out of the car, I heard a shout. 'Oi, Wells, what are you doing here?'

I looked up. A head was poking out of a first-floor window. It was Lt Hickson. 'Hi Craig,' I shouted. 'I'm back, actually on the course this time.'

He came down to give me a hand unloading the car and then we went for a cup of tea in his room to catch-up. At least this time I wasn't covered in scabs, although I had put on almost two stone after eating pizza every night in Italy.

Wandering about College Hall again was fantastic, savouring all the pomp and ceremony.

There were plenty of friends from officer training on the course and loads of familiar faces from my earlier time at Barkston Heath, so it felt a bit like coming home.

I realised I quite liked that sense of belonging, rather than the feeling of being an outsider and a very small fish in a big pond like I had on 29(F) Squadron.

Even though this was the official start of our RAF flying training, we'd all done loads of flying by now so most of us were pretty confident, which contributed to the feel-good factor at the start of the course.

What did catch me out was the fact I was now a student, not a member of the Barkston Heath staff, as I had been before. I had rocked up and breezily greeted old colleagues with, 'Hi mate, how are you?' Half of the staff were civilian but this meant the other half were military. Craig pointed out I should now be referring to ranks of Squadron Leader and above as 'Sir'. Being a Navy man, and an instructor, courtesy dictated that this meant him too. It was a good wake up call.

To keep everything official we still had to undergo six weeks of ground school before we were able to take to the skies in the Slingsby T67 Firefly – a fun, agile little twin-seat trainer with a propeller up front.

This was back-to-basics stuff, covering everything from flight theory, simple electrics and hydraulics, meteorology, air law, air traffic control, radio transmissions, morse code, parachute drills and physical training.

When we were allowed to get airborne, I went solo on trip four before we moved onto instrument flying, navigation and medium (2-3,000 feet) and low level (500 feet) flying. We did lots of land-aways at places like RAF Benson south of Oxford to practise different types of navigation, including transiting between radio beacons.

We also took our first steps in formation flying and tail chasing, following a leader as closely as possible as he jinked and turned every which way.

We were scored for every trip, and out of six I was generally a pretty solid five, but that didn't mean we could get complacent. Ours was the first course that was streamed, which meant quite early on you would be assessed as to whether you could continue towards fast jets or you would be diverted to fly multi-engines or helicopters.

My good friend from UBAS days, Vossers was having a clash of personalities with his instructor and faced a chop ride. This means that if you do not make the grade you would fail the course and have to take up a ground branch. Fortunately, Lt Hickson took him back up to get his confidence back and he progressed with us.

Another guy, Rich was informed he was going to be streamed onto multi engines and decided in the end to leave the RAF completely. He was such a loss to the RAF.

Generally, though, it was a really fun, sociable time. We all had new name badges made, some with more humorous 'bar' names to wear in happy hour. At six feet tall and in a nod to Sesame Street, I was named... Big Bird! Not quite the dynamic pilot callsign that I was hoping for.

At the graduation ceremony I was handed the leadership prize and several other awards for formation flying and navigation. It was great to have a bit of silverware behind me.

My flying career was taking off but emotionally I was all at sea. It was clear Craig and I had a connection and were getting on well. But as a member of staff it was an absolute no-no. We fought it, but at the end of the course, during a celebratory evening we had a farewell kiss. It was as if we had opened the flood gates.

My next posting was going to be to RAF Linton-on-Ouse near York for basic flying training in the Tucano. Before then I had a few weeks leave and I had arranged to go travelling to India with my university friend Liz.

Hard as it was, Craig and I agreed this should be the natural end of our liaison. Driving out of Cranwell for the final time I followed him out onto the A1. He pulled into a Burger King at the first service station and I was right behind him. We were both sobbing as we hugged for the umpteenth time that day.

What was I doing letting go of this lovely, special man? I must, I reasoned. Flying planes was proving to be much easier than real life.

CHAPTER 5

LEARNING FROM MY MISTAKES

India was a complete eye-opener. I thought I was reasonably well-travelled but I wasn't prepared for the beauty, rawness, reality, humanity and contradictions of life over there.

There was the poverty and suffering in Delhi; staying on a beautiful ornate houseboat on Dal Lake with a background noise of explosives and small arms in what turned out to be a war zone in Kashmir; the startling generosity of an Indian family on the overnight train when we didn't have any food; picking up an inevitable dose of the runs in Pushka; the utterly arresting Red Fort and Taj Mahal; and being ogled and leered at by groups of local men on the beach in Goa.

But something else happened in Agra that left a bitter taste in the mouth.

We often went to the same café for breakfast and we met this lovely chap who wore cricket whites and said he was educated at Oxford University. He treated us to banana lassies and gave us loads of tips for visiting the sights.

One day he invited us to his house for dinner to see the 'real' India. His family was all there and we chatted to 'and gave us loads of tips for visiting the sights.

During the conversation his uncle said new laws, which were making life very difficult, had hit the family carpet business. They had previously exported their carpets to the UK to sell at craft fairs but now the import duty was too big to make it viable. Our livelihood is dying, he said. Would we like to see some of their carpets? Of course we would. We wandered around the corner to a shop where they kept the most beautiful rugs and carpets I had ever seen. Seeing as you are nice people who we trust, said the uncle, would we mind taking some back home for them to get around paying the duty? All we had to do was buy some rugs now and they would send them over. When we received them back in England we were to call their representative, who would meet us, refund our cash plus a little bit per carpet for our effort, which would go a long way towards paying for our flights, and then they could sell the carpets at the craft fairs as before.

It all sounded fairly plausible and we'd had a lovely dinner, and the rugs were very nice, and yes, please I'll have five. Here are my credit card details.

I said goodbye to Liz in Goa and flew back to start Basic Flying Training School at RAF Linton-on-Ouse near York.

I was trumping like a trooper and so was everyone else.

We were all giggling but I was trying not to catch anyone's eye because I knew that would set me off even more. I had to calm myself down.

I was sitting in a hypobaric chamber with six others at RAF North Luffenham in Rutland. I was on a three-day aviation medical course in preparation to fly at higher altitudes in the Tucano we'd be training on during basic flying training at RAF Linton. We were getting fitted for g-suits and learning about hypoxia, caused by a lack of oxygen.

Hypoxia makes you feel drunk and slightly euphoric, apparently much like drowning. In the air if you become hypoxic you start to make really poor decisions and it can be really dangerous. The decompression chamber is a way of getting you mildly hypoxic to experience the symptoms so if they happen, through a faulty oxygen supply, you can recognise what is happening and do something about it. Eventually a lack of oxygen in the system can cause altitude sickness leading to potentially fatal complications such as high-altitude pulmonary oedema and high-altitude cerebral oedema, as experienced by mountain climbers.

A friend of mine once became hypoxic whilst flying his Harrier over the North Sea. He noticed he had fuel problems, but thought, 'Well, that's fine. It's a lovely day.' Suddenly he realised what it was, went through the correct set of drills and pulled on his emergency oxygen. He felt better straight away and was able to react to the fuel issue. But it's very insidious and creeps up on you.

The trumping begins when the pressure is lowered in the chamber to simulate climbing to higher altitudes.

I was giggling behind my oxygen mask and from the crumpled lines around their eyes I could tell the others were too.

When we had reached the pressure equivalent of 10,000 feet, the safety observer got us to take off our masks and sign our names. So far, so good, although the smell in the chamber was foul. Then they held up flash cards with pictures on and motioned to us to draw them on a pad on our knees. I produced a very passable flower and I was even more pleased with my airplane.

As were climbed higher we were asked to write down the answers to some simple sums on our pads, followed by more drawing. In the debrief later it turned out I was scribbling all sorts of gibberish, although in the chamber I thought I was doing well. Eventually it got to the point when I couldn't be bothered to write anything down at all.

Above 40,000 feet, breathing 100 per cent oxygen isn't enough to offset the effects of hypoxia. This is because the partial pressure of the oxygen in the atmosphere is lower.

To counter this, you wear a mask which pumps oxygen into your mouth at a higher pressure than the ambient pressure. The force of the oxygen means every time you open your mouth it fills with air and expands like a balloon. To speak you have to keep your mouth very small.

Now we were asked to make pretend radio transmissions while doing pressured breathing. I accidentally caught Vossers looking my way. We both started to laugh. But with my great sucking roar I was drowning on oxygen. This set everyone else off. The staff had to stop the pressurised breathing session while we all calmed down.

Rocking up to RAF Linton-on-Ouse a few days later I felt like my flying career was really about to take off. This was where those of us who had advanced in the fast jet stream took another step towards getting our wings at RAF Valley.

I had been flying similar piston-engine propeller aircraft for my entire aviation life so far, but now I would be learning to fly the Tucano, a two-seat turbo-prop trainer. It still has a propeller but its powerful turbine engine can take it to speeds nearing 300 knots – double the speed of the Firefly. The instructor's seat is behind the pilot, not side by side, which I had been used to up until then. The Tucano is basically a cross between a propeller plane and a jet and the perfect stepping stone.

RAF Linton is about ten miles north west of York, which made it feel like the centre of the universe compared with what I had been used to in sleepy old Lincolnshire. Having a big city so close screamed nightlife, shopping, entertainment and life outside the RAF.

The atmosphere on the base was buzzing with loads of pilots, instructors, trainers and students all there to fly Tucanos. Even the smell of the place was different. The jet fuel, or Avtur, the Tucano used had a more pungent, exciting, racier nose to it than the petrol of the piston engines. Like moving from a youth wearing Brut to a real man rocking some sort of Gucci Italian love potion.

As usual, 155 Basic Flying Training course began with ground school, but whereas the JEFTS course was about teaching flying to beginners, this was very much type-specific, so it was all about learning the intricacies of the Tucano and about high-speed, high-altitude flight.

About a week in I got a call from Liz. She was back from India and something horrendous had happened. She had had a call from the Royal Mail to say her three carpets had arrived and there was an import tax of £180 per carpet to pay.

She was shocked but coughed up and repeatedly called the number the guy had given us but there was no answer. She was beginning to smell a rat and feeling terrible about the whole thing. Shortly after, my first package arrived at Linton. I paid the duty, but when I unwrapped it, I felt sick when I saw a thin, polyester rug like a prayer mat. Nothing like the beautiful carpets we had seen in Agra. I was so upset. I couldn't believe we had fallen for the scam. It all seemed too long-winded and elaborate not to be true, but now here we were having paid about £500 for some worthless tat plus the import duty. It would end up costing more than the whole holiday. Every couple of days another rug would arrive in the mess to add to my dismay.

I told the guys on my course and in true RAF fashion the floodgates to the harshest banter were opened. That is the great thing about the military; you can't dwell on misfortune for very long. You have to crack on with the next thing. One of my rugs even ended up in the mess's Christmas Draw as a prize, just to ram home the joke.

Towards the end we transitioned to the simulator, an exact replica of a Tucano cockpit, housed in a big dome on the airfield. You climbed up into it, fully kitted out for a flight even down to having maps in your leg pockets. The cockpit was dark, save for the lights of the instruments, and outside the canopy window was a projection of the local area, which moved as you flew. We began with the basics, going through instrument flying, and then practising emergency procedures, such as the loss of an engine or instrument failure.

It was so realistic that if something went badly wrong you could get to a point where you had to eject. Not that you would physically fire from the seat but to the extent that was the only course of action left open to you.

But simulating ejecting caused the whole machine to freeze and it took ages to get it back online, so I was always urged, 'If you must eject, just say you're going to do it. Don't pull the bloody handle, please.'

At the end of ground school, we went on a week-long combat survival course back up at Otterburn. In full combat kit and camouflaged up to the eyeballs we yomped into a huge forest and learned how to build shelters from sticks and moss and live off the land.

The instructors gathered us in to demonstrate how to set snares for rabbits and then gave us a lesson in dispatching them. Not much science to this one – find a big tree, smack their heads against it until dead. Skinning was the fiddly bit.

That evening, when the staff had left us to it in our little camp in the woods, we sneaked into the top of a steeply sloping field and placed a series of snares in the hedge.

It was a warm, early summer's night and the clear sky was turning to a purple dusk. We circled back around to the bottom of the field and fanned out in a long line. We walked slowly up the hill, clapping our hands and shouting, hoping to drive any rabbits towards our traps. It worked like a dream and we found half a dozen rabbits tangled up in the snares.

Back in camp, I wasn't too keen on the head-tree-wallop manoeuvre but I didn't mind getting stuck into some skinning.

I had finished two when there was a lot of shouting and commotion. We had been told we would be 'attacked' at some point that night and should be ready to escape, but we'd assumed it would be in the middle of the night.

I scooped up the two skinless rabbits, stuffed them down the front of my combat jacket and dashed off into the woods.

We had been told that when the attack came we should go to ground and stay there until a whistle sounded to signify the end of the exercise. I bounded through the undergrowth and after running for about two minutes I dived into a little hollow underneath a holly bush and made myself comfortable. Time passed, the light dimmed and everything was quiet, save for the natural sounds of the forest.

The rumbling of my empty stomach was threatening to shatter the silence.

My position was pretty hidden and in my pocket was my small Hexi burner. I reckoned the staff had gone back to their camp for some nosebag and had left us to an evening in the open. I figured if I could shield the flame from the outside of the hollow I would be OK. I pulled the rabbits from down the front of my jacket and took out my penknife. I lit the burner and hacked off a chunk of flesh and held it in the flame. The sizzling seemed ear-splitting in my paranoid state, but the smell... mmm. I scoffed both of the rabbits virtually to the bone and nestled down to sleep on a blanket of leaves and moss, cradling my aching belly.

For the last couple of days of the exercise we would be going on the run in the wilds of Otterburn.

I formed a trio with DK and Batters and armed with only a map, a set of coordinates, our newly acquired survival skills and a bit of guile, we were to navigate to various checkpoints while evading a hunter force from the Black Watch, then part of the Royal Highland Regiment. These were regular army hardnuts who were hell bent on bagging some junior RAF officers and aspiring fast-jet jocks.

We tootled off into the night, half jogging, half fast walking and found the first checkpoint after about an hour. We checked the map under a poncho to keep the light hidden and set off for the second checkpoint. We emerged from a wood and used its backdrop as cover to skirt around the edge of a grassy field. Stealth was the key.

But an almighty roar erupted from the grass in front of us.

'GO, GO, GO... GOT YOU, YOU RAF PONCES ...' The whole earth seemed to lift up and start chasing us.

My heart surged as if someone had applied a pair of electric paddles to it. I bolted towards the wood line, adrenaline coursing through my system, and jumped up onto a barbed wire fence following Batters and DK who had beaten me to it. But whereas they got clean over and scampered into the bushes, I snagged my trouser leg on the wire and was left hanging upside down on the opposite side with my face on the ground.

Seconds later, some great big oaf with coffee and cigarette breath wrestled me off and manhandled me the ground. He knelt on me with most of his weight and dug me in the ribs with his elbows as he pulled off my balaclava. 'Hello. We've got ourselves a flipping girlie,' he said. 'Where's the rest of them?'

He sat me up and barked a few questions at me, playing the hard man act with swearing ever other word for added clout. To be fair, when you've just been jumped in a field on a dark night, it's quite effective.

There were about five them, all big, in combats with black balaclavas with just the eyes peering out. Coffee breath told me to sit with my legs crossed, my back straight and my hands on my head, the classic stress position.

'Right, we know you're out there, we've got your mate. If you don't come out now, we'll shoot her,' he shouted into the darkness.

The rules of the game were that teams had to stick together, so I knew, and he knew, that Batters and DK would be nearby, skulking in the bushes. There was no immediate movement, so he turned his attention back to me, giving me a small boot in the ribs just for kicks.

'Fellas, you know the rules, now bloody well come out,' he tried again.

Twigs and branches snapped and leaves rustled as DK and Batters emerged out of the darkness. They were immediately pounced on and taken down, like lions on baby zebras. They were both forced into a stress position and we were all blindfolded and made to sit there for what felt like ages.

I could sense the Black Watch guys pacing around us, but under the hood I couldn't make out any of their whispers. Eventually we were hauled up and escorted down what felt like a muddy track. An engine sparked up out of nowhere, startling me, and I was bundled into the back of a vehicle, perhaps a Land Rover.

'Keep your hands on your head,' roared a voice.

We were driven, more like bounced, around for a while before the vehicle stopped.

'Get out.' It's not that easy with a hood on and I banged my head on the roof of whatever it was.

Outside, my hood was whipped off and when my eyes had adjusted, I saw Batters and DK next to me in a clearing. The big burly Black Watch guys slammed the door shut – I was right about the Land Rover – and came over to us with a map.

'You're here. Now scarper.' And with that little dose of scaremongering we were back in the game.

We celebrated the end of ground school with a night out in York. We ended up in a nightclub, and I was introduced to a tall, good-looking guy called Jason. Hello ladies, I thought. I was flirting away, just for fun and told him I was training to be a fast-jet pilot. He didn't really say what he did and I forgot to chase it up.

I was trying hard but getting nowhere. I switched to the emergency banter frequency, hoping to make some kind of impression, but he was having none of it.

On Monday morning I walked into the 2 Squadron crew room to meet my instructors for the flying part of the course. Obviously, Mr Friday Night was standing there grinning. Hello, Mandy. Trainee fast-jet pilot, I seem to remember? I'm Flt Lt Jas Hawker, I'm one of your instructors.

Genius. Nice one, Wellsey.

'Oh, Sir, I'm really sorry, I was just on a high after finishing ground school.'

'Don't worry, it was a fun night. Look forward to flying with you.'

Jas went on to become the Officer Commanding Red Arrows.

My first instructor was Wing Commander Orton, the chief instructor for the whole station. The first time he took me up we raced off over the North Yorkshire moors flying so fast and so low I was convinced he was breaking the rules. It turned out he was right on the money at 250ft. I just hadn't reset my visual image of what flying at this speed and this height was now going to look like.

It was the first aircraft I had flown with a retractable undercarriage, so every time I had to say 'gear up, flaps up' after take-off made me feel like the real deal.

Moving onto advanced instrument flying we were made to attach a helmet visor: essentially an eye shield which obscured any view out of the cockpit but allowed us to see the gauges and dials inside.

We then had to fly radar instrument patterns blind, relying on our trust in the instruments. The instructor in the rear seat could see if we lifted our heads up to peak out and cheat.

Our training sorties took us all around the country, landing at different airfields for practice. With various instructors I went up to Edinburgh, Cranwell, St Mawgan in Cornwall, RAF Leeming in north Yorkshire, RAF West Freugh in Scotland and RAF Leuchars near St Andrews, where I did a talk to the air squadron cadets.

After about ten days I was ready for my first solo, but because the circuit at Linton was pretty busy, they sent me off to Dishforth airfield, just north of Linton.

I flew up with Wing Commander Orton and did a couple of circuits before landing. He got out to go and watch from the air traffic control tower and then I taxied back out. 'Dishforth Tower, Lima Oscar Papa 44 ready for departure, runway one niner.'

I took off again, flew four circuits, taxied round and then did four more before coming in to pick him up.

The first time I taxied out I made a potentially dangerous error which taught me a valuable lesson.

When Wing Commander Orton had got out, I had put the seat pin in, so the ejector seat didn't accidentally fire me out. It was all a bit different to the usual routine, so when I re-taxied and did my checks I missed something. I took off, flew the circuits and came back to land. As I pulled up in front of the tower, I realised the ejection seat pin was still in, which meant it wouldn't have worked if I had needed to eject in an emergency.

Oh. My. Gosh. Obviously nothing happened and I was fine, but it was a massive wake-up call.

It's not that I was being blasé, I was working as hard as I could, but it was the first time I fully grasped the importance of the routine in checks.

I felt sheepish and embarrassed and climbed out of the aircraft like a furtive dog, which knows it's done something wrong. I didn't even file a safety report because I didn't want to look stupid. Why say I messed up when nobody else knew? Phew, got away with that one.

But as a trainer now looking back, not to alert others to the potential pitfalls is at best bad practice. How bad would I have felt if somebody else had done that and had to eject, and I hadn't mentioned it? It makes me quite sad that this was the frame of mind and the culture that existed at the time.

It had been an evening full of pomp and ceremony, with the best silverware, smartest uniforms, haggis, neeps and tatties, speeches and military drinking. It was Burns Night and the Officers' mess at RAF Linton had gone big.

I was in my smartest gear, the No.5 dress uniform, which consisted of a long skirt down to the ground. This was no good for dancing. Swaying demurely, yes. But not dancing. Not how I do it anyway. Hitching it up a bit helped but rolling it up a few times at the waistband gave me far more freedom. That was more like it, now I could really groove. Get down on it... do... do... doo... Oh... what... a night...

On Monday morning everyone in the mess was still buzzing from the bash. The talk of the town was the punishment meted out to toast-master Rich P for pausing nine seconds between saying 'Ladies and Gentlemen', and... 'The Queen' during the loyal toast. It was a cult and much-anticipated game but pushing the pausing record out to nine seconds was stretching things a bit. It felt like a lifetime and did not go down well. He'd been given mess duties for two weeks including two weekends. Not good.

I was minding my own business at my desk when I was called to the boss's office. No big deal, I got on well with this one. Bring your hat, added the messenger. Oh no, a hat-no-coffee chat. I was in deep dwang here. I was wracking my brains to work out what I'd done wrong. Other than a few cheeky gags during my lassies' reply to the lads' speech, one of the cornerstones of Burns Night dinners, I couldn't think. The evening got a bit hazy after that. I knocked on his door and waited to be called in.

'Don't sit down, Mandy,' he said.
Oh. My. Gosh. What is this?
'So, talk me through Friday.'
My mind was racing. Which bit?
'My speech?'
'No.'
'In the bar?'
'Not exactly.'
'Er...'
'Anything to do with your uniform?'
Crikey. Did I set fire to it?

'It's been reported to me you altered your uniform by lifting up your skirt to an indecent level.'
  'With all due respect, Sir, have you ever tried dancing in one of those skirts? It was still below the knee.' Only just.
  'It's not particularly feminine and not particularly professional. And you were heard swearing.'

'Oh.'

It's not like I was the only one.

'So what would you like to do?' He was fishing now.

'Sorry, Sir, I don't quite follow you?'

'Would you like to volunteer to do anything, Mandy? Mess duties, perhaps?'

I thought, if you haven't got the balls to order me, I'm not going to offer. And anyway, all the men around me were swearing. Why should I be singled out just because I'm a woman? Is it so un-ladylike to let off a few f-bombs in a bar late at night? The busybody who reported this must be a sad case.

'Well, no, not really, Sir.'

The boss leant back in his chair and glanced out of the window. Turning back to me I could trace the outline of a grin.

'Oh, just get out, Mandy.'

CHAPTER 6

NEW FRONTIERS

 loved the Tucano. It was a fantastic little airplane: agile, fast and smooth and felt like flying a mini fast jet.

Twice the speed at half the height equals four times the rush. That's what it feels like flying low level in a Tucano for the first time.

My previous low-level flying on the Firefly had been restricted to 500 feet because it is a civilian aircraft whereas the Tucano is military and is allowed to drop to 250 feet at nearly 300 knots.

Trusting the altimeter for low level is not always the best policy because it's not sensitive enough for such fine margins. It gives you the height above the mean sea level, not the ground.

So initially you had to do it with a visual picture. The rule of thumb was pretty simple. At 500ft you could see the legs of cows but you couldn't see the legs of sheep. When you got down to 250ft you could see the legs of sheep. It was very technical.

We began our low-level training up over the North Yorkshire moors. Jas would take it down to 250ft and hand it over, but I would subconsciously start climbing back up before I could programme my brain to be comfortable down in the weeds.

'Mands, you're creeping up, get back down.'

It was all about keeping your head out of the cockpit, flicking your gaze from left to right, forward and back, keeping an eye on the terrain and anticipating what was coming. One thing to avoid was ridge clipping. You could become so focused on the big hill coming up you failed to notice the smaller hill in front of you and could be in danger of skimming the surface.

At this stage our flying also became a bit more tactical. We'd go up to the North Yorkshire moors, the Dales, the Pennines or the Lake District and fly routes using the valleys for protection, not just in a straight line from A to B. Working out timings became even more important.

I loved the challenge of planning a route. I liked going into the big operations room at the side of the taxi way at Linton and working out all the timings and turning points on a route, getting the weather, speaking to the engineers, walking to the flight line and seeing twenty aircraft all lined up, climbing in and taking off on a mission.

One early problem I struggled with was over map-reading, which generally occurred when you didn't have faith in the techniques and your planning. I was very guilty of crawling my finger along the map, rather than having my eyes out of the cockpit.

My habits were quickly solved by Dick Shuster, known as the 'The Shu', who was one of our instructors, an old and bold pilot and a real character.

He took my meticulous flight plan and map and disappeared before coming back with a small sheet of white paper with a few numbers written on it in thick purple felt tip.

They were headings, timings and turning points. That was it. No map, nothing else, just basic numbers.

'There's your map Mandy, let's go,' he said.

'But Sir...'

'This should cure your over map reading. There's nothing to look at.'

Sure enough, we flew the sortie into Northumberland with the route as good as scribbled on the back of a fag packet and guess what? It went fine. It was proof the system works. I've never over-read a map since.

Basic formation flying was another key skill to master and we'd go up in a two or three-ship to practice keeping station on your mate's wing. Or we did tail chasing, taking it in turns to be leader and twisting and turning all over the sky while the chaser tried to stick to you like glue.

The part of the course I liked best was night flying. This was the first time I had been up in the dark and I loved the serenity of the night sky. The bustle of the working day at the airfield had died down so there was only us about and there was very little radio traffic, so it felt very calm. By its nature you need good weather for night flying, certainly in training, so the nights we went up were always clear, stunning and filled with stars. On high-level navigation exercises you could often see coast to coast. It could be disconcerting, though, because of course it was basically pitch-black outside, which meant a lot of trust in your instruments, especially on landing.

One trainee on the course in front didn't like flying at night. The story goes he taxied off and hid his aircraft behind a hangar and made all the radio calls he would use during the circuit from there. You can imagine the air traffic controller, slightly puzzled going, erm, I can't quite see him but he's requesting clearance to land. Apparently, he taxied back forty minutes later, still keeping up the deception. He was only rumbled when the engineers realised no fuel had been used.

Towards the end of our time at Linton we were tasked as a course to organise an expedition. It was trumpeted as an exercise in logistical planning and team building.

The course ahead of us had gone parachuting in Florida. Right, we'll have some of that, then. But our plan was soon scuppered when the budget was slashed.

We opted instead for a week in Norway, an outward-bound expedition combining cross-country skiing and a bit of arctic survival.

We went on the overnight ferry from Newcastle to Stavanger and got a bus up to Hovden in the rocky Setesdalsheiene mountains.

We spent the first couple of days learning to telemark ski with an adventure training instructor, hiking uphill on the skis with seal skins attached to the bases to stop us sliding backwards before pointing them downhill.

It was hot work, and I had kitted myself out in a stores-issue purple ski jacket and trousers with fleecy liner. Anytime I moved I sweated buckets. With a bright red face and sweat-matted hair I looked like Waynetta Slob from the Harry Enfield Show.

We did some wilderness hikes and learned how to drill holes in the ice on the lake to catch fish. One day we made snow holes and were supposed to sleep in them that night, but we were bonding very well as a team and persuaded the instructor that another session in the bar would be more useful.

Back at Linton to round off the course the staff organised an aerobatics competition. We were each given one practice flight and then it was show time. I started with a half Cuban, then pulled a one quarter vertical roll into a Noddy stall turn, a one quarter descending vertical roll to align with the crowd line, a slow aileron roll, a stall turn left to reverse the direction into a barrel roll, a stall turn right, a Canadian break and a Prince of Wales to finish. Have some of that boys.

I got through to the three-way final with DK and Rodders and went through the routine again for the chief instructor to judge. This time I had to settle for second behind DK.

In the background I was still in turmoil over Craig. I had tried desperately hard not to contact him when I got back from

India but I failed, miserably. Almost the first phone call I made was to him. We met up a few times but we had to keep it top secret.

We both admitted we were struggling badly and didn't think we could bear to be apart. But it was messy and complicated and shouldn't be happening for all sorts of reasons. Love is rarely straightforward and it was a very turbulent time. I experienced the most intense feelings I'd ever had. We went through so many enforced split ups only to get back on the phone again a few days later.

Towards the end of our time at Linton, Vossers asked if I was seeing Hicko. I couldn't meet his eye and blushed. I just couldn't think of how to answer a straight question. I knew the game was up. 'Yes.' 'Oh, great because he's a top man and we all love him,' came the reply. Little did they know the turbulence we'd been through. I felt like a weight lifting from my shoulders that we could now be open and no longer had to conduct our relationship in the shadows.

I graduated near the top of the course at Linton and felt like I was at my flying peak. The Tucano was an aircraft I loved and very much within my capacity. I was relaxed and enjoying it.

As I moved on to Hawks and then the Tornado everything got more complicated, more intense and twisted my melon far more.

Before going to RAF Valley to start my fast jet flying course I was posted to Boscombe Down in Wiltshire for another spell 'flying a desk', the expression for pilots who have been lumbered with an office job.

I'd requested Boscombe Down as I was now officially seeing Craig and living in Winchester, which was only half an hour away. We moved into his sister, Vanessa's flat and it gave me a wonderful opportunity to get to know Elliot and Chessie, Craig's children a bit better.

Boscombe Down, near the village of Amesbury in Wiltshire, was home to the RAF's Empire Test Pilot School (ETPS). It also housed elements of the RAF's School of Aviation Medicine, Fast Jet Test Squadron (FJTS) and the Strike Attack Operational Evaluation Unit (SAOEU).

The great thing about the posting for me (and Vossers who'd also requested Boscombe) was that we were Johnny-on-the-spot if anyone had a spare backseat during test flights.

Even better, our mate Rodders was on the FJTS ops desk upstairs. He was able to hand out Hawk trips like Robin Hood dished out venison.

My first ride in a proper fast jet, as opposed to the Tucano, was in a Hunter; a big, robust, historic aircraft.

I went up with Flt Lt Justin P and when he put full power on and took the brakes off, the acceleration was like being in a souped-up dragster. I was pinned to my seat, gurning ridiculously but loving it. It was everything I hoped it would be. Faster than anything I'd been in before, with bags of g-force. It was the first time I'd worn a g-suit.

The g-suit is like a pair of chaps that cowboys wear around their legs, except these come up over your waist and have bladders in them which inflate. You plug them into the aircraft's anti-g system when you climb in and when you are pulling g – or accelerating fast – they inflate around your legs, squeezing your blood vessels to stop the blood pooling in your lower limbs, which can cause you to black out, lose consciousness and ultimately crash. If you are in a g turn, as most are in the Hawk, it can narrow your vision and make it turn monochromatic.

There is also a bladder around your middle and the instant you pull g you have to tense your stomach muscles because it feels like you are being punched in the guts when it inflates.

I couldn't believe what a whack it gave me. Woah there, what the hell was that...?

'Fancy a go?' asked Justin. 'Too bloody right I do.' I just did some level flying and general handling but it felt like I had come home.

A few days later I bagged a ride in a Jaguar, the RAF's supersonic attack fighter. It's normally a single-seater and reserved for the real Top Guns but this was a training version with a backseat. The pilot took us off to Wales for some low-level flying. 'Might as well give you an experience to remember,' he said. Flashing through the valleys at 250ft with the hillsides racing past in a blur of green and brown above us was the best rush I'd ever had. It was also the most physical flying I'd ever done with the g-suit giving me a real beating up.

One of the highlights was a flight in a Harvard, the old snub-nose twin-seat war-horse with a long canopy my grandfather flew in the Second World War.

With at least another six months before Valley was due to start, I asked the authorities whether it would be possible to take some time off to go travelling. I thought this would be my last chance for an extended trip before my career and my relationship really took off. Or didn't, depending on how I did.

My request was duly refused, but later that day someone from Strike Attack OEU put his head into our room and said he heard I was keen to go travelling. Did I fancy coming to Las Vegas with them to work as an ops clerk for three months?

These guys would be trialling new bombs and weapons systems for Harriers, Jaguars and Tornados and they needed a driver and general dogsbody.

It sounded brilliant but I didn't really fancy the full three months. I rang Matt Lindley, who was holding at HQ, and asked him if he wanted to split it, six weeks each. He was bang up for it, and the Strike Attack guys agreed to it.

I flew out with the ground crew in a Hercules, via Goose Bay in Canada, to Ridgecrest in the Arizona desert.

Ridgecrest was a Hicksville town in the middle of nowhere with a huge two-land blacktop running through it, surrounded by red dust. To pop into a shop over the road you had to get in your car: there was no way of nipping across on foot.

My job was pretty mundane, picking up and dropping off the pilots, delivering packed lunches and helping with flight planning, but it was all good experience working with different parts of the RAF, meeting new pilots and getting further immersed in the world of military aviation.

I had every weekend off, so I made the most of it. Once a group of us drove to San Diego and one of the guys hired a yacht to go out sailing. Another time we flew up to San Francisco for a couple of nights.

After a month in Ridgecrest we spent the last few weeks in Las Vegas where the unit would be using the Nevada bombing ranges.

In my downtime I sampled a bit of Vegas life and went to the Grand Canyon. It was a great trip and it had just made my travel itch worse.

I asked again if I could take some time off, using all the leave I'd saved up. This time, bingo. Six weeks off. Australia here I come.

I flew into Cairns, and stayed at a cheap-as-chips backpacker joint for ten dollars a night with dinner and a beer thrown in.

Even though I was earning a decent wage I wanted to meet some fun, like-minded people, hence joining the backpacker circuit.

I travelled on the Oz Experience bus, a regular service where you can get on and off whenever takes your fancy. I could be as sociable or as quiet as I wanted to be and could be whoever I wanted to be. Word seemed to have spread though, and quite often new people would greet me as the "laughing pilot" before I'd had a chance to introduce myself.

I did all the usual backpacker stuff; a PADI diving course on the Barrier Reef, a tandem skydive over Mission Beach, white-water rafting, a four by four trip to Fraser Island and I joined the crew of a maxi yacht to cruise around the Whitsundays for a few days from Airlie Beach. My best friend from school days, Sarah Sellers joined me for part of it and acted as a courier for my tandem sky-diving video and dropped it off to Craig in Winchester. As I was waving to the camera, falling through the sky, Elliot and Chessie were frantically waving back at the television not realising I was on the other side of the world.

I was wandering through the market in Byron Bay one morning when a wrinkled, heavily tanned lady asked if I would like to have my palm read. I was feeling suitably bohemian so said 'sure, why not?' By now I looked like your typical backpacker with sun-bleached hair, wearing a short blue sundress and sandals. No jewellery, no watch. Nothing could have suggested I was an officer in the RAF. She turned over my hands and stared at my palms.

The first thing she said was I was very run down. Oh, there's a surprise, I thought. I'm a backpacker and I've been burning the midnight oil all the way down the east coast of Australia.

'You're seeing someone a lot older than yourself.'

Erm, ok, how did she know that?

'There are two children already... you're going to be with him forever... There'll be two more, but not yet... You're in education of some sort...'

Here we go, butted in my cynical self, she hasn't got a clue now.

'... But it's not normal education is it? You're in... have you taken a sabbatical? I can see trees whizzing past you very quickly. You're not a pilot are you... I'm thinking military?'

I didn't say a word but I was quite floored. How did she know? I'd been careful not to give her any clues. She carried on.

'At thirty-eight you'll have a huge career change...'

Well, actually you're wrong there, I thought, I only signed up for a short-service commission taking me until I was thirty-two. Ironically, I did stay in until I was thirty-eight and did have a complete change of life.

'I can see you helping others.' This didn't tie in with the usual post-RAF pilot life of commercial flying.

'You're very close to your mum and older sister, but you also have a younger sister (that would be my very sweet half-sister Frances who'd just started at secondary school).'

I was completely blown away by it and went to sit on the beach to mull it over. It made me believe there is a bigger picture out there. Some other spirituality. It made me wonder whether life is mapped out as obviously as that.

Back at Linton I had to put my flower-power travelling days behind me and dust off my RAF officer persona. I logged another twenty-six hours in the Tucano to sharpen up the flying ready for the biggie.

RAF Valley, fast-jet training. Hawks. Make or break. Bring it on.

CHAPTER 7

THE JET STREAM

My eyes were opening wider by the minute. We were all laughing, but my bravado was only on the outside. I'd been at RAF Valley less than an hour and the horror stories had already started.

The worst of the lot was the one about the Air Vice-Marshal's son who was chopped two flights from the end. The clincher to the tale was that his dad was going to be the one handing out the wings at the graduation parade.

I sipped my wine as if to dislodge this growing lump in my throat. I noticed my knuckles had turned white.

Oh my gosh. It's that brutal. It doesn't matter who your dad is, if you dip below the standard, you're out. If it can happen to him, it can happen to anyone. Especially me. That summed up how the next ten months of my life were going to be. Living on the edge, only a couple of bad days in the office away from losing my dream.

Valley is the RAF's training centre for fast jet pilots and search and rescue helicopter crews. With three runways, it's the busiest military airfield in the UK, flying 100s of sorties a week.

It's a long way from anywhere, a bleak, remote outpost on the western edge of the island of Anglesey in north west Wales.

Driving over the bridge crossing the Menai Straits on Sunday evening was like a symbolic step into another world, every mile further on down the old A5 felt further from civilisation. Valley's stark, characterless buildings did little to put me at ease.

At least I was surrounded by familiar faces. All my chums from the Tucano course were there – Rob, Chris, Tristar, Andy, Rich and Neil. I'd been through officer training with most of them and had been bumbling around with the same crew for three years. These guys were my best friends, real brothers in arms.

Plenty of other old faces on courses ahead of us poked their noses into the bar at some stage that evening. We were all going through this big sausage factory and getting churned out at different times. That's how the horror stories filtered back.

I hardly slept that night because of the thoughts bouncing around my head like a game of pinball. What if I get found out? What if they rumble my rubbish navigation? What if...? Then I'd gee myself up. It's all there for the taking. What an amazing opportunity. It's yours, go get it. Dream it, do it, become a fast jet pilot. I'd wake from a half-sleep revved up and raring to go, only for the worries to seep back.

Even though I had won awards for my flying, I still had a deep-seated anxiety about not having passed my aptitude tests to be an RAF pilot. I was aware I had been taken on as a sort of test case. That had become a bit of a burden to me. If you're taken on to see how far through the system you can get before you fail, then in some ways you are set up to fail and are always waiting for the end. Whereas, if you're thinking you're there to pass, it's a very different mindset.

Oh, and of course, I was the only girl, so I stuck out like a sore thumb anyway, which at times was quite challenging. In many ways the drab dawn of Monday morning was a relief from my nocturnal head spin.

But before the glamour of whizzing a Hawk at low level through the valleys of Snowdonia or the Lake District, waving casually to the punters on the hillside and looking cool in aviator shades, I had six weeks of ground school to look forward to. Six weeks of theory and tights, back in my beloved blue No.2 uniform.

The first few weeks in the drab lecture hall were spent purely learning about engines, electrics, hydraulics and how does a Hawk even fly anyway?

I was never that technically minded. Nothing to do with being a woman, just not very interested. Has it got an engine? Great. Does it work? Fingers crossed.

As far as the theory goes, I'm not that far beyond your basic suck, squeeze, bang, blow. I was surrounded by guys who were positively frothing at the inner workings of a Rolls-Royce Turbomeca Adour engine. It didn't really float my boat.

There were two guys on our course who were Cambridge aeronautical engineering graduates. They had so much capacity, photographic memories and could absorb all this technical information. I would have to spend hours and hours just reading to cram this stuff into my brain

A large proportion of our time in those early days was spent in front of our old favourite, the cardboard cockpit, chair flying in our rooms after dinner.

The Hawk – the jet of Red Arrows fame – in those days was the T Mk 1, which had a quite old-fashioned analogue cockpit, so lots of dials and gauges and navigating with paper maps, a stopwatch and a compass.

Nowadays they train on the Hawk T Mk 2, which has a similar cockpit to the Tornado or Typhoon with a moving map and Head-Up Display (HUD). That's the green writing that is projected onto a glass screen in the front of the cockpit, with information such as heading, speed, altitude and angle of attack.

The good thing about our Hawk was it was fairly simple and could be started up in about fifteen minutes. That's fairly similar to the Tucano so it wasn't a massive jump up in the amount of checks we had to go through. Still, you had to know them better than the back of your hand.

In the second half of ground school we added sessions in the simulator. Strapped into the replica cockpit, with the gauges glowing blue in the dark and Valley's virtual runway spread out below me, the Hawk felt within spitting distance.

I was close to my dream of flying a fast jet but first I had to get past the ground school exams, which meant noses pressed into books every night.

The stuff was going in, but unlike the air being forced into the Hawk's engine, not very quickly.

When we weren't up to our eyeballs in engines, avionics, pre-flight checks and simulators, we still had to exercise our bodies in a steady stream of healthy outdoor pursuits. There were other aspects to being fast jet pilot we had to learn, such as what to do if you ditched in the sea. For this we boarded a boat and took to the cold, grey waters off Holyhead. Dressed in a full immersion suit with flying kit over the top, plus boots and helmet, we each had to jump in and be pulled along in the wake to simulate being dragged by your parachute after ejecting and landing in the drink.

'OK Mandy, whenever you're ready...'

Already shivering in the autumn morning, I took a deep breath, inflated my lifejacket, folded my arms across my chest and took a big step into the Irish Sea. The cold shock hit me like I'd been punched in the stomach and I surfaced spluttering and sucking at the air. I felt the yank on the harness as the slack was taken up and I was pulled face first through the water by the boat, like a giant fishing lure. Knowing I had to act quickly, I heaved myself over, so I was lying on my back and spread my legs like a starfish to make a more stable platform.

I scrabbled to find my harness clasp and swallowed mouthfuls of spray as I fiddled with the release mechanism. Come on, you little blighter. Yes, done it. The harness flew off with the boat and I came to a stop. I grasped the line attached to my waist that was trailing my personal survival pack and started hauling it in.

This was the base of the ejection seat, which you released to dangle below you when you were parachuting down. I grabbed the box and pulled the black and yellow handle on top. Nothing happened so I did it again, while kicking my legs furiously to stay afloat.

Suddenly it burst open to reveal the single-seat orange life raft that would be my lifeline. When it was semi-inflated, I flung my arms over the side and tried to pull myself in but my saturated flying kit weighed me down. I half squashed the side and kicked like Michael Phelps to get over the edge. I flopped into the bottom like the world's most ungraceful seal. Done it. Blimey. If I had any kind of injuries from ejecting, likely to be some sort of arm issues from flailing on exiting the cockpit, I would have serious problems getting in. Especially if the sea was rough. It goes to show why you've got to be in good physical condition in the first place.

I'm staring down the west runway at Valley. The slate-coloured strip stretches to the horizon, with grass on either side. Over the far fence is the sea. In front of me the instruments are alight. The high-pitched whine of the jet engine makes the whole machine feel alive. I've finished my checks and get on the radio.

'Good morning, Tower, this is Victor Yankee Tango (VYT) 76 ready for departure.'

'Victor 76, you are clear for take-off runway one three, climbing flight level 200, turning right onto heading 190 contacting departures stud three.' Studs are the pre-set radio frequencies for various airfields.

I repeat the message back word for word. I give the pronounced nod that says I am about to go and push the throttle forward with my left hand. The noise builds to a roar and I ease my feet off the brakes. The jet lurches forward like a catapult, slamming me into the seat. The thrust...oh my gosh. That's why I wanted to fly fast jets. My eyes flick down to the speed gauge and when we hit the pre-set take-off speed I pull back on the stick with my right hand. The nose twitches and then lifts into the air.

Gear up, flaps up, I say, cool as you like. We climb out to the west over Cymyran beach and lines of white water from breaking waves. The gunmetal grey of the Irish Sea is spread out below.

I rock the stick over to the right and we cut a tight arc back around towards the Welsh coast. The g-force pins me in my seat and I feel the suit tighten around my legs.

This is exactly where I want to be and I can't take the smile off my face, mainly because the g-force has stuck it there. But it could be permanent, a fast jet thing.

I pull back hard and the jet responds instantly, tipping us onto our backs with our feet pointing in the general direction of space. We roar upwards, slicing through wispy cloud into brilliant clear air. I pull a bit more and the nose gently tilts over the top. Inverted now, I can see the whole of Anglesey below me. I bring the Hawk slowly round until we complete the loop and achieve level flight again.

I look all around me to check the sky is clear before pulling back the stick as before. This time, about five eighths of the way around the loop I push the stick to the left and we roll from being inverted to level flight, going in the opposite direction. This is known as a half Cuban eight. To make it into a full Cuban I do the same manoeuvre to end up flying back the way I was going in the first place, effectively completing a figure of eight.

I'm relishing the speed and agility of the Hawk. The Tucano we had just been flying had a normal operating speed of 240 knots, nudging 300 knots all out. Now we would be flying at about 420 knots and sometimes up to 500. The air speed indicator finally read as a Mach number: you could hit over Mach one in a dive, and that's faster than the speed of sound.

If the Tucano felt like a sedate family car with a propeller right in front of you and a long bonnet, the Hawk felt like you were driving a souped-up mini. The view was better and suddenly you could see over the front edge. With that came a heightened feeling of speed across the ground, added to the fact you were doing twice the speed of a Tucano at take-off – 110 knots.

After nine logged hours of flying with an instructor I was let off the leash. My first solo trip was brilliant and simple. Take off in a fifteen million pound jet, leave Holy Island to my left, fly as fast as I can around Anglesey and land back at Valley.

That first solo was like taking the stabilisers off your bike for the first time. Climbing out of the cockpit that day I had the same swagger as a five-year-old with their new-found freedom.

I felt confident. I could handle this. I belonged here.

The bar was packed that night for a tradition known as the 'solo barrel', a macho, willy-waving, how-much-can-you-drink celebration of our first solo trip in the Hawk.

All of us who had gone solo up to that point chipped in for a barrel of beer, hence the name. But this wasn't a pleasant summer evening spent sipping ale politely on the lawn.

In our flying suits, we were lined up and handed a succession of shots. Downing them in one was the only option. Crème de menthe made for a cheeky opener, followed by a smooth hit of Baileys and then in a convenient nod to the squadron colours, Blue Curacao and banana schnapps.

We washed these down by necking a pint of beer and then a glass of milk. Strangely, this was what caused all the problems for those with less than cast-iron stomachs.

I was given absolutely no quarter for being a woman. I suppose I had been yearning to be one of the boys, so I couldn't really complain. Suitably sozzled, we shook hands with the boss and were awarded the squadron's diamond-shaped embroidered cloth badge to wear on our left arm.

After Ground School, joining 208 squadron felt like growing up a bit.

We could wander around in our green 'growbags' again and no longer felt like the new kids on the block in the mess. We were issued with a name badge and light blue squadron T-shirts with the crest on the left breast.

The squadron dated back to 1916 and its official badge was a crown at the top and a picture of the Sphinx in reference to its Egypt days and the motto 'Vigilant'. To be part of an historic squadron put a little spring in your step.

The unofficial motif was of a kneeling naked blonde woman with the perkiest of bosoms, looking over her shoulder. Above her it said '208' and below was the word 'Penetrate'. Classy. Not. Technically, this described the squadron's role, but it was later scrapped by a new station commander for being in bad taste.

The main diet of our flying for the next few weeks would be circuits. Imagine an oval racetrack suspended above an airfield. That's the circuit. You spend hours and hours taking off, flying a circuit and landing, all the while avoiding other aircraft, talking to air traffic control, checking your fuel and keeping an eye on the weather.

Each time you alter the parameters; speed or altitude, simulating flying with your flaps stuck down, flying low level to simulate bad weather, gliding in to replicate a loss of engines.

These drills were all intended to build your capacity. Sometimes you would fly on your own to practice, every so often an instructor would jump in the back seat to assess your progress and see how you're adapting to the next step. If you're not quite up to scratch, you were deemed to have failed a flight.

You'd be given a couple more trips to practice before facing what could be your chop ride. In theory, this could be your make or break moment. Potentially the end of your flying career in the RAF.

We progressed from the confines of the circuit and started to fly around the local area, moving on to advanced instrument flying and navigation.

The great thing about the Hawk flying at 420 knots is you know that you're covering seven miles a minute. You have to be very quick on your mental arithmetic, so that if you slow down to, say 360 knots, you can work out instantly how many miles a minute you are doing now.

We mainly flew over Wales, which is perfect for training. It is fairly rural, there are not too many towns where you can annoy people, and the flying is stunning with deep valleys and mountains. Sometimes we would go to the Lake District and roar up Lake Windermere, or head up to the Moffat Valley and St Mary's Loch in the Scottish borders before circling out west and flying back down to Anglesey over the Isle of Man. At various points we had to be careful of paragliders as we often flew under them as they soared on the thermals rushing up the sides of the valleys.

One of the favourite areas in Wales is the Machynlleth Loop, known as the Mach Loop. This is a circular route around the valleys in the shadow of Cadair Idris mountain about eight miles inland from Barmouth between Dolgellau in the north and Machynlleth in the south. It operates a strict one-way system, so jets can only fly around it anti-clockwise.

We used this a lot to practice low-level flying, down to 250 feet – that's the height of an electricity pylon. But 250 feet is also the mandatory all-around clearance, so you had to stay in this envelope away from the steep valley sides, too.

The Mach Loop is a well-known honey pot for aviation fans. At various points around the circuit – Cad West or East, Corris Corner or Bwlch – you get gaggles of plane spotters waiting for the jets to come thundering through. Given the depths of these huge glaciated valleys the aircraft often roar past below the snappers, who can be literally looking down into the cockpit.

It was always quite funny waving at unsuspecting walkers as you scream past and scare the hell out of them. They can't believe you've seen them whilst going that fast, but you've had them in your sights for ages. It's just that your sound hasn't hit them yet.

Sound was a bit of an issue so to practice flying at Mach one we would head out at night over the Irish Sea to avoid sending a sonic boom down on Wales. Climbing to 40,000 feet we'd tip the nose and push the throttle forward, using gravity to help us plunge down until the instruments nudged up to more than 660 knots. It was a wild eye-popping, face-stretching, head-crushing ride as your g-suit squeezed like a boa constrictor. Completely electrifying, too, but faintly scary if you stopped to think what you were doing.

The weather always had to be perfect for night flying which meant you got some brilliant views. The country looked so much smaller in the dark. You could be flying at 25,000 feet in the middle of Wales and could clearly identity the glows of Chester, Manchester, Liverpool and Birmingham. Often you could see coast to coast, too. It was the strangest feeling, very calming and almost otherworldly as you flew about in the blackness peeping down on the real world. Talking to air traffic control felt like you'd been allowed access to some secret midnight high-altitude club. Even the squadron had a calmness about it when you were getting ready as everyone else had gone home.

A lot of it was about instrument flying but it was easy to get disorientated up there when you were doing manoeuvres. Glittery stars are very similar to the faint lights sparkling from houses on Welsh hillsides.

If we weren't actually in the air at Valley, we would be briefing, hanging out in the crew room, either studying around the large communal table or lounging around in the RAF-issue saggy armchairs drinking endless brews of tea.

Most weekday nights were spent studying but we might have one night off for a game of squash or a quiet drink in various hostelries around Anglesey to reboot our brains. Occasionally we'd go across to the mainland, to go to the cinema in Bangor. That felt like a real treat.

A few months into the course I felt a strong urge for my own space. I had been in the air force for nearly five years and couldn't see why I shouldn't leave the mess and get my own place. I did some research and got quite excited at the idea of my own little flat in, say, Rhosneigr that I could get on a six-month contract. Craig could stay to save us squashing into my poky little room in the mess if he visited on a weekend. It would be perfect.

I wrote a letter to the station commander, carefully laying out my arguments. 'I know you wouldn't normally allow it on a course like this but I wonder if you'd give me special dispensation to move out of the Officers' mess to rent a flat? As one of the only women on the squadron I feel it is really important for my well-being.' I posted it and went off to work with a warm glow. The next day I got my reply. A categorical 'No'.

The gist of his answer was that it was all down to camaraderie and living with the guys. I was gutted and angry. It seemed so unfair. It was a perfectly reasonable request and from my point of view, made logical sense.

His decision was about to have a dramatic effect on my RAF career but I couldn't have foreseen at this stage just how much.

Around this time I had another brush with the boss through no fault of my own. One day, Rob and Tristar took me to one side and said they weren't happy with how some of the instructors were talking to me.

'Sorry?' I said. 'What are you talking about?'

They said they had both noticed it and felt uncomfortable. Apparently, every day I was getting comments such as, 'We can spot which jet is yours, it's not parked straight,' or 'Wrong time of the month, eh?' or 'Off to apply your lippy, are you?'

Undoubtedly, this was all meant in humour, and bizarrely, that's exactly how I had taken it and thought nothing more of it. After all, this was an era when Miss World, lads mags and page three girls were still prolific in a very male-dominated society, despite having had a strong female prime minister. It's shocking how I had normalised this behaviour to simply 'get through' and yet interesting that the behaviour had become unacceptable to my good friends.

But the guys pointed out there were about twenty instructors on the squadron and if each of them made just one little remark, that was twenty derogatory comments a day. The guys asked if I minded them talking to the squadron commander. I said, well, OK, but I don't want it to sound like I'm the one moaning. I was really worried that it would put people's backs up. I wanted to blend in and keep my head down.

Later I got a call to go and see the boss. Crikey, what's going to happen here? As soon as I sat down in his office, the squadron commander apologised. I insisted it had not been a problem for me but he said these comments were not appropriate and that he had spoken to all the instructors. Afterwards, they all came up to me and said sorry, too. They just hadn't clocked it. Far from turning into a big thing, that was the end of it. I felt a bit awkward about the whole thing at first but I was really touched the guys wanted to stick up for me.

CHAPTER 8

THE TEAM WORKS

 could feel the pressure ramping up. Each sortie was getting more complex with new learning piled on top of what we were already supposed to know.

The instructor in the backseat would throw in emergency situations for you to deal with, a technical problem or a weather alert which meant you had to plot a new route to arrive at the waypoint on time or navigate quickly to the nearest airfield.

If I wasn't flying or eating, I was studying and practising my procedures. Even with more than sixty hours now in a Hawk, it never felt like I could do enough.

I sensed my grip slipping and my confidence was getting knocked as I struggled to absorb all the extra information. I felt like I was starting to get behind the jet, as if I was at the end of a water ski tow, desperately trying to keep up.

Every day my head felt like it was being squeezed a bit more and one more extra weight placed on my shoulders, in a precarious and seemingly unsustainable tower. I was missing Craig intensely and we were barely seeing each other. There was one other girl on the course in front, Mitch T. Sometimes we would chat just for a bit of female company, but talking to her made me feel worse, she was doing incredibly well and I didn't feel I could share my insecurities about my fear of failing with her.

I was on a downward spiral, feeling a bit like I was getting sucked underwater.

I struggled to sleep because I was worrying about everything and then I was so tired I couldn't get my head around some aspects of the flying and worried more. The classic catch-22.

My entire career, everything I had ever dreamed about was on the line. My anxiety had become intoxicating. The final straw was a rash which broke out down my arm. I tried to ignore it but it wouldn't go away. I went to the doctor. 'I think I must have changed my washing powder or something...' He saw straight through it, looked up and down my arms and said, 'Hmm, yes, are you stressed at all?'

NOOOO, I wanted to scream out sarcastically, of course I bloody well am! But I thought this might act as a siren to grab one of those white coats with the straps around the back, so I just said meekly, 'A bit.' I didn't realise stress could cause a physical ailment.

Sometimes I had to vent to my mum, dad or my sister, reassuring voices on the other end of the line that knew what it meant to me and constantly offered soothing words and guidance. My sister Sarah was a junior doctor so she could certainly empathise with the stress levels.

Every flight was becoming a real challenge. Every trip passed was a huge relief off my mind... for about ten seconds before my brain fizzed onto the next one and the crush on my skull pressed a little tighter.

On my third trip from the end, the instructor was throwing in emergency diversions and navigation problems. I was aware I was getting behind in my decision-making.

The first thing to go when you hit maximum capacity is your hearing and when you are slow to respond to radio calls the instructor can tell you are nearing overload. He had to interject at one point in the emergency procedure. I felt a sense of doom, like I'd been caught in the act of a crime. There was minimal chatter as we flew back to base. It was horrible. I still had to negotiate re-joining the circuit above the airfield, always one of the most stressful parts as there were lots of aircraft and pilots in different stages of their flying careers.

We landed and he said, 'OK Mandy, get yourself a cup of tea, I'll meet you in the debrief.'

We ran through the flight, and when we got to the navigation emergency he said, 'Tell me what happened there?'

I explained as best as I could but I didn't really have a solid excuse. The main reason was my confidence was shot and I was flagging. 'OK, so for that reason, that's a fail,' he said eventually. 'I just feel you need to do that one more time to convince me.' I felt like I had been booted in the stomach.

I was given a couple of flex trips, which meant I could go back up and practice, before I had to take the check ride again.

On a normal day this would be nerve-wracking. On this day I woke with a knot in my stomach and way too many butterflies to be able to fit in breakfast as well. A major error when you are flying as you always should have something in your stomach. It turned out to be a fascinating exercise in man management. It was a beautiful sunny day and I was assigned to fly with the chief flying instructor, Wing Commander Ray L.

'Right, Mandy, here's the route, you've got an hour and a half to plan the trip,' he said. He pointed to a location on the map and suggested I might want to contemplate a plan of action if I was to lose an engine around there. Normally, you have no idea where the emergency is going to happen so you can't mug up on the nearest airfield, but now I knew I need to be thinking about aborting to Hawarden, a small airfield just south of Chester.

I felt a sense of calm as we took off and I stayed on top of it the whole trip. He turned to me as we taxied in and told me I had passed. I could have wept in relief.

I asked why he hadn't overloaded me and tried to make it more difficult. He smiled. What he had done was look at all my previous scores and he knew the only reason I was struggling was my plummeting confidence. I was talking myself out of passing the course. I know you can fly and I know you can navigate, he seemed to be saying. It's not an easy ride but why fail you when we don't have to? He said if I could just get my confidence back there was no reason why I couldn't progress.

I could see why he was the top instructor. It was the mark of an incredible teacher that he knew how to get the best out of somebody by not breaking them. My respect for him soared, just like my jubilation at passing the latest hurdle.

By now, the rest of the course had graduated and were spending most of their evenings in the bar. However, I still wasn't quite home and dry. To pass the course and get my wings I still had to satisfy the staff I could fly the final few sorties, which consisted of learning how to fly battle turns.

These are changes in direction when flying with a wingman in battle formation, three-quarters-of-a-mile apart.

It's not quite as straightforward as all just turning at the same time because the aircraft on the outside would be out of position and unable to catch up. Often it meant the wingman had to switch to the other side of the leader and required some maths to work out what was required for each heading.

If we were approaching Anglesey over the A5 pass, say, we'd have to have worked backwards about five turns from the airfield to make sure our wingman was on the correct side to re-join the circuit.

The arithmetic wasn't inherently difficult, but it was obscuring what I needed to do in reality.

I could feel the panic and self-doubt returning. Not only have I failed the navigation test so that the spotlight is firmly on me, I'm now struggling with these bloody battle turns. I'm supposed to be getting my wings in two weeks but now it looks like I'm one of those who just might not quite make the grade. Blooming heck, this is terrible.

I was sitting in my room after dinner, desperately trying to work out angles using my hands as props, like a downhill skier at the top of a racecourse, tracing the air with their hands to visualise the track. If my normal self had been watching, she would have laughed out loud at the ridiculousness of the scene. But my normal self had gone AWOL and the figure sitting here was fast running out of mojo. I was despairing that the numbers wouldn't go in and generally feeling sorry for myself.

There was a knock on the door. I got up slowly, slightly cross that my ever-diminishing time to nail this was being interrupted. I opened the door to see Rob, Andy and Tristar grinning.

'Come with us Mands, we're taking you out.'

'Not now guys, I'm not in the mood. I'm bricking myself over these turns. I've just got to get my head around them.'

'Just trust us,' they urged.

I glanced at each of them and saw their eyes imploring me to go with them. I shrugged and thought well, why not. I'm not getting anywhere here. Maybe taking my mind off it for a bit would give me the clear head I needed. I followed them down the stairs and out to the bike sheds. I presumed we were going to the pub. 'Where to?' I said. 'You'll see,' came the reply. We unlocked our bikes and cycled around the block until we came to the parade square. It was in darkness but lights from the nearby buildings gave it a warm orange glow.

Out of the shadows emerged several others milling around with bikes. What on earth...? I was told in no uncertain terms we were going to practice battle turns and we were not leaving until I'd nailed them. Bloody battle turns. They were going to be the death of me.

I got on my bike and was told to follow Tristar, acting as his number two in a pretend two-ship formation. The others paired up and we all started circling the parade ground. Someone then called out 'Thirty port' or 'Forty-five starboard' or 'shackle' (how two jets swap positions in the same direction), or 'rotate' (how two aircraft turn through 180 degrees).

My head started whirring with the maths as I wobbled my bike vaguely across Tristar's path. I sneaked a look at the others. They were crossing confidently and took up their new positions without a fuss. It was like a scene from a cheesy film, and must have looked very odd, but it was actually happening. Tristar pointed to where I should be and I got into position for the next one. My brain was a blur, but the more we did, the less I thought about the numbers. I was just concentrating on positioning. It was not exactly the same as doing it in the jet, there was no vertical separation after all, but the penny was finally dropping.

We spent hours out there until I swore I understood what a battle turn looked like and could I go to bed now please. I slept soundly for the first time in weeks.

The next morning, I got my weather briefing at 0730 and was airborne an hour later. It was a piercing blue–sky day.

My mojo put in an appearance for the first time in a while and I caressed the controls. My decisions were clear and confident. I was actually enjoying it, flying in sync with the instructor flying the other jet. I stopped focusing on the numbers and started to see the bigger picture, just like we had on the bikes.

After I landed the instructor said, 'What the bloody hell was that, Mands?'

'What do you mean?' He said it was like flying with a completely different pilot. Like I'd put in a different cassette or had re-wired my brain.

It was true, it was as if the mist had cleared and the whole concept of the battle turn was spread out before me. I told him the story and he was blown away. He said he had never heard of a course coming together like that.

They had seen another way of doing it, while I was so focused on the task, I had complete tunnel vision. I really don't think I would have graduated without those guys, and the camaraderie we had built up between us. What they did for me was amazing. They didn't have to do it, they could have spent the night in the bar, but they did it for me. Technically, we were all in competition too, which made it all the more remarkable. The slots to fly the front line aircraft were precious and sometimes limited. I realised then the true essence of teamwork was acting selflessly. Going the extra mile for those around you when you have nothing to gain.

I reflected back to the letter from the station commander, he was absolutely right about not moving out of the mess. Your team is everything.

Earning my wings as an RAF fast jet pilot was everything I had dreamed of since I first started flying.

I had been through a hell of a lot to get here and I barely slept the night before, I was so excited.

My mum and Stanners (my step-dad), dad and sister were coming to watch the wings parade; Craig had flown up in his own Hawk from Yeovilton which was quite cool.

The family were so excited being shown around the buildings and hangars and then being allowed to sit in a Hawk.

Dad, resplendent in his dickie bow, didn't say much but I could tell he was very proud by the way his eyes kept on tearing up. Sarah's first reaction was 'Oh my gosh, it's bloody tiny, it looks like a Tonka toy.'

They were allowed to sit at the back and listen to our final briefing before we treated them to a nine-ship fly-by.

I was flying as number two, which meant I was on the leader's right wing. By now I was pretty skilled at formating on someone's wing but now there was the added pressure of two others formating on me. I'd better not mess this up.

We did one pass, turned around and came back. Not quite the Red Arrows but thrilling for all of us. Afterwards I changed into my No.1 uniform for the formal ceremony in the presence of then Air Vice Marshall Philip Sturley.

It was held in the dining room of the Officers' mess. We sat on chairs in front of the rostrum with our families at the back as citations were read out about each pilot, praising our strengths and our key attributes. There were prizes awarded for many things; best academic, best team player, person you'd most want to go to war alongside. I won the award for outstanding leadership. I marched up, saluted the air vice marshal, he pinned a brevet onto my chest, we shook hands, I turned around, flashed a cheesy grin for the photos and marched back to my seat.

I had been in the RAF since October 1994 and had nothing tangible to show for it until now.

Whatever happened from here on, no-one could take away the fact that I was now a fully winged-up, qualified RAF fast jet pilot.

CHAPTER 9

CREAMING AND STREAMING

ingo. That will do. I was scanning Teletext (no internet in those days) for cheap holidays to the sun. An all-inclusive package deal to the Dominican Republic. We're in. I legged it down the corridor and told the guys. There were six takers. Caribbean sun, here we come.

We'd lucked in with a juicy seven days off on account of bad weather delaying the course in front of us. No point in mooching around here. We're going to the beach.

It was my first experience on holiday with just men and I learned an interesting lesson. We soaked up the sun in the day and went out partying at night. What an eye opener. It was fascinating to watch the single guys in full pulling mode.

The women just melted into their arms when they said they were fast jet pilots. When I tried it on a few guys in the club, just for fun, it seemed to act as the biggest repellent in the world. I crashed and burned every time. When I resorted to saying I was a secretary or a nurse, immediately there was interest. The men seemed much happier. 'Oh, really, that's interesting.' The usual dynamic had been restored and suddenly they felt very manly again. It was a fascinating piece of psychology. In the flirting arena there was clearly a big difference between being a male fighter pilot and a female fighter pilot. It was a good job I was smitten with my man at home.

Even now if I'm out with a group of girls and they tell some guys that their mate over there was a fast jet pilot, the men will generally respond with wisecracks like, 'Yeah, and I'm an astronaut.'

Refreshed, albeit with liver damage, we turned up back at Valley to start 74 (R) Squadron.

If I thought I was at max capacity before, I was about to realise there was a whole new level. We were set to learn the tactical aspects of advanced flying, learn about weapons and bombing, study air-to-air combat and do it all as part of a pair or sometimes a four-ship in battle formation.

Bombing was first and for that we went on a two-week detachment to RAF St Athan in South Wales.

We began by learning the basic technique of how to drop three kilogram practice bombs onto bundles of barrels painted white in the dunes of Pembrey range in Carmarthenshire. We'd fly around in a circuit and then come in on the bombing run, trying to get the height and speed exactly right and factor in the effects of the wind to get the bomb in the right place. When you were happy, you flicked open the cover on the bomb switch on the control stick to drop the bomb. Spotters in the control tower radioed to tell us how accurate we were. Or more accurately, how far away we were. 'Correct right 300 yards in three o'clock position' or '100 yards to the left.'

Then we did 'pop-up' or 'loft' attacks where you came in on the target at low level, pulled up in an upward trajectory and rolled over the top, releasing the bomb at a certain altitude so it travelled up and forward first. This was for when you didn't want to fly low over the target and wanted to avoid any bomb blast effects.

Another important element of this detachment was strafing – firing your guns at a target on the ground. You started at 1000 feet, then dropped down and pointed your nose at the deck. You gently squeezed the trigger on the back of your control stick and unleashed merry hell from the 30mm Aden cannon – drrrrr, drrrrr, drrrrr, drrrrr – firing in four-second bursts before you pulled up into a four g recovery so you didn't get hit by ricochets from the ground.

I messed up on one run and started firing well before I should have done. Watching back on the video, the instructor said, 'Oh, Mandy, you're a bit far out there, you opened up a bit early… please don't tell me you didn't fire again… Oh. You did.'

Keeping your finger on the trigger until you get a bit closer is a no-no, apparently.

I was sitting in a classroom back at Valley, twirling two planes on wooden sticks around in the air. Everyone else was doing the same thing. The mass quoting of lines from Top Gun was like a group audition for the sequel.

We were starting the air defence module which meant learning about air combat manoeuvres.

This was known as dogfighting, your classic 'bandits in my six o'clock' stuff. It was the essence of the Battle of Britain, when crack Spitfire and Hurricane pilots scrapped it out with Germany's Luftwaffe aces in the skies of southern England.

There was a lot of theory and strategy to learn first. Hence the planes on sticks. Then we would take it airborne against a 'real' enemy.

We were paired up with a fighter controller on the ground, who would give us the vector to the approaching bogey, one of our course mates, and talk us onto contact.

We took off and flew in different directions about twenty miles apart. Then we turned and came roaring back towards each other for the 'merge', like two knights facing each other for a joust.

We had been given a block, from 12,000ft to 20,000ft, and could come in anywhere we liked in 1,000ft increments, as long as number one – me – picked an odd altitude and number two – him – took evens.

The classic thinking, if you have the sun behind you, was to stay high and use the golden orb as cover, swooping in on him out of the glare.

Of course, there was a good chance he or she might have twigged that's what you were thinking and be high too. Or they might want to be high to avoid looking up for you into the sun. It was like a huge game of 3D aerial spoof. Or rock, scissors, paper. What's your play?

Flying at 420 knots gives a closing speed of 840 knots and there was a smattering of fluffy white cumulus clouds to keep us on our toes. I was at my ceiling and my eyes were flicking back and forth across the horizon and scanning up and down.

I couldn't see the bandit yet but my heart was thudding. The man-on-man nature of this had really upped the ante. It was only training, plus my opponent was on my team and we weren't actually going to shoot each other down, but every nerve was fizzing. It was one thing trying to coordinate a battle turn with an instructor sitting behind you but this was on another level.

What was that? I caught a speck off to my left. Bugger these clouds, no, maybe not... yes... I clocked him, screaming past my left flank about 1,000ft below. Game on. Right, come on Wellsey. I dropped the nose and broke hard left, trying to get in behind him without him seeing me. The name of the game was to get in your opponent's 'six' to use your weapons.

We were both trying to fly our aircraft to the limit of its abilities, mindful of aerodynamics, physics and geometry.

It was a trade-off between air speed and altitude. The former was a bird in the hand in the form of kinetic energy. The latter was potential energy, in other words, speed in the bank with the help of gravity.

If you were up against another aircraft type, you could try to exploit differences in performance to get an edge. Because we were both flying Hawks, we were just hoping our chess player's instinct and grasp of dogfighting tactics would give us an advantage.

Like chess, there were myriad manoeuvres, switching between offence and defence; barrel roll attack, high yo-yo, low yo-yo, lag roll, guns defence, defensive spiral. The key was to have these downloaded in your brain but fly naturally, rather than flying by numbers.

My opening gambit seemed to be working as his course stayed constant, in and out of the clouds. Then I lost him. 'Bugger, where have you gone?' I was swivelling my head all around the cockpit, trying to get eyes on. Panic was rising, like losing a toddler in a supermarket.

There... got you... he was up high, climbing to the left. Oh no you don't. I pulled back and followed him up into the blue.

He seemed to stall and spin and now he was dropping down towards me. I yanked the stick right back, so I was flying upside down and then slammed it over to the right. Maintaining your spatial awareness, in other words knowing where you were in the sky, was crucial.

My neck was already getting sore from constant swivelling, trying to keep a visual. I was like a polo player concentrating purely on the game rather than focusing on how to ride the horse. Each time I pulled a big turn I got a kick in the stomach from the g-suit. Oof. 'Where are you now?' 'OK, got you again.'

He was diving below me. What have you got up your sleeve? Maybe he was getting ready for a big steep climb over the top. I tried to anticipate where he might end up and pulled into a tight corkscrew hoping I might pop out behind him. Making spaghetti trails in the sky like this was so physical. I was getting beaten up by the g-suit.

I was inverted when I saw him flash across my nose. Oh gosh, that was close. But it did mean that if I pulled hard and levelled out, I might be able to get a shot in. I was flying totally on instinct now, not taking my eyes off him as I brought the aircraft around. A bit more... a bit more... I was on his tail now and he knew it. He started rocking left and right. He was trying what was known as gun jinks to avoid being shot down. I anticipated his rhythm. Hang on... hang on... FIRING! I leased off my virtual guns and gave the official countdown... three, two, one, splash. 'Yeehah, Jester's dead!'

'Knock it off, knock it off, knock it off,' came the instruction on the radio. That was the signal for the end of the fight. What a rush, but bloody hell, I felt drained. We flew off over the horizon and re-set for another bout.

Once we got to grips with singleton dogfights, we built up to two on one, you and a wingman against an instructor, or even multiple bogeys. On the one hand having a wingman was easier because you could look out for each other, but it was also super hard because of the added communication needed while trying to push your aircraft's envelope.

The key, if you knew there was definitely only one enemy, was to try to occupy the bandit while your wingman peeled off. 'I'm in a rolling scissors, heading out to the west.' 'Visual.' When he had crept into position, you banged out of there and he'd be in a prime spot to go to weapons and nail the enemy.

Everyone was buzzing after an aerial combat sortie. It was such an adrenaline high but exhausting, too. My legs and stomach looked like zips had been sewn into them where blood blisters had formed because of the constant tightening of the g-suit.

Some people utterly loved the gladiatorial nature of it. I enjoyed it but I was happier down in the weeds – flying low level. I got more satisfaction out of finding and hitting targets in ground attack and bombing mode.

One week during the air combat phase the weather was really bad which shut down operations out of Valley. To keep up our trips we flew the jets to Norwich and booked into a hotel. It was funny operating out of civilian airport, wandering through in flying kit and carrying helmets while people were going off on holiday.

I landed after one trip and the detachment commander called me in to his makeshift office. He told me that my mum had been in touch to say grandpa was really poorly and may not see out the day. He asked me if I wanted to be with him. Of course I did but I didn't want to mess up the trip. He said what is important is that you're with him. Someone went back to the hotel to get my kit and my instructor Archie and I flew the Hawk up to Humberside airport. My mum picked me up, which was quite amusing in its own way as I can just imagine her boasting to all and sundry in Arrivals that she was there to pick up her RAF pilot daughter.

Mum whisked me off to see grandpa at his home in Hull and I was able to say goodbye before he died that evening. It was very sad but lovely to be with him. As an RAF man himself he was very proud of me and knew I had got my wings. It just reinforced to me that the air force was a family and incredibly caring. It would go the extra mile to get you somewhere. It is so often the acts of the man in the middle, who makes on the spot decisions, that mean so much. That single act bought no end of loyalty and goodwill, more than any pay cheque would ever offer.

There were other perks, too. The journey back to Winchester from Valley on a Friday night could take six hours. If I left work on the dot, or before, at five p.m. I would get home at midnight. I'd then have to leave again at tea time on Sunday to get enough sleep in to fly on Monday. Because of that I only did the journey about once a month, which wasn't brilliantly conducive to maintaining a relationship.

But then I chanced upon a great ruse. One of the instructors offered me a lift home in a Hawk. We would use it as a training flight, except instead of landing back at Valley we would land at RAF Benson in Oxfordshire where Craig would pick me up. We'd then fly back up on the Monday morning, incorporating another training flight on the way back up. It was an excellent learning opportunity taking the jet into a different airfield at the same time. Genius.

Back at Valley the training continued at a frenetic pace. We were now getting used to bombing missions in pairs and taking it in turns leading a two-ship.

On one low-level sortie I got the fright of my life. We were flying as a pair down Lake Bala in Snowdonia, one on one side, one on the other for camouflage. Flying down the middle would be too obvious if you were in a combat situation. My eyes were flicking left and right, near and far, scanning for threats. Across on the far bank I spotted an aircraft coming in the opposite direction. 'Aircraft on your nose,' I shouted to my wingman on the radio. No sooner had my eyes switched back to the front I saw the looming shape of a Jaguar almost filling my cockpit. WOOOAAAHH! I pulled back harder than I ever had before, virtually sticking my jet on its tail and giving it full power as we climbed to the moon. Holy Moses. My pulse had soared almost as high as the aircraft. Thank goodness the Jaguar hadn't seen me because chances are, we would have both pulled up and gone smack. He was the wingman for the jet I saw across the valley, but because we were on an exact collision course there was no obvious movement in my scan pattern, other than getting bigger, until the very last minute.

'Mandy, where are you?' my wingman said on the radio, oblivious after avoiding his threat. 'I'm at 20,000ft. I've almost soiled my flying suit. I'll come down now.'

It was just bad luck. Now there are electronic systems where you can plug in your intended low-level route and check if there will be anyone else in the area.

The final stage of the course pulled every aspect of our learning together in Simulated Attack Profiles (SAP). There were ten levels to the SAPs, a bit like a computer game, starting off relatively easy and building up into more and more complex missions throwing in multiple bombing targets and evasion from enemy 'bounce' aircraft.

Every flight pushed me to my absolute limits and I spent every night pouring back over the details of the trip. By now I lived and breathed flying the Hawk. There was nothing else in my world. My head didn't have the space for it.

A really good friend on the course in front was on the verge of quitting two trips before the end because of the pressure. Fortunately, given my wobbles on 208 squadron, I was managing to keep my stress levels under control.

Sometimes if I wasn't flying, I would hop in the backseat of one of the bounce aircraft just to build up more operational experience without touching anything.

We were in a fast-jet hot-house but Christmas put the festive brakes on before we'd finished all the levels. I spent the holiday both trying to remember and trying to forget the last few intensive months. But back at work I jumped back on the

Hawk highway and had a couple of days in the backseat before the final mission.

This was a massive melon twister which involved flying low-level, in battle formation, navigating a route, attacking multiple targets at set times with a combination of guns and bombs, dropping live bombs on a range and all the while avoiding the 'bounce' aircraft flown by instructors. Bonkers.

Somehow, I got through unscathed which was something of a miracle. I'd done it. My training was complete. You couldn't have taken the smile off my face even with an industrial laser.

Once they knew who had passed the course, the instructing staff met for the Role Disposal Board to decide our fate. This 'creaming and streaming' would decide what we would go on to fly and therefore where we would be posted.

When we had been asked for our preferences, I had put in for the Tornado GR4. I wanted to fly ground attack rather than the Tornado F3 fighter version. The staff would also decide if anyone was good enough to be recommended to fly a single-seat jet, the Harrier or Jaguar. I knew I was only a twin-seat recommend anyway – both on ability and desire after my Italian experience – so it was a toss-up between GR4 or F3.

In true RAF tradition, instead of just sticking these up on a notice board, the news was dished out during a drink-up. We were told to report to the bar in flying suits and I met some of the others milling about outside the locked door. We could hear voices and laughter coming from inside, however a few polite knocks didn't seem to register.

We shrugged and carried on chatting but I could sense a few nerves in the air. Then the door eased open and the eight of us we were ushered in. We were greeted with a big Wheel of Fortune-style spinning wheel in the middle of the room. All our instructors were gathered around and we were handed pint glasses, which were quickly filled up from a jug. On the wheel were photos of different fast jets, plus a picture of a jug of cream. This, we were told, indicated you would become a 'creamy' and stay at Valley as an instructor with the chance to go through selection again for single seat.

Each pilot in turn took to the floor to spin the wheel. If it landed on your designated aircraft first time, all well and good. If it didn't, you had to neck a pint.

When it was my turn, I landed on a Jaguar twice, a Harrier and the jug of cream. To huge roars from the baying mob, the first two pints went down fairly swiftly. University sport socials did have their uses. The third was a struggle; the fourth took forever. That left only GR4 or F3. I paused for a huge burp, and then gave the wheel an almighty yank. 'Come on, be the one, come to Wellsey,' I yelled, fully in the spirit. The pictures fizzed past in a blur, although that could just have been the beer. The wheel slowed, the Jaguar went past, the GR4, the cream, Harrier, the F3... a couple more pictures ticked slowly by and the pointer settled on... Tornado GR4. Time froze. I looked searchingly at the master of ceremonies. Another pint or...?

'Congratulations, Big Bird, that's what you'll be flying.'

'Yesssss!' I punched the air in true football fan fashion.

The room erupted in cheers. The boys piled onto the floor and danced around like loons, interlocking arms with me and chanting 'GR4, GR4.' It was going to be a big night.

CHAPTER 10

TORNADO TIME

'd like to say I was relaxed, focused and fully prepared for the next stage of my career as I arrived at RAF Lossiemouth in Scotland to train on the Tornado. I'd like to, but I can't.

I had stuffed my little Peugeot to the roof with kit and set off from Winchester, bound for the far north of Scotland. I was filled with equal parts excitement, uncertainty and apprehension. And not just because it dawned on me it was a blooming long way.

Excitement, because this is what I had dreamed of – flying fast jets for a living; uncertainty, because who knew what lay ahead and how long it would take; and apprehension, because at any stage I could be cut from the course and my hopes dashed.

Poor old Percy Peugeot. The baggage of my life was too much. He wheezed and spluttered his last few miles into a service station just outside Manchester. It turned out the head gasket had blown – not that I had a clue what that was – and I got him towed to my dad's house. He loaned me his car, an incredibly powerful Audi. Compared to my little run-around, you barely had to waft your foot over the accelerator and it would leap forward. I might have been a super-slick aspiring

Tornado pilot but I wasn't quite ready for the Audi.

Pointing my new rocket north, I sped off up the M6, past the Lake District, past Glasgow and Perth and onto the A9 through the Cairngorms, past Aviemore, turned right before Inverness... and only got flashed at by three separate speed cameras. I'd have to get the car back to dad the following weekend as well.

After 600 miles of driving, one blown head gasket, nine points on my licence and sixteen hours since I set off, I pulled into RAF Lossiemouth.

Ah, Lossie. The 'Jewel of the Moray Firth', the tourist blurb calls it. I call it a typical grey Scottish town looking north over the water, bounded by the golf course to the west and hugging the River Lossie to the east.

It was ten p.m. on the Sunday night, but this being May, early Scottish summer, it was still light. The base sits right on the edge of town, and I drove through the gate and pulled up in front of the red-brick officer's mess.

My spartan room contained a single bed with a thin mattress and the usual white and green striped pillows. It had the same standard-issue blue RAF carpet, with a desk, a bedside table, a wardrobe and a sink in the corner.

Once I'd unloaded, I went for a poke about. The dining room and bar were in exactly the same place as every other mess I'd ever been in.

And almost in the same places in the bar were some familiar faces from Valley. After 'carmageddon' it was lovely to flop down beside Chris and Rob and catch up again after our various holding jobs. I'd spent three months at RAF High Wycombe doing a duller than dishwater admin role, a bit of a come down after a year thrashing a Hawk around Wales at low level. They introduced me to Ian 'Radders' Radford, a navigator who I hadn't met before. We'd heard there would also be two overseas pilots on our course, and it didn't take much detective work in the bar to track down American Steve W and Aussie Mark N.

The next morning, in our shiny No.2 uniform, we assembled in front of one of the jets for course photos with the new squadron boss Wing Commander Simon 'Hobbo' Hobbs. We were, after all, the first course on this operational conversion unit (OCU) after it moved to Lossiemouth to be a national course rather than the tri-national outfit it had been at RAF Cottesmore.

Starting ground school always reminded me how much there was to learn. It was a good job we were young and our brains were agile because once again the info dump was massive, like plugging your head into a super-computer and hitting 'download'.

The thought of a deep dive into a Rolls-Royce RB199 turbo engine didn't exactly light my afterburners, but it's essential a pilot does understand what is going on. If you have an emergency, you need to know what is happening to be able to sort it out. But everyone learns differently and I'm definitely a practical learner – I find it hard to just absorb information by reading about it.

For six weeks life revolved round the inner workings of a Panavia Tornado GR1, a twin-engine, swing-wing, multirole combat jet designed for low level penetration of enemy defences. The Tornado was going through a huge upgrade programme to become the Tornado GR4, which brought in software upgrades but also the addition of a forward-looking infra-red (FLIR) sensor under the fuselage. We would be flying both types as it went through this transition period.

We were at it from 0830 until 1700 with an hour for lunch, broken up by PE two or three times a week. Most nights involved a run, a trip to the gym or a game of squash and dinner. We'd generally pick the early sitting in the mess because you could wear your work clothes.

If you were going to the bar you had to keep an eye on the traffic lights. These were red or green cards, which were posted to signify what the dress code was at a particular time. Red meant there was a high-ranking officer in or a function on and you had to wear a suit. Green meant you could lose the tie although you still had to be in your smart-casual gear.

But mostly our evenings involved study. And as well as the technical stuff we were also beginning to learn how to fly the jet. Or at least switch it on.

Cue the cardboard cockpits again. The Tornado cockpit was a different world to the Hawk with virtually double the dials, switches and buttons. That in turn meant hundreds more checks to do.

We were issued flight crew checklists which were laminated flip cards the size of a brick to be kept in the thigh pocket of your flying suit. These listed every check that was needed, including the correct challenge and response where necessary.

There were initial checks to make sure switches were safe and ready for starting, external checks, starting checks, taxi and system checks, take-off checks, after take-off checks, a host of other airborne checks such as before entering low level, and descent, landing and after landing checks.

There was never an excuse for not knowing the checks – only that you hadn't spent enough time and effort learning them. We would go to each other's rooms and go through the checklist with one of us pretending to fly. The other would chip in with things like 'No, you've missed one, you've forgotten to put the X-drive clutch to open.'

Rock 'n' roll, these nights were not, but I managed to cram a load of technical details into my head in the same way a teenager tidies their bedroom – by randomly stuffing things in drawers and cupboards – and somehow passed ground school.

Newly armed with an encyclopaedic knowledge of the GR1, I was finally going to be taught how to get the thing up into the air.

Not in an actual Tornado yet, though. At £35 million a pop, the real ones were off limits until we'd proved our mettle in the sim.

The sim, inside another nondescript red brick building near the mess, was an exact replica of a Tornado cockpit, only on jacks which moved it around.

The whole process was very real, as close to an actual sortie as it could be without taking off.

In full flying kit, including helmet and g-suit – with leg pockets weighed down by manuals and checklists – you climbed up the stairs and lowered yourself into the cockpit.

First you checked the ejection seat exactly as you would do in a real aircraft – this involved checking everything was connected as it should be and then removing the pins to make it live.

Strapping in, you connected up your g-suit – although in the sim it didn't inflate – and attached the leg and arm restraints.

Next you checked the miniature detonating cord (MDC) which is the dark zig-zag line you see in the top Perspex of the canopy. This exploded when the black and yellow ejection seat handle was pulled to get rid of the canopy, as you don't want that anywhere near you when you're being fired out of the jet like a human lunar lander.

You stowed the MDC pin and the canopy jettison pin and clipped into the seat, attached the life support system, which provided oxygen, and connected into the communications lead. You were pretty well in now.

There were at least fifteen minutes of checks to go before you could even think about pushing the starter button to fire her up.

Now to run through the drills you'd rehearsed hundreds of times in your room.

It was about making it an automatic process, so your hands and eyes ran around the cockpit. It was all done in patterns, starting in the back-left corner, moving up to the front and across to the right making sure every switch was in the right position.

Once you got into the groove it was better. You remembered that needed to be off, but the next one was on, that one was in the left position, that one right. It was all about remembering a flow.

The instructor in the control room played the part of the navigator and chipped in when needed. Eventually, when you were ready, you circled your index finger in the air, like a well-rehearsed dance move, to signify to those on the ground you were ready to fire up.

You reached forward to the left side of the console to press the engine start button with your left hand and watched the dials come alive. You heard the engines spooling up and once they reached certain parameters you could open up the throttle a certain amount before bringing it back to idle.

Next up it was the hydraulic checks. The workload was intense.

Once you'd worked through these you indicated to the ground crew to take away the chocks from behind the wheels – hence that well-worn flying phrase 'chocks away' – and took the brakes off before powering up ever so slightly.

Taxiing a Tornado in the sim for the first few times was quite funny. It was like getting into a new hire car and taking a while to tune into its whims. I kept meandering left and right over the centre line on the tarmac while trying to keep it straight. Or I'd power up the throttle too much and shoot forwards and then tap the brakes too hard and lurch to a stop. 'Oh no, a bit more, oops, bugger,' as I careered down the runway looking like a youngster on roller skates for the first time.

Once you were cleared for take-off you went through the final challenge and response checks with the navigator.

'Hydraulics?'

'Left ON, right AUTO.'

'EPS.'

'Auto, light out'.

'Pins.'

'Stowed, four front, two rear.'

You had to make sure you gave the right response to every question. It was really easy to fall into the trap of saying what you thought you should, rather than what was actually happening. For instance, when you put down your landing gear and say automatically, 'Three greens' to signal three wheels down because that is what you always say but actually it's two greens and one red.

One of the real dangers of flying is it's all about motor programmes – you are wanting people to operate an automatic process, with drills and checks, but at the same time they have to be vigilant and spot if something is not where it should be. Plenty of times I've looked at a switch and thought, 'Hang on a minute, I'm about to skirt over the fact the batteries are off.' You become so used to the routine of saying it. That's why a lot of aircraft crash – people saying what's not there.

You then radioed the tower. A voice came back, 'Roger, Mitre One, you're clear for take-off runway two three, climb to 3000ft, contacting departures on stud four.'

With your feet on the brakes, left hand on the throttles and right hand on the control column, you eased the two throttles forward, through the 'dry' range of power until they clicked. That was the burners lighting, one, then two. There was no thrust in the sim, but you could see on the gauges they were lit. You inched the throttles forward by another three centimetres.

Then, as we used to say to the bus driver when setting off for an away netball match at university, 'Floor it, drives.'

In the briefing you'd worked out the specific speed – known as the V speed – needed for take-off given the load of fuel, recon pods and weapons. As you raced down the virtual runway you kept an eye on the speedo. At about 150 knots you pulled back on the stick to raise the nose wheel off the ground. A bit more, keep going... there's 170 knots. You pulled back a bit more and you were airborne.

'Landing gear up, lights out.'

Through the canopy I could see us lifting over a fairly good digital representation of the Moray golf course just by the beach and we climbed up over the sea.

I was flying a Tornado. Or at least a big metal box that looked and acted very much like one.

The early sims were a chance to learn about the manoeuvrability, get used to the systems and flying with a Heads-Up Display (HUD) in front of you. That was the green writing that was projected onto some glass just in front of the cockpit, so you didn't have to look down at your instruments. It had information such as heading, speed, altitude and angle of attack on it.

In many ways flying a Tornado was easier than flying a Hawk because you had a HUD, as well as a moving map telling you where you were, and someone in the back seat to help. It was more operational, whereas the Hawk tested your capacity to fly the thing in the first place.

As time marched on the sims got harder as the instructors introduced you to more kit, harder scenarios, such as instrument approaches and more emergency situations. You were fully focused for the entire two hours in the sim; it wasn't like double maths at school when you could drift in and out.

Turning over the meaty flight crew reference cards you'd find the emergency procedures checklist. It covered everything from tyre failure on take-off, premeditated ejection, engine malfunctions to engine fires, fuel system failures and landing gear issues, each with a set course of action dependent on the symptoms.

These also had to be learnt. How I longed for an evening reading Jilly Cooper instead of this stuff.

You were desperate to avoid the dreaded beep, beep, beep of the alarm to signal you'd crashed. In aviation parlance that would not be good. But, of course, that was the whole reason for the sim, to get all this learning done in the safety of a hangar just next to the ground school.

The eighth sim was the last virtual trip before we got airborne for real. This involved a whole heap of fun and games and emergency situations to deal with, all designed to keep us on our toes. I was thinking so hard, and trying to process information so quickly, my mind was sifting through what needed to be done now and filtering out what could wait... albeit by only a split second or two.

Just when you think you'd cleared your plate and could get back to straight and level, there was always another problem to solve; an engine fire, bad weather, a request to divert to a new airfield or bogeys in the area.

Imagine driving up the motorway at 100 mph, trying to remember off by heart a deck of cards while someone fires maths questions at you, and then tells you your engine's on fire and what are you going to do about it? All in the dark.

The two hours seemed to whizz by in about five minutes. My world had narrowed to about two feet in front of me and I had to concentrate extra hard to climb down the stairs of the sim properly. I walked very deliberately to the crew room, like a drunk trying too hard to stay in a straight line. I made a cup of tea on autopilot as I came down from the mental rush.

In the debrief my instructor adopted a measured, reserved tone. Unusual for him, I must have cocked it up, I thought. He was toying with me. Well done Mandy, excellent sim. That's a great pass. I slowly exhaled. Next step Tornado.

It was an intense working week, not just for us, but throughout the station. There were plenty of other courses going on, such as Jaguar operational conversion units, or senior bodies going through flying training as well as the operational squadrons based at Lossie. Friday evening happy hour in the bar was always a great buzz and you could feel the sense of relief. People would hit it large. Sometimes we would go into nearby Elgin later on. There were some good bars, all full of RAF personnel given RAF Kinloss was just down the road, so we knew an awful lot of faces.

The actor Ewan McGregor's brother Colin was one of our instructors and one night Euan came out with him in Elgin. Euan had just appeared as a young Obi-Wan Kenobi in the Star Wars film Phantom Menace. Fuelled by the force, plus several pints of heavy brew, I sidled up to him in a bar and pulled out my pretend Star Wars light sabre and did the 'zzzzhh" noise of the blade swishing through the air. He looked at me, raised an amused eyebrow and went 'Hmm' and I just walked off. I never even spoke to him but I was rather pleased with myself.

CHAPTER 11

SLAYING THE IMPOSTER

O ne bright morning, or to give it its official title, 8 June 1999, I climbed into a minibus bound for the operational side of the airfield. This was a world away from our sheltered ground school life of classrooms and sims and back to the mess for tea and toast.

This was where the squadrons worked, with jets lined up on the flight line, operational staff busy with this and that and lots of people buzzing about. I'd been through it with the Hawk, but this felt different. This was everything I'd worked for, five years of training to get to this point.

My first flight in a Tornado. I grinned all the way across the airfield, happy but nervous, like a small child moving up to big school.

We'd been to this side of the airfield a few times for mass briefings. On the last occasion we left chastened and feeling unworthy. One of the pilots addressing us decided to take a hard line. He had that real fast-jet jock mentality and began firing questions around the room. We were still in ground school mode and not quite 'on it'. None of us covered ourselves in glory and he tore us apart.

He basically went ballistic and started really shouting at us. 'How dare you bloody well come over here and not know any of the answers...' It was like being back to square one at school. I was scared witless, thinking, 'Oh my goodness'. Of course, he was being tough because he was trying to make sure we were completely switched on. We did know our stuff, but it just wasn't right at our fingertips waiting to be blurted out to the room. It was a bit of bluster really, but we had been duly warned and were under no illusion we needed to get our heads back in the books.

This time I did feel switched on. I knew all the details, facts and figures and I was eager for the first flight. I was down to fly in the second wave. The first wave had been planning since 0630 to get airborne around 0930.

I was having a cup of tea in the crew room, waiting to see if I would get airborne. There could be any number of reasons why your flying may get binned for the day, such as bad weather, the jet becoming unserviceable, or other flights taking priority.

Eventually I got a call from Squadron Leader Tom Mac. 'Mandy, we're good to go.'

We went into a small briefing room with a big whiteboard and an overhead projector. Sqn Ldr Mac ran through what we were going to do on the flight. This wasn't the pre-flight briefing; this was just the pre-briefing briefing. Then it was my job to plan the mission, down to timings, navigation, weather and communications, before we joined up again to brief properly for the flight.

The last task was to run through the out-brief with the ops team. They asked questions such as 'Are you fit to fly?' 'What are your diversions?', 'Are you fatigued?', 'Are you on any medication?', 'Have you had any alcohol?', 'Have you signed all the required forms?'

Paperwork done, I wriggled into my g-suit, grabbed my helmet and followed the squadron leader out to the flight line.

Standing beside my Tornado I developed an instant

attachment, like a child hugging their horse on the merry-go-round. I was so excited it's all I could do to stop myself patting it.

Sqn Ldr Mac began the walk around, showing me how to conduct all the exterior checks of the aircraft.

We did the fast-jet equivalent of kicking the tyres and moved around to the rear. At which point... THUD! I walked smack, bang and bloody wallop into the taileron, whacking my un-helmeted forehead really hard. It came from nowhere. The rear of the taileron tapers to quite a fine point and were at exactly the same height as my eyes. I just didn't see it. I started to feel faint and saw cartoon stars before my eyes. It was so painful but I couldn't let on that I'd nearly knocked myself out cold before my first ever flight in a Tornado.

I didn't think he'd seen me so I tried to concentrate and pretend I was fine, but when I put my helmet on it was really pressing in on the welt.

Somehow, I got to the end of the walk around and climbed in. I shook my head to try to clear any remaining fug and took a few deep breaths. Luckily, the cockpit felt completely familiar because of all that sim time.

Soon I was pressing the engine starter button. The sound of whirring and whining as it spooled up brought a grin to my face. With your helmet on it's not overwhelming but you know it must be deafening outside. I gestured to the ground crew and taxied out, talking to the tower.

I'd got so much written on my knee pads to sound good on the radio I could barely read it.

I lined up, cleared for take-off, put the footbrakes on, eased the throttles through the gate, checked the burners were lit, full power and ...WALLOP! Oh yes, there it is, that's the sweet spot. That's the moment you go, 'Oh, my golly gosh, this is so flipping different from the sim.'

I was slammed back in the seat as the whole airframe leapt into life and we rocketed forwards. We hit 148 knots, stick back, 160 knots, nose up, wheels clear, gear up, flaps up.

'OK, let's go flying,' the squadron leader said in smooth RAF style.

We climbed up over the Moray Firth for a bimble around the area, practising a few turns, left a bit, right a bit, just to get a feel for the aircraft in the actual air.

For take-off and low-speed flying, the Tornado's wings stick out at twenty five degrees but when you nudge up to higher speeds you can swing the wings back through forty five to sixty seven degrees to give the jet a more aerodynamic form, the distinctive dart shape you get with paper aeroplanes.

It felt so different to a Hawk. It felt heavier and there was the sensation that there was so much more power underneath you. The Hawk felt like a throw around sports car in comparison, a Mazda MX5 as opposed to the full, throaty, maniacal muscle of a F1 car.

I'd done 560 hours flying in the RAF up to this point, plus forty hours to get my PPL, so I had been building up to this for some time. So even though I was sitting in a super high-tech weapon, it was in fact just an airplane like many others I'd flown, albeit one with two fire-breathing, face-tightening afterburners.

It was an incredible feeling and I was absolutely loving it.

The squadron leader was chatting like we were on a trip to the seaside. 'Lovely day up here, isn't it?'

He pointed out a few local landmarks and showed me the old disused World War II airfield of Milltown that had confused plenty of pilots in the past. It had the same orientation as Lossie and a number of pilots had tried to land there. The radio chat would have been priceless. 'Hello Lossiemouth, we're on final approach, are we clear for landing?' 'Er, are you sure you're here, because we can't see you.' 'Bugger, maybe not, then.'

Coming back into land was where flying an actual jet obviously differed from the sim. It was that very real, very fast looming contact with the ground.

I was guided in by air traffic control on a precision approach radar (PAR). They essentially talked you down a virtual glide slope set at three degrees, so at three miles out we were at 900ft, two miles out 600ft, one mile out 300ft.

There was another heap of checks to do. Wing sweep, twenty five degrees. Airbrakes, in and locked. Flaps, mid. Landing gear, down... I was working hard, knowing the instructor was in the back with his hands poised over the dual controls. I could see the runway down there, over the fence, beyond the golf course but I was absorbed in the numbers, trying to hit the parameters.

Steady, Wellsey, steady. Here we go then. I touched down the main wheels first and then gently eased down the nose wheel. Pulling the throttles back to reduce power with my left hand, I then pushed them both to the left, known as 'rocking outboard' to deploy the buckets that covered up the afterburners. When I could see from a dial on the right of my cockpit that the buckets were deployed, I powered up again by pushing the throttles forward. This fired the thrust in a forward direction and I jolted hard into my straps as the reverse thrust slowed us down.

We slowed to taxi speed and I talked to the tower as I brought the jet back to the squadron apron.

So, that'll be me then, just back from flying a Tornado.

There were a lot of smiley faces at dinner. We were all on a real high still, swapping stories and tales of cock-ups. 'I forgot to swing my wings coming back in,' or 'I nearly knocked myself out on the tail fin.'

Despite the RAF's love of a good knees-up there was no time for celebration. This was work mode and I retreated to my room early to write up my notes from the debrief, jot down points I wanted to work on and go through the brief for the next flight.

I had just stepped on to a fast-moving conveyor belt where every day I'd be handed another huge stack of information. Where did I put it all? It was like the TV game show Supermarket Sweep where you had to collect as many goods off the shelves as you could in a certain time. Stuff always gets dropped, sometimes the lot.

From now on we would be flying four trips a week. The ante would be upped on each one. We could still fail.

The sun shimmered off Loch Ness as we screamed down the Great Glen. Chrrr. The engine hummed its contended tune, as happy as me to be skimming down the valley on a clear summer morning. We were low, 250ft off the water. Low enough to see what the fishermen had in their sandwiches. My eyes were out of the cockpit, looking ahead. Now and again they flicked inboard to check the altimeter and fuel gauge.

Patches of forest and fields separated by stone walls slipped by on either side. Browning upland stretched to the sky above. Down to my right the ruins of Urquhart Castle flashed past. Roaring on down Loch Lochy, the huge hulk of Ben Nevis loomed on the left above Fort William.

We were heading out towards the Firth of Lorn and the Isle of Mull. We would make a big, sweeping right turn over the sparkling seas on the backside of the island before heading north towards Skye and the Western Isles. From there we'd chase the corrugations of the swell back towards the coast to enter the highlands at Loch Morar. We'd nip up Loch Arkaig before hanging a left back up the Great Glen and climbing out of low level at Inverness for the return to Lossiemouth.

Yesterday we went north from Lossie across the Moray Firth, dropped into low level at Wick and cruised around the far north coast of Scotland.

The flying was spectacular. The islands out to the west are like giant jigsaw puzzle pieces. The inlets and bays studded by white beaches and turquoise waters, like diamonds surrounded by sapphires. If I didn't have the pressure of having an instructor in my backseat watching my every move, I'd just gawp and daydream. But I do, and I'm grafting. I just happen to have the most idyllic office view in the world.

I was learning to fly the jet I could go to war in. That might sound bloodthirsty and gung-ho but professionally it was like passing your final exam in order to practice in your chosen field.

Each flight was like another chunk being chiselled off the impostor syndrome lodged on my shoulders. We often think of ourselves as being a less worthy and less able than our colleagues see us. We all have those inner voices that say you can't do it. That nagging feeling that you'll be found out soon. They'll realise it's just little old me, you think, not some hotshot fast-jet jock. I was far more aware than anyone else of my history of failing those initial aptitude tests but each flight I passed took me closer towards my goal.

I never really doubted I could do it but you never really believe it until you have done it. Now I've proved I can fly a Tornado, I'm ready to learn how to fight one.

We quickly progressed from simple circuits and general handling to basic navigation, low-level navigation and instrument flying. After seven trips I flew my instrument-rating test, which meant you could fly on just your instruments and land in bad weather. They stuck a visor on your helmet so you couldn't see anything of the outside world, just inside the cockpit. You're expected to fly around and then do your final approach with no view out. At 200ft you flip up the visor as if you've popped out of cloud for the landing.

Each flight was a bit more complex than the last. You needed to give each one your maximum focus, but you needed to keep half an eye ahead too. It was like the build-up to the first of a series of exams at school, you don't want to focus solely on the first one and then realise there's another two straight after it.

Often, we'd fly a trip with an instructor pilot in the back seat and then fly it again with a navigator to get used to working as a crew. The navigator instructors would sometimes make deliberate mistakes to simulate being a new student nav and see how you responded. They'd be looking for you to be proactive and ask for information ahead of time rather than them just spoon-feeding you the data.

Planning for an hour-and-a-half sortie began about four hours before you went up and could take two to three hours. After landing it took half an hour or so to taxi back in and close the aircraft down. Then you climbed out of your kit, grabbed a brew and debriefed for an hour. So the whole process was about six hours for one flight.

The met briefing might be at 0730 but you might not be scheduled to fly until 1630. Some days you'd get scratched because of bad weather, or the aircraft became unserviceable, or another course with higher priority than you needed the jets. It was quite demanding trying to stay focused all day, not quite knowing if you would go up. I spent a lot of the time in the training rooms with the cardboard cockpit going through the mission in my mind, or swotting up on the various manuals, chunky 400-page tomes covering everything to do with aircrew, operational details, electronic warfare systems and preparation for the front line.

Once we had become instrument, navigational and low-level whizz kids we moved onto formation flying. Battle turns, the whole nine yards. Just like riding a bike, I thought, as we sat in a briefing going through the theory. Thinking back to the evening I'd spent with my course mates at RAF Valley, practising battle turns on our bikes brought a smile back to my face... it seemed so easy now.

My first bombing mission came on my seventeenth trip. We used Tain range, a short hop across the Moray Firth on a promontory poking into the Dornoch Firth south of Dornoch.

To begin with we practised basic 'lay' bombing, flying in at 150ft and 500 knots on a level approach, armed with three kilo practice bombs stuffed with concrete. The navigator would be watching his radar paint a developing picture as you got closer to the target, which could be a bunch of barrels or just a mark on the ground. Once he knew he had identified it, he input it as a green crosshair, which showed up on the pilot's HUD.

The pilot could move the nav's mark if they thought they could get a better one, which was a sure-fire way to hack off the back seater. They had done all the hard work, then at the last moment you took the glory... or not!

But your main job as pilot was to keep the jet flying at the correct speed, altitude and heading and press the big red weapon release button on the top of the control stick at the right moment.

I was listening to the range controller on the radio. What I wanted to hear, of course, was 'direct hit'. But when he said '100m at six o'clock' I knew I was dropping 100m short and needed to correct for next time. It was all about flying the jet to the exact numbers worked out beforehand to drop that bomb on target and on time. The instructors were watching to see how accurately you could fly. For 'loft' bombing, the onboard computer did all the projectile maths, so you just needed to press the button. You didn't even need to press the button at the right moment. 'Pickling' was when the bomb dropped on your command, so when you've pressed the button. But 'committing' allowed the computer to decide when it would actually drop, given all the parameters, as long as you'd given it permission. It was completely different to the Hawk and actually much easier. Loft bombing on the Hawk felt a bit Heath Robinson. 'Oh, that looks about right... and press.' The Tornado's weapons systems were telling you not that it looks about right, but that it was right.

1984, Sarah and I represent the Girl Guides at their 75th Anniversary at Buckingham Palace.

1987, 318 Sqn Air Training Corps.

August 1991, my first flight as a qualified pilot taking my family flying in a PA28 from Blackpool airport.

1994, Celebration after winning the De Havilland Trophy on UBAS at RAF Cosford.

A big smile after winning the aerobatics competition.

1994, Graduation Day from the University of Birmingham with Mum and Dad.

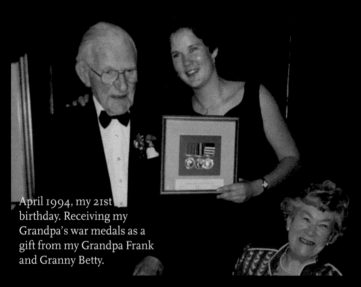

April 1994, my 21st birthday. Receiving my Grandpa's war medals as a gift from my Grandpa Frank and Granny Betty.

1994, Field Leadership Training, Officer Training with John and Mark.

6th April 1995, RAF College Cranwell Graduation parade.

Left: Suraya and myself, exhausted in NBC kit on Operation Peacekeeper, Officer training in 1995.

A proud moment outside College Hall with Granny Betty, Sarah, Grandpa, Mum and Dad.

16 JEFTS Course at a ball at RAF Cranwell.

1996, Survival Course, cooking up rabbit.

August 1996, 155 Basic Flying Training Course. RAF Linton on Ouse.

1998, Advanced Flying Training. Landing in the Hawk after a 9-ship wings parade flypast for family and friends.

/37 Course gain their RAF wings.

208 Squadron 'Penetrate' Official Crest. RAF Valley.

Award for leadership.

Sarah, Craig, me, Dad, Mum and Stanley

1998, celebrating
Vossers and Mattly's
Wings parade.

May 1999,
No.1 Course of the
National Tornado
Operational
Conversion Unit
(NTOCU) at RAF
Lossiemouth.

1999, Craig and I at
the Summer Ball at
RAF Lossiemouth.

Sea drills at RAF St Mawgan.

Left: 2000, first combat mission on Operation Bolton.

Above: 2000, Conduct After Capture Course.

2002, after returning from a successful attack mission on Operation Resinate South.

Above: 2000,
II (AC) Squadron on
Operation Bolton at
Ali Al Salem AFB,
Kuwait.

Left: Last flight in a
Tornado GR4.

Michel and myself
enjoying sitting on
a Tornado with our
names written on it.

Top: 2002. Duke of Edinburgh's Award presentation at St James' Palace, London.

Bottom: Opportunity of a lifetime, flying with the Red Arrows in 2011.

April 2008. I finally get my man! Craig and my wedding day.

Elliot and Chessie when I first met them.

Above: 2008, Craig and I, Jack and Jamie.

Trying to tempt Jack and Jamie into a life of aviation.

2015, Jack, Elliot, Chessie and Jamie.

2015, Air Experience Flight as a RAF volunteer reservist flying Emily.

2018, photo shoot for a magazine.

2019, Sarah, Dad, me and Frances.

5 female aircrew that have flown the Tornado GR4 at a hangar party 2019

Sarah, myself and Mum, 2015.

CHAPTER 12

SWISS CHEESE

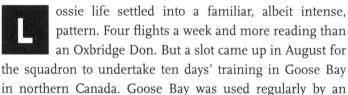

Lossie life settled into a familiar, albeit intense, pattern. Four flights a week and more reading than an Oxbridge Don. But a slot came up in August for the squadron to undertake ten days' training in Goose Bay in northern Canada. Goose Bay was used regularly by an assortment of national air forces for low-level training and although we were moving on to air combat, the boss decided it was too good an opportunity to miss.

To partake in air combat in a Tornado GR1 was a last resort. As a low-level ground-attack aircraft, if you got dragged into a dogfight in a Tornado something had gone badly pear–shaped. Still, it was worth practising the skills just in case.

The instructors couldn't believe their luck at getting a Goose Bay trip and flew out with the jets while myself, Rob, Chris, Radders, Steve and Mark piled into a transport aircraft with the ground crews for the trip across the Atlantic.

Happy Valley-Goose Bay is a remote outpost on the Churchill River near Lake Melville in Newfoundland. The low-slung, frontier-like town was spread out across the flats, with wide highways flanked by clapboard houses, diners, shops, pornography shops and bars. We were billeted on the base in the British block, one of four two-storey buildings for visiting international aircrew with an Officers' mess and bar in the middle.

According to the old hands, in winter it was so cold that all the base buildings were linked by underground passages, so you didn't have to go outside. But you needed the sense of a meerkat to take the correct staircase to pop up inside your chosen building.

Our first couple of flights were just familiarisation rides to get used to the local area, a vast flat featureless plain of 130,000 km square – bigger than Iceland – covered in pine forest, tundra and frozen lakes.

One stormy morning, on my third sortie of the tour, I was pitted against Rob in a series of merges designed to test our offensive and defensive flying against a single bogey. For the first time out there, I was flying with a navigator in my back seat, a great instructor called Jason P.

There were big thunderhead clouds around and in technical speak, the weather was hideous. We'd had a couple of engagements but the air was heavy and dark and it looked like we'd have to abort the mission. To make it count as one of our required flights we decided to push for one last merge.

We got into our dogfight, made some nice trails in the sky and then knocked it off. I radioed the tower. A voice told me there was a huge thunderstorm coming through and we should be prepared to divert to Halifax several hundred kilometres south across the Gulf of St Lawrence in Nova Scotia. I told them we were right on the fuel minimum, so they gave us the green light to try to land back at Goose Bay.

The cloud was thick and we were to come in on a precision approach radar (PAR) with air traffic control talking us down.

So far, so good, but then the tower asked if I would accept a PAR from a trainee air traffic controller. Without thinking I said yes. Second mistake. After pushing it to squeeze in the final merge, fuel was already tight and I needed the very best team on hand to get this aircraft down on the first attempt.

Normally on a PAR approach the controller would direct you to alter heading 'one degree left' or 'come right two degrees', 'slightly higher'. This guy was saying, 'five degrees left.' That's quite a lot of heading change at this late stage of an approach. Then he said, 'Ten degrees right.' I was doing my best in thick cloud and heavy turbulence but I was thinking, 'This must be really bad flying if I'm ten degrees out.'

In the back of my mind I was aware that at Goose Bay the runway is quite wide and divided in two halves. The left side was smooth, but the right side had a series of ridges in a ripple effect to stop water pooling from the frequent thunderstorms.

In our initial briefing we were told if it was wet, do not land left or centre, land on the right side.

The trainee in the tower was giving me five degrees this way, ten degrees that way and when we popped out of the cloud at 300ft, I saw in horror we were lined up with the apron where all the aircraft were parked.

I knew we were flying on fumes and didn't have enough fuel to go back around so I did a massive bank to the right thirty or so degrees to line up with the runway and then back left ready to slam it down on the centre line. I was thinking, 'Aren't I the girl?' for rescuing what could have been a disaster. Mistake number three. Avoid the centre line in the wet.

I slammed the main wheels on the tarmac and then eased down the front wheel. Gently, easy does it. My left hand pulled the throttles back to the idle position and I rocked them outboard to engage reverse thrust and powered up again to slow us down.

But suddenly, the left wheel started aquaplaning on the pools of water and we whipped through ninety degrees. Now we were skidding sideways down the runway at 150 knots.

I screamed, 'Loss of control' into the intercom and my left hand snatched back my throttles to idle. As soon as I had said the words out loud, my brain and hands reacted on automatic pilot, I'd practised this before in the simulator, so that when things do go wrong, you could 'just' follow the emergency drill. My left hand did what it was meant to do, cancelling thrust reverse and I rocked the throttles inboard.

But we were still sliding at a serious pace. I was pumping my foot pedals to try to straighten us out, but the jet was aquaplaning too fast, like a car on a sheet of ice. At the far end of the runway, but getting closer very quickly, was a German Tornado that had overshot and crashed earlier in the week. Bugger.

At this point I heard Jason shout, 'I'm not ejecting yet.' Oh my gosh, he's thinking about ejecting. It hadn't even crossed my mind. I instantly grabbed the handle between my legs. Am I ejecting?

Time had stopped. I was a bystander, watching fate decide my future. My eyes were staring. My open mouth locked in a frozen contortion under my mask, like the stupefied corpses of bodies in Pompeii. Our skid was taking us towards the right side of the runway.

My heart was pulsing and my right hand gripped the control stick like it was my only lifeline. By somehow not letting go of this meant everything would be OK I seemed to be thinking. Not that I was thinking. I was completely maxed out. My situational awareness was zero. But the drier ridges on the right side of the tarmac began to slow us down and my brain inched back from the brink as I sensed the slide coming to an end. Eventually we came to a stop. Miraculously we were lined up exactly with the taxi way to exit the runway. The knuckles on my left hand shone like white lights as I slammed the throttles forward to power up the engine. We surged backwards with a great roar.

I shouted to Jason, 'Why are we going backwards? We must be caught on something.' He replied, in an incredibly calm tone, mastered from years of flying with new pilots, 'Mandy, you've got reverse thrust on.' Oops. I disengaged thrust reverse, clicked into dry power to pull forward and we eased off the runway.

After a pause, Jason came up on the intercom, 'That was a bit close, then.' We both started laughing manically, out of shock more than anything.

All we got from the tower was, 'You're cleared to ground, taxi off, stud two.' That was it, no acknowledgement of our spin, nothing. Unbelievable.

Once the initial spike of adrenaline subsided, I began shaking. A near miss in the air happened in a heartbeat, but when you'd had thirty seconds of thinking, 'Is this it? Am I about to die?' it took a bit longer to get over.

Hand on heart, I had total mental overload. That's why I couldn't think why we were going backwards. When I shut the jet down, I just sat still in the cockpit for a few moments to gather my thoughts. I could hear Jason bustling around behind me but I just stared at the instrument panel. When the ground crew pushed the steps up to the side of the aircraft and climbed up to open the canopy, I shook my head like a dog after a swim and climbed out.

In those days although there was a safety reporting system, it was not well used and a blame culture existed which put people off from reporting mistakes. Jason and I talked about it walking in and we decided that we needed to share with others what had happened. As a student still in training I didn't want to look stupid but if this could happen to us then it could happen to anyone else. At least I had learned the lesson from when I'd forgotten to remove my seat pin on my first solo in the Tucano. It's so important to share anything like this so you can all learn from it.

It really hit me that evening. Bloody hell, that was your closest shave yet, Mandy. You could easily not be here now. I rang Craig and told him about my close-to-death experience. It was, however, only by the grace of God we came through unscathed. Ejecting from a spinning aircraft on the ground is not considered a Good Thing.

I was also cross with myself. 'Was it my fault? How did I let it get to that position?' In fact, it was a perfect storm of factors that came together. It was the classic Swiss Cheese Model, proposed by Professor James Reason, where all the holes align, opening up the likelihood of an accident.

With twenty-twenty hindsight I could have done so much differently. I should have been more proactive. To break this error chain, my advice now would be that if you hear yourself saying 'just' then stop. 'Just' normally means 'can't'. If you're driving down the motorway and you think you've got 'just' enough petrol, you probably haven't. Even if you have, you'll spend the next thirty miles panicking. It's the same with flying. If you think the weather is 'just' about all right, it's not. Have a reassess.

Our decision to squeeze in the last merge and air traffic's request for a student to talk me down on minimum fuel in extreme wet weather should have been like someone waving big red flags in front of us, saying 'Stop'.

I'm a firm believer that people have to learn but in hindsight it was totally inappropriate for air traffic control to even put me on the spot. There were plenty of safer times for that. Having half a runway ridged and half smooth was also ridiculous – a classic threat. Apparently, my incident wasn't that unusual. The crashed German Tornado at the end of the runway was proof.

You would think I failed the sortie, but actually it was a semi-textbook example of how to handle an emergency loss of control on the ground – ignoring the bit about not knowing why we were going backwards.

It's such a cliché but these emergency drills are drummed into us so much during training so they become automatic.

If you lose control on the ground the first reaction is for you or the navigator to say, 'Loss of control'. Not 'Oh my goodness' or 'Look, we're sliding'. Hearing the words is the trigger for your hands to go into the drill. It is like doing your times tables, so as soon as you hear 'four sevens,' for instance, you know the answer is twenty-eight.

The system works and the training has pulled many a pilot out of a scrape.

It was however, the first real time I had the feeling that I was not invincible.

Away from the flying, Goose Bay was proving to be a fun trip but it was also quite challenging. All the instructors had that feeling of being on detachment, not exactly in holiday mode, but operating under 'detachment rules' where playing hard at the weekend was priority.

The reality for us was we were still on the operational conversion unit under training, so we had to balance joining in with being under assessment.

The Canadian summer was lovely when there weren't thunderstorms in the area and we had plenty of team barbecues and sport and water skiing on the lake.

Nights out were spent at a place called Trappers' Cabin, a roadside diner that turned into a nightclub later on. Sometimes we'd go to The Bulldog, an infamous all-ranks bar on the base, with cheap beer and the propensity to get messy.

For a change we sometimes went to the tip. It might

sound like we were going stir crazy but it was the best place for spotting bears. We'd drive in slowly and put the headlights on. Being conscientious fast-jet pilots, we always made sure we had a wingman or a back seater checking our six o'clock position for bandit bears sneaking up on us, but we'd often get to watch a few bears rummaging through the rubbish.

One Friday night we were standing around the snooker table in the mess bar playing a game called 'Tanks' which involves strategically sending the white and black ball to one end or the other to try to get each other 'out.' On more than one occasion it turned combative and caused more bruises than a game of rugby. The boss walked in and said, 'Right, I've got your postings.'

These were the squadrons we would join when – and if – we passed the course.

We had put in our requests a while ago and I'd asked for RAF Marham in Norfolk. It was the most southerly option in the UK, otherwise it was staying at Lossie, or going to Germany. The boss ran down the list to general murmurs of approval until he got to me.

'Mandy, you've got II(AC) squadron, RAF Marham. Reconnaissance.'

Chris spat out his beer and the others erupted in cackles of laughter. I looked at him. 'What?'

'Well, you're not exactly the air force's top recce star, are you?'

He had a point.

Whenever we did recce training, I always ended up as the butt of the jokes. My recce skills were absolute rubbish. Often the training would be as simple as holding up big sheets of paper with the outline of an aircraft on it.

The instructor would then ask, 'Theirs or ours, Mandy?'

'Erm, theirs, looks too punchy to be ours.'

'So, you would shoot it down, then?'

'Yep, absolutely.'

'It's ours, Mandy, it's a Nimrod.'

'Right, ok.'

To me, one big tanker looked like another. Now, recce was going to be my specialisation.

To be fair, I knew Marham was a recce squadron but it was the best way of seeing Craig and maintaining some semblance of normal life. I was thrilled.

If Sir David Attenborough was voicing tonight's sortie in the skies above Lossie it would go something like, 'The Tornado, here in its natural habitat... stalking its prey at low level, in the dead of night, its bristling weapons primed for a lethal strike.'

There was no moon. There was nothing to see out of the cockpit, although I was faintly aware of the dark hulks of hills high above us on either side. We were somewhere west of Wick in the wilds of northern Scotland. There was virtually no man-made light down below. Even patches of water had lost their sheen despite being only 250ft above them.

We were flying blind.

I was studying the E-Scope, a little screen with a green display high up on the left of my cockpit dashboard. This housed the terrain-following radar, which, when coupled up with the autopilot kept the jet tracking the ground at a prescribed height. From the profile I could see what was coming up. I gave a running commentary.

'High ground ahead, expecting pull up in one, two, three – aircraft responding, over the top, nose down, levelling out at 250ft.'

My navigator, Radders chipped in with, 'Right turn, two o'clock, coming up in four miles...'

We were utterly absorbed. It was intense and needed total concentration. There was no other chat. We had to trust the equipment completely. The radio was quiet. The only voices were ours. I felt like we were the only two people left on the planet.

CHAPTER 13

DARK DAYS

In the late summer sunshine Lossie was beautiful, with stunning countryside and amazing beaches. We'd go sailing, with dolphins swimming around the boat and see seals sunbathing on the rocks. Sometimes the guys living in married quarters would throw parties or we'd hit Elgin for a knees-up on a Friday night. Craig would come up once a month and I would try to head down south to see him, Elliot and Chessie too. I was loving life and had never felt quite so content.

We were now into a dive-bombing phase, practising different profiles of attack over Tain range.

Every so often we would take an instructor pilot in the back seat for a check ride, before moving onto the next phase. There was a great story doing the rounds about a navigator on another course who was so scared during a strafe attack – when you dive towards the ground and unleash merry hell from your 27mm mauser cannon – that he yanked so hard on his radar stick thinking the pilot wouldn't pull up that he snapped it completely off.

Ignoring the intense pressure we were under to pass every flight and succeed in our dream, life was progressing well.

But on 14th October 1999 our world was rocked to the core.

There was a QWI (qualified weapons instructors – pronounced cue-why) course going through and I was helping in the planning room by photocopying maps for them. The QWI course was basically the best of the best, pilots and navigators, from various squadrons.

Eight of them took off for the mission, heading south from Lossie down towards the vast range at Spadeadam between Carlisle and Newcastle in the north of England. With my role in the mission planning done I went to the crew room for a brew and a chat.

The first I heard something was wrong was when one of the staff came in and told us the ops room was out of bounds and we had to stay put where we were. It seemed one of the four jets hadn't yet returned.

Course mates and instructors sat together in the crew room in a stunned silence. We had no other information and were in the dark for hours. The longer the lock down went on, the worse it seemed. Helicopters can crash land and the crew still be OK. But not fast jets. If no parachute was seen, that means there was no ejection, that's the reality. It was clear they weren't suddenly going to be found.

It was the worst feeling, just waiting in silence. No-one spoke, no-one did anything. I just sat there feeling sick, staring at the floor, the walls. Not wanting to make eye contact with anyone in case it set me off howling. Just waiting. Waiting.

Eventually one of the instructors, Richard, a lovely chap known to all as Deano, came in and blurted out,

'It's crashed. There are no survivors.'

It was blunt and a terrible way to reveal the news, but the poor guy's eyes were full of tears and his voice was strained.

Eight of them went out and two – Flt Lts Richard (Dickie) Wright and his navigator Sean Casabayo, both 30 – never returned. In bad weather they lost radar contact. The search and rescue helicopter was sent out and found wreckage near Newcastle. The jet had totally disintegrated.

It was utterly horrendous. I was just numb. I didn't move from the crew room. I was absolutely shocked that two guys at the top of their game hadn't come back. I just couldn't process it. It was really tragic, more than sad. Being on a squadron when you lose somebody is one of the worst feelings you can imagine.

That evening we all filed into the bar in a sombre and reflective mood. Their bar books were opened up and all drinks put on their accounts, which would obviously get chalked off at the end of the month.

I sipped at a beer but there was no taste, no enjoyment, just the tang of melancholy and disbelief.

As the alcohol kicked in so did the tears and raw emotions. The other guys on their course were all big characters and experienced second or third tourists in the Gulf, but they were in pieces.

The booze flowed and we toasted Dickie and Sean long into the night.

At some stage, as tradition dictates, the mess piano was wheeled outside and set on fire while someone was playing it.

That's the way it's always been done in the RAF. It's almost like this release. Moments like this bring about all the fragility and vulnerability of life and how dangerous the job is you're doing. The reality is, you do lose people.

I thought a lot about the effect on my family and friends if something happened to me but reconciled myself with the fact that driving down the motorway was just as dangerous.

We were given the Friday off and I flew back down to Winchester. I spent most of that weekend in a delayed state of shock. My raw emotions never far from the surface.

The atmosphere was still very subdued back at work on Monday. People knew life had to go on but it was difficult. It was even harder for the guys on their course.

That week there was another serious incident at Lossie when the station commander, Group Captain Alan Hudson, had to eject from his Jaguar over the Moray Firth after the jet suffered complete failure of its hydraulic systems. A Nimrod in the area immediately began searching on his beacon signal but couldn't find him. That's because he was just above them floating down in his parachute. He narrowly missed the Nimrod and was plucked from the sea by the search and rescue helicopter shorty after.

Two days later, I was flying a low-level trip up in the glens with Deano.

We heard on the radio London Military were trying to contact a Hawk from 100 Squadron based out of RAF Leeming in north Yorkshire. There was no response. They tried again. Nothing. It wasn't that unusual; they could have been out of range. Then we heard they had launched the search and rescue helicopter from Valley. I got a shiver down my spine. Oh no, this didn't sound good. It crossed my mind Craig was flying a Hawk that day. Deano and I fell very quiet save for operational chatter. I was trying desperately hard not to let my mind drift and to focus on the job. Fortunately, I was flying at nearly 500 knots at 250ft trying to locate different targets, so it wasn't hard to stay engaged with what I was doing.

When we landed, I heard a Hawk had crashed near the village of Shap, between Penrith and Kendal in Cumbria. The pilot was a friend of mine, Steve Todd. He died along with another pilot, Squadron Leader Mike Andrews. Steve and my paths had crossed many times. He was a top guy, lanky, very quick-witted and everyone's mate. He was a high-flyer and had won the sword of honour for the top student on his course at Initial Officer Training at RAF College, Cranwell. My sister had flirted with Steve at our Graduation Ball and Craig had been his instructor at Elementary Flying Training.

As soon as I could I hurried back to my room. I threw myself on my bed and sobbed and sobbed. They say that things come in threes, but this really was the final straw.

The final SAP (simulated attack profile) phase of our flying at Lossiemouth was like minestrone soup. A bit of everything we had learned, all mixed in together.

Each of these final flights simulated a different type of attack, building up towards precision formation navigation at low level to arrive at certain waypoints exactly on time. There would be various different bombing scenarios on Tain range, on targets out in the Moray Firth or on a sea stack south of Skye.

The bombing now was not just a case of hitting a target. We were told specifically what each target was, such as a bunker or a building or an enemy convoy and we had to then plan what weapons and fuse settings to use to suit each attack, whether it be a bunker with a three-metre thick concrete roof housing fibre optics, or a soft target like tanks. You needed the right weapon for the job and then the right fuse setting, so the bomb exploded at the optimal moment. For a deep bunker complex, you'd want a delay of maybe half a second, so the bomb had time to penetrate, rather than exploding on the surface.

We were getting close to being operational and the whole point of the trip was to destroy the target, so you had to start thinking about bigger things.

We also did electronic warfare training at the Spadeadam range, about 9,600 acres of forest and moorland dotted with a variety of radar threats representing different surface-to-air missile systems, gun-related radars and moveable weapons such as Scud missiles. It's perfect for practising tactics, manoeuvres and electronic counter-measures.

Every sortie was progressively more difficult, but it wasn't boom or bust because by this stage the RAF had invested about £3.7m in your training. If you did fail, chances were they'd backtrack you and give you another chance.

My final check ride was an hour-and-a-half mission leading a two-ship formation at low level down the glens, through the gap between Glasgow and Edinburgh and along the Moffat Valley to bomb various targets while evading the radar installations hidden in the trees at Spadeadam.

This one took mega planning, more than two hours pouring over maps.

I had to factor in lay bombing, dive attacks and strafe attacks. We had to take into account various ground threats from radars and work out evasion plans and co-ordinate attack and defence plans for the bounce aircraft that would be hunting us. Obviously, they wouldn't be shooting us down but they would test our air defence skills and try to disrupt our timings and give us fuel problems.

It was a massive capacity-sapping exercise and we hadn't even got airborne yet.

I had that, by now, familiar feeling of tension and apprehension. I wasn't worried about failing, I'd done well on this course and had proved myself to be capable and resilient. None of the wobbles of Valley here. But this was the big one, in a good way, and I wanted to show them how good I could be. This felt like the icing on the cake, a chance to really excel. It felt like the staff were willing us to do well, too, rather than trying to catch us out.

After we had planned the mission, we all came together for the final mission brief. I stood up at the front, looking at the formation of course mates and instructors. The bounce aircraft joined us too, as it was important that they knew all the details of the trip. They then disappeared off to work out the best places to intercept us and how to wreak as much havoc as possible.

I laid the slides out on the overhead projector. I took all the questions that came up well and felt ready to go... this could be my last sortie in my lengthy RAF training and I was raring to go.

Climbing out of the jet that afternoon I was drained but I felt confident. We'd hit our targets on time, worked well together and I couldn't really think of anything screamingly bad. I had a funny feeling in my stomach as I walked across the apron to the debriefing room. For all I knew I could have failed the flight on some minor technicality, but I just had this sense I had flown my last trip at Lossiemouth. I looked back towards the jet and down the runway, just taking it all in. It was like the last day at secondary school, sad it's over but exited for what's to come next.

I stowed my helmet back in the locker and took my lucky chair next to the radiator in the debrief.

'How do you think you got on? '

'Well, I, er...'

'Congrats, Mandy, you've passed.'

Relief, jubilation and pride washed over me. All the hard work had finally paid off. I had never given up on my dream, even when the going had got tough. I'd learned so much about myself, about my strengths and my weaknesses, but I'd also seen the difference an amazing team could make. Although I was only the second woman to go through the Tornado pilot training, I never considered myself to be a trailblazer because I was always just one of the team. I am under no illusion that if it weren't for my family, course mates and my mentors who had been uncompromising in their support I would never had just heard those magic words.

I'd been in the RAF for just over four years and on 8th Nov 1999, I'd finished the operational conversion unit with seventy-nine hours in a Tornado. Shame not to get to eighty in a way, but no big deal.

Lossie, thanks for the memories.

CHAPTER 14

SHINY TWO

T he car was packed again and I was heading to Kings Lynn in Norfolk for a date with 'Shiny Two.' My new squadron, II (Army Co-operation) Squadron, was the oldest fixed-wing squadron in the RAF, based at Marham. It's historic and a lot of the air force's top brass came from it, hence the nickname.

Rocking up at the gates of RAF Marham on a crisp November morning as their first ever female pilot was technically another historic moment.

I was proud of myself and excited to be joining my first operational squadron, my dream job as a tornado pilot. Neither I, nor the squadron were quite prepared for what was to come.

Up until now in my career I had been surrounded by people who knew me, most of whom I'd been through training with from the beginning. We had confidence in numbers. To my mates I was just Mandy, Big Bird, another aspiring fast jet pilot, no different to anyone else for being a woman. And there were other women on some courses too. Even on the OCU at Lossie we lived in our little bubble.

Now I was out in the big wide world. I was joining a squadron of about 250 people, with about forty in my immediate sphere of whom I knew one – GB – who was six months in front of me.

I felt under the microscope like never before.

Marham was very different to Lossie. As an operational airfield there were loads of big semi-circle roofed sheds made of reinforced steel with grass growing on top so you can't see them from above – known as a HAS (hardened aircraft shelter).

The operations building was in one of these and you felt as if you were hidden away from the world, which I suppose was the whole point of them. There was no flight line as I had always been used to, each HAS was the home to a different aircraft.

When I walked in on my first morning, I saw that on virtually every wall in the Junta (junior aircrew) crew room was a calendar of naked women, the classic Pirelli jobs. Plus, I quickly found out, all the screen savers on the computers were of naked women, too. I let this pass for a couple of days and then I surreptitiously changed them all to pictures of scantily clad men. Surprisingly the next day they were all miraculously scenic landscapes. I had made my first mark!

I was nervous enough anyway, but this threw me a bit more off kilter. It was a very testosterone-fuelled atmosphere. You could smell it in the air.

The first week was spent moving into the mess, meeting as many people as I could and reading piles of books on the squadron and the Tornado. I took a couple of sim rides and got airborne the following week with an instructor in the back seat.

As a squadron we would be deploying to Kuwait in April 2000 to patrol the southern no-fly zone in Iraq as part of Operation Southern Watch. My priority was to be combat ready by then, although with Christmas looming, this would likely have to wait until the new year.

One day I was flicking through the squadron diary and I noticed we were down for Exercise Red Flag in Las Vegas in February.

This was a joint exercise involving lots of different air forces practising for a coalition war. It's a massive war game, a combined operations training mission. It just happens the Arizona desert is a very decent replica of Iraq.

I knew I wouldn't have enough hours to actually fly in it, but on asking around, I was told I would be going as part of the operations team, helping to plan for the missions.

It seemed I'd landed on my feet here. 'Lucky cow,' was the general consensus. Red Flag is a bit of a golden ticket and lots of people don't get to go in their entire career. Here I was, having just waltzed onto the squadron getting a Las Vegas gig straight away.

Even though I wouldn't be flying it was exciting because it would be good to be working backstage and logging some experience of mission planning. Plus, it was Vegas, baby, and should be fun.

We flew out there by VC10, one of the big transport aircraft, and landed at Nellis airforce base in the Nevada desert in piercing sunshine.

We were bussed to a small hotel on the outskirts of Vegas. No Bellagio's or Venetian's for us. Apparently, the RAF can't have personnel on exercise exposed to all those slot machines and that gambling. Oh no. So, we were put in a tin-pot little joint with a tiny pool on the edge of town on probably twice the rate the big hotels could have offered us.

I was so excited driving into Nellis the next morning. I'd heard so many stories about it. I felt like a tennis fan on their first trip to Wimbledon or a golfer going to the Masters at Augusta. Oh my goodness, we're actually here. I was in awe of the whole thing and felt very proud to be part of it.

Nellis was the busiest fighter jet airfield in the US – the epitome of aviator cool. Very modern, very clean and very American, with big, wide roads, lots of grass and even more sprinklers, like a golf resort or country club.

It was a stark contrast to the rather more raffish downtown Vegas, with single story modern buildings and replica airplanes on stands outside. 'Red Flag' was daubed everywhere just in case you'd forgotten where you were.

Aircraft of all descriptions were parked on the aprons and aircrew of myriad nationalities scurried about.

On the first morning we filed into an enormous briefing room, like a theatre with banked seating. On the stage was a lectern in front of a giant video screen.

The place was packed with buzz-cutted aircrew. A square-jawed American stood up at the front and a hush went around.

'Hi, my name's Ninja and I'm the commanding officer...'

Once he'd done his bit another identikit American took to the lectern.

'I'm Tomcat, and I'm the best goddamn navigator in town.'

It was totally Top Gun.

After several corny call-signs and much American self-adulation, it was the turn of one of our squadron members. He casually strolled onto the stage, looked up, paused and said, 'My name is Biggs. I'm called that because I have a fondness for large women.' We all cracked up. The Americans had been so serious and pleased with themselves and the Brits just stole the show.

Milling about Nellis was like a massive reunion for me, with loads of friends from training days in various squadrons, either on the C130 Hercules or the Tornado F3. As I was still finding my feet and my identity on the squadron it was brilliant to have that connection.

Red Flag was a massive game of war played out over the Nevada desert and in the canyons and valleys to the north west of Vegas in an area half the size of Switzerland. The philosophy is that you train harder than you will ever have to fight for real.

It was a huge jigsaw puzzle to organise. The goodies

were the blue force, made up of British Tornado F3 fighters looking at air threats, our Tornados there as bombing and reconnaissance, another GR4 squadron, plus American F15s, F18s, A10 bombers, alongside air forces from France, Portugal, Spain and Turkey. The bad guys were the red force, made up of various US Air Force units, principally using F16s as the 'enemy.'

It's vital to learn to work with people in different roles in a coalition theatre of war to co-ordinate attack and defence. For instance, if you're going near a surface to air missile (SAM) emitting at your frequency you need the help of IX(B) Squadron, who could suppress the radar, jam the frequency and get the threat off your back.

Different individuals from various countries and squadrons were made the mission lead on any particular day.

Each air force would submit their training requirements, such as wanting to drop a 1,000lb bomb and it would get factored into the plan.

Once we had the big picture, we covered everything from weather to exact timings and deconfliction plans. The planning stage could easily take up to six hours for one mission.

In the mornings I'd go for a swim or a stroll down the strip. Nosing about some of the famous spots, I couldn't get over the fact that the people were still gambling or starting this early. The ching, ching, ping, ping noise of the slot machines and the casinos lit up like Christmas trees drove me crazy.

I would go into the base about lunchtime and plan all afternoon and early evening. The aircraft launched when it got dark and the mission would run from about eight pm to ten pm, then we would debrief and be done by about midnight.

It was an intense Monday to Friday but slightly different to your average working week. Friday nights tended to be a big blow out in the Nellis bar, a buzzing multi-national knees-up.

One evening I'd organised a squadron dinner in Vegas. We were being picked up from outside our hotel in a stretched limo. I decided to make a bit of an effort, which merely involved putting on a dress and some make-up. It was nothing over the top, just something a bit more feminine than my green growbag.

I walked down the stairs into the lobby and Michel, a French navigator on exchange with the squadron, said: 'Mandy, you look beautiful this evening.'

I was just about to utter, 'Why thank you,' when Rich M blurted out, 'You can't say that to Mandy, she's one of the boys.'

Michel replied, with a Gallic shrug of the shoulders: 'Pah, You Brits, you know nothing about women.' We all roared with laughter.

It summed up how the rest of the squadron saw me, which was both good and bad. Good, because I was seen to be integrating with the guys, bad because they were neglecting the fact that I was a woman and therefore intrinsically different.

My friend Suraya was also in Vegas as a navigator with a Tornado F3 squadron. We had been friends at university and at initial officer training together but because she was a navigator and her training was a little shorter, without all the lengthy 'holds' the pilots had, she had reached a front-line squadron much quicker than me.

She is also very talented and one day was appointed as blue force mission leader.

It was a huge honour and a big job, she did brilliantly and the mission went well. I felt so proud of her, standing on the stage, briefing the huge auditorium full of testosterone filled aircrew. She came across as so incredibly professional, a great role model for female aircrew. (As testament to this Suraya is now the highest-ranking female aircrew in the RAF.)

She and I were on a high at the end of it and decided to go out into Vegas together, just us girls.

We went to a place called the VooDoo Lounge on the roof of the Rio Hotel. This place was 51 stories up and had fabulous views across the whole of Sin City.

We weren't messing about and ordered a Witch Doctor, an enormous goldfish bowl cocktail full of spirits. Smoke from dry ice swirled about the top to make it look like some devilish potion bubbling in a cauldron. Which, in effect, was exactly what it was.

With a smile on our faces we went down to 'Boogie Nights', a nightclub in the basement, which was rammed with a lively, dressed-up crowd.

At one point they turned the music down and a guy got on a microphone to announce a dance contest with $1000 prize for the best couple. A grand just for dancing on the stage? Stick us down for that. We launched ourselves up there in a flash.

There were ten other couples and one other all-woman pair. Everyone was grooving away to cheesy disco music. Some were dancing properly as a couple, doing twirls and spins and even the odd lift, while others just jammed loosely opposite each other. If you weren't up to scratch the guy tapped you on the shoulder and you were out in time-honoured dance-off style.

We ramped it up to avoid the chop with some Dirty Dancing inspired moves and got down to the last four couples. Kool and the Gang's Ladies Night came on and we moved in closer.

With a belly full of Witches Brew we were ready to take it to the next level and began really grinding together. It was all getting a bit steamy in a hilarious kind of way.

Two other couples were given the heave-ho, leaving us and the other all-girl team, who were both stunning.

All four of us were really going for it. I executed a particularly gymnastic manoeuvre to end up on the floor, and Suraya climbed on top of me, grinding away to the music. We were grinning madly at each other, lost in the moment, but not forgetting the $1000 carrot. Then the other girls got their breasts out. Ah, er...

Fortunately, that seemed to do it for the judge and he tapped us on the shoulder. We escaped, cashless, but dignity just about intact. It didn't matter anyway as we didn't know anyone in the place. It was just one of those very funny impromptu nights but nothing bad happened and we didn't break any rules.

The next day at work I had to give someone a lift, so I took a pool car and drove down to the flight line where all our aircraft were. The ground crews were all beavering away, and as I got out of the car I was met with a wave of ovation, 'Wayhay, ma'am.'

I turned around to see who had appeared behind me. Then I realised all eyes were on me. They'd all been in Rios. I felt very hot all of a sudden and didn't quite know what to do. Should I wave? Inside I'm thinking, 'Well done, Mandy, you utter muppet. How to embarrass yourself, step forty-two.' I grinned inanely and tried not to look sheepish.

But actually, I seemed to have garnered a new-found respect. 'Welcome to the squadron,' seemed to be the message.

At the end of Red Flag, I was allowed to help begin flying the jets home. GB and I as junior pilots took off with a navigator each in the backseat from Nellis bound for the Tinker Air Force base near Oklahoma City, and then down to Savannah, Georgia. It was a great little trip and gave us each a two or three-hour leg to fly.

We had a free night in Savannah, so we went with a few of our ground crew to a place called the Blue Oyster. It was like a joint out of a deep-south backwater movie. We were all on tequila and it got pretty messy but for some reason I was fine.

Someone later sent a cartoon of me standing at a bar, with a load of blokes at my feet and the caption, 'And that, gentlemen, is how you drink tequila.' My reputation, for better or worse, was growing.

The next day we took a Hercules – the world's most uncomfortable form of transport, a bare empty shell with just netting for seats – to Goose Bay. Some Tornado F3 guys had just flown in and were laughing at our jaded and, in some cases, very hungover state.

The Herc crew had money for rations and had been to TGI Fridays for nachos and mud pies which helped soak up the tequila. We landed in thick snow and had a steak at Trappers and an early night. The F3 guys, meanwhile, went out large. Settling down for a nice comfortable ten-hour fight back across the Atlantic in the Herc the next day it was our turn to laugh. They were green and about to be met by bright-eyed wives and some crazy kids at the other end.

The clock was ticking on our departure for Kuwait. I had a month back at Marham to complete my combat ready work-up.

That meant intensive flying, sixteen trips in March, including air-to-air refuelling sessions and trials of the TIALD (thermal imaging airborne laser designator) pod. This was the system used for the laser-guided Paveway bomb we would be using in the Gulf. Usually one jet in a two-ship formation would laser the bomb onto the target and the other would actually release the weapon.

The TIALD put a lot of workload onto the navs who had to locate targets and then make sure they had the right codes for the laser and the right codes for each weapon.

My respect for the navigators grew daily when you start to realise that in many ways the front-seater pilot is just a taxi driver. The pilot just creates a stable platform for the navigator who doubles as the weapons operator. You really need to be working as an efficient team, trusting each other to do the job to the best of their abilities.

I also had to cram in some night flying to get my hours up. One of the reasons I couldn't fly at Red Flag was because I didn't have enough night-flying experience. But here I was about to be sent to a conflict zone where most of the sorties would likely take place at night. Figure that one out.

Alongside the practical flying, I had to get my head in the books again to swat up on the hardware we were likely to encounter out there and whether it was friend or foe.

There was absolutely masses to learn on electronic warfare and weapons.

The surface-to-air missile system SA-6 was common in Iraq at the time so it was key to learn what it looked like – like a tank with three great big missiles in a rack on the top – what the signal of its associated radar 'Spoon Rest' looked like and what our receiver would be telling us when it spotted one.

My final sortie was to drop a live 1000lb bomb on a range in Cardigan Bay off the coast of Wales near Aberporth in Pembrokeshire.

I was paired with a navigator called Bax who was also on his first squadron.

Bax and I geared up and set off, knowing this was a biggie.

The practice bombs we had been dropping up to now just went 'puff' and made a little cloud. Real bombs go bang and cost an awful lot more money.

From Marham we climbed to 20,000ft to cross the country in one of the air corridors before dropping into low level over Wales.

The target was to be an orange raft somewhere out in the bay, parts of which are a designated range for the military.

It was a blustery, greyish kind of a day and we set up our bombing pattern over the sea. The waves were enormous and the wind was whipping their tops into a foamy froth.

Bax was peering intently into his screen, trying to pinpoint the raft as the radar painted a picture of the seascape speeding up at 500 knots in front of us.

Each time he thought he had it, the raft miraculously disappeared. Bax was struggling to get a decent mark.

'Thirty seconds,' I said into the radio, indicating our time to the target.

'Continue,' he replied, meaning he hadn't positively identified it yet.

'Fifteen seconds.'

'Continue.'

'Ten seconds.'

'Captured.' He's got it. Phew. 'Sure?' 'Think so.'

'Switches live.'

'Five seconds.'

'Captured.'

'Committing.' That's me thumbing the bomb release button on my control stick. The weapon drops and I pull away in a wide arc to the right for the long trip home.

Back in the debrief room at Marham, the weapons instructor played back the onboard video.

Watching the grainy footage, I gripped my mug of tea tightly as a gnawing feeling spread up from my feet. What we thought was the raft was actually the crest of a wave breaking.

It did look a bit like a raft from the way the radar was painting it on the screen. Then again it could have been debris on the sea. Either way, what it wasn't was a little orange life raft that was our target.

'Guys, you've just wasted a 1000lb bomb here,' said the pilot QWI (Qualified weapons instructor).

It was disappointing as there was a big pressure to deliver. However, we were two very inexperienced crew flying together and we both felt the pressure to drop the weapon.

We had talked ourselves into seeing what we wanted to see, not what was there. We'd decided that because we were on target, because we were over the sea... because, because, because.

What we should have done was bring the bomb back.

If there is any doubt, there's no doubt. You don't drop. If you have not got the target acquired, you are not dropping that bomb. It was a good wake-up call and a harsh lesson in not succumbing to personal pressure. If there was a time to learn this lesson, then over the Irish Sea was probably as good a time as any. It was a lesson I would never forget and one that held me in good stead for my operational time in Iraq.

CHAPTER 15

QUEEN OF
THE DESERT

I couldn't wait to get there. Judging by the energy fizzing around the squadron, nor could anyone else as our departure day ticked closer. It might sound mad, it makes me sound like a war-mongering robot, being desperate to get out to a military theatre where there was a very good chance of being shot at, but I was looking forward to it with the same butterfly-inducing anticipation as a summer party with a hot date lined up. I wasn't fearful or scared. Just keen to go and do the thing I'd been training to do for seemingly ever, like a footballer desperate for a game.

The female emotions you might have assumed I would have about going to war just didn't happen. I was more nervous about flying in a huge coalition of aircraft from different countries. It was more about not embarrassing myself. More about getting it right, for me and the team, and not letting them down.

Our job as part of Operation Bolton, in turn part of Operation Southern Watch, was to defend the no-fly zone over southern Iraq, almost up to Baghdad. From our intelligence reports we'd learned there was no actual air threat from the Iraqis but we didn't want them rebuilding their air force, or massing weapons, or putting fibre-optic communications underground. We wanted them to keep their telecoms visible so we could gather intelligence on any build-ups of troops and equipment.

Despite my eagerness, in the back of my mind I wondered what was really the point of us being out there? What were we trying to achieve in the big picture? The 1991 Gulf War had long finished and the newspapers had even gone a bit quiet on Iraq. Still, orders are orders. I tried not to make too much of my departure among family and friends, just a breezy 'see you in a couple of months,' like I was off on my travels.

I turned up at RAF Brize Norton for the flight to Kuwait dressed like everyone else in our civilian equivalent of uniform. Chinos, blue checked shirt and a blazer. I was wearing exactly the same as all the other guys in the mess. It occurred to me I should try to maintain my identity. It was great to be part of the team, but I was a woman, I loved being a woman and I needed to be true to myself and not just gently morph into the masses.

We were allowed one big RAF kit bag for our personal stuff but I had no idea what to take. I am a prolific reader, and this was before Kindles or tablets, so I loaded my bag with fourteen massive novels. That should do me for eight weeks I thought, although they did take up a large proportion of the bag.

I stuffed in a couple of flying suits and long johns to wear under them, despite the heat. My g-suit, helmet, and life-support jacket all went separately.

We were taking over from 14 Squadron and we'd be using their jets, which were already out there, so we trooped onto a VC-10 for the ten-hour flight to Ali Al Salem Air Base, in the desert about half an hour's drive west of Kuwait City.

As we began the final approach, I peered out of the window to get some sense of my new home. It didn't take long to make my first impressions. Yellow, brown, empty, almost certainly dusty. Definitely hot. I could see the glinting glass and steel of the capital's skyscrapers packed in a tight thicket next to the coast, with lower-rise districts petering out into the vast, beige nothingness of desert beyond. Ali Al Salem was a concrete island in the sand just under thirty miles from Iraq's southern border.

Stepping off the airplane was like walking into a fan oven. It was about thirty-five degrees with a warm wind blowing. It even smelled hot and the inside of your nose tingled as you breathed in.

Driving across the base I was struck by how huge and flat it was with line upon line of identical single-story prefabs.

I had a lump in my throat as reality began to hit me. Oh. My. Goodness. I signed up to do this. To spend months at a time in this dump. What was I thinking?

Home was a flat-roofed hut, exactly the same as the hundreds of other huts in a row, which all slept forty people, each in their own cubicle of a room.

A corridor ran down the centre of the hut, with a tiny kitchen in the middle and a set of toilets and three showers at each end, which were now going to be mixed, because of me. It never actually occurred to me this was anything unusual. I never gave it a second thought.

Opening the door onto my 'cell' I was greeted by wall-to-ceiling pornography. Naked girls in various poses and states of undress, and other things. Nice. Not.

I was never sure if that room was given to me deliberately, owing to the lovely decor chosen by the previous occupant, or whether it was done bespoke for me as a standing joke.

I just stripped it all off, dumped it outside my door and yelled, 'Porn's up, boys'.

The first time it really hit me that I was on a real-deal, life-and-death tour of duty, and not just on a dusty training detachment, was later that day when I walked past a huge sand bunker outside the briefing room. I asked someone what this was for and I learned it was a safety backstop for loading and unloading your personal weapon.

Now we were on operations we would be flying with Browning 9mm pistols. You could choose whether or not to fly with yours loaded. I had a bit of a think and chose not to. I just didn't like the thought of flying with a bullet in the chamber of the gun, whether the safety catch was on or not. We were also issued with a new sandy pink coloured flying suit with no name badge on it, just a small Union flag.

I lay awake for most of the first night – and plenty afterwards – contemplating my new world and my role in it.

We were 200-strong supported by the RAF Regiment, but there are so many trades out there contributing to the effort you realise that even as a fast-jet pilot you are one small cog in a big machine.

Mostly, though, I just lay awake bemoaning the sketchy air-conditioning system.

It either didn't work at all, in which case I broiled in my own sweat and couldn't sleep, or if it did come on it was so loud the walls shook and my ears rang.

Ali Al Salem was split into two halves, with the Brits on one side and the Americans on the other, and never the twain shall meet. We had to be invited over, and it was worth buttering up the yanks we met as they had fast food, McDonalds, ice cream parlours, cafes, even a huge duty-free shop.

Our catering facility, on the other hand, was a large canteen, but we did have wonderful catering staff who managed to pull together some incredible meals on limited resources. But an outpost of modern American consumerism it was not. Having said that, after a few weeks I spotted more and more of our American friends (especially the fire-crews) who just happened to find themselves on 'duty' on the British side of the camp, particularly on Sundays when the comforting wafts of a full roast dinner drifted on the desert breeze.

The first couple of flights out there were just to acquaint ourselves with the area and get used to flying in these conditions and operating in hot temperatures. When the air is hotter it is less dense and so the performance of the aircraft goes down. It's why all the runways in the Middle East are longer.

There are lots of different operational aspects to get your head around. For instance, you have to learn about tyre limiting speeds – tyres would get too hot, so you had to taxi, and then stop to let your tyres cool down before you could continue, otherwise they would burst.

In the lecture room, the QWI pushed us hard from the word go and he ran extra briefings for us junior guys.

We were quizzed constantly on weapons systems, SAM systems, radar systems, anything and everything to do with electronic warfare and weaponry.

'Mandy, what is the radar associated with a SA-8, what frequency does it operate on? Come on, quickly, quickly...'

I felt sure I was being singled out but put it down to being the newbie and tried to crack on with the job.

Another mind bender was the HaveQuick radio. This was a frequency-hopping system to keep our radio comms secure. You couldn't fly over the border unless it was working.

You had to put in twenty different codes to make it secure and the pressure to get it up and running was enormous.

Imagine sitting in a greenhouse with the doors shut in thirty degree heat. That's what it was like when the hood came down on the cockpit. The Tornado did have ECS – environment control system – as you couldn't have the avionic equipment overheating, but it was rubbish. The fans were directed down to cool the avionics, not into the cockpit so there was no air con until you were airborne.

If we didn't have enough on our plates trying to get over the mental obstacle course of the pre-flight checks, while strapped fully clothed in a sauna, we had to go through the hassle of the loading the frequencies into the HaveQuick radio. Everyone else in the team would be waiting and listening on the net so I was desperate to sound really professional.

I'd be just thinking, 'Please let this work, please...' After a short but agonising time it goes beep and you know you can go secure. For me that was almost the most stressful bit of the job.

The learning curve in those first few weeks was utterly vertical. I'd got my wings and was on my first tour with an operational squadron, so you'd think I was doing well and going places. The reality was very different. I was like the classic swan, trying to look calm and serene on the surface but paddling like hell underneath just to stay afloat.

A handful of mornings into my new life I filed into the briefing room clutching a mug of tea expecting another routine training flight.

We sat in two rows – five pilots and five navigators – in front of a big projector screen.

John Packer, known as Pacman, was on his second tour and was the mission lead. He waited as we settled down. 'Today's mission is a retaliation strike. The targets are two anti-aircraft batteries in southern Iraq, which have been causing us some problems.'

So not training then. Not a spot of gentle reconnaissance to take some aerial snaps of SAM sites. No, instead of a little sightseeing, my first mission into Iraqi airspace as a pilot on a recon squadron was to drop live bombs. Oh, gosh.

My eyes enlarged to the size of saucers and my insides surged as if someone had plugged my chair into the mains. Electricity danced around the room. A live bombing mission was a big deal even for the experienced crews.

We'd be going over the border in a four-ship, in battle formation – two aircraft in front, two behind in each flight – with a spare aircraft sparked up and ready on the runway in case any of us couldn't take off.

After the initial brief to set out the big picture of the mission we split up to begin the detailed planning.

I was flying number two in the first wave with Andy, a really experienced navigator, in my backseat.

As the most junior pilot my role in the planning was to assist anyone and everyone, from photocopying maps to working with the navigators on the routes.

The formation leader had all the mission-specific information and delegated duties to the team: The lead navigator planned the route; the QFI (qualified flying instructor) was tasked with calculating all the right speeds for take-off, given the temperature and our payloads; another pilot focused on the targets – what weapons to select, what should be the fuse settings, how should they be deployed; someone else was in charge of investigating all possible threats in the area.

We had a man responsible for comms and radio frequencies, someone on weather duty, and another responsible for speaking to the Americans to find out what else would be up in the airspace. They had a whole collection of aircraft likely to be patrolling about up there, from F15s and F18s to A10 tank busters and the Prowlers, electronic warfare specialists and we didn't want to get in a tangle with any of them.

The planning was intense and took all morning. Armed with all the information we'd need we came together again after lunch for the main briefing.

The briefing covered every single 'what if?' scenario.

What if you lose an engine here? What if you had to eject here? What's the RHWR (Radar Homing and Warning Receiver) tag of a SA-10? What's the missile engagement range of a SA-6?

One radar facility was called Big Bird – my nickname – so I couldn't forget that, but I was right on the edge of my capacity.

All the questions seemed to be coming to me, like a contestant under the spotlight in Mastermind. I felt under pressure to perform, to not show myself up, to hold my own.

I was under the cosh, but I thought I did OK given the circumstances, although I was a bit confused as to why I had to field every curve ball. I just assumed this was how it always was with the junior pilots and put it down to testing out the new girl.

The briefing lasted more than an hour, ending with timings working backwards from the target. So, we're dropping the bombs at 2005 which gives us a take-off time of 1805 which means walking out by 1705 so we'll suit up at 1620. It was so precise it almost factored in what time we had our last wee.

We had a couple of hours before we had to put on our war faces so I retreated to my room and lay down on my bed.

I'd thought about having a nap but my head was too restless, my mind spinning as quickly as the ceiling fan I was staring at, but not as noisy.

Anxiety nibbled at the inside of my head: about the reality of a live mission with a real, tooled-up enemy waiting for us; about what could go wrong; about making a basic mistake; about letting down the team. I knew I was ready for it and I knew I was more than capable but there is always that nagging doubt. What if, when it comes down to the precise, defining moment of my career so far, I come up a bit short?

Suiting up in the crew room and seeing the faces and the cool but determined attitudes of the guys gave me a lift. I'm glad I'm on their team, I thought. Walking out in the residual heat of late afternoon alongside Andy, I felt reassured to know I was flying with a top man.

I climbed into the cockpit and strapped in as a member of the ground crew pulled down the lid. I felt the heat build immediately.

My hands went to work, flicking quickly over the switches.

I came up on comms and soon started the engines before easing us off our blocks bang on time.

My heart was thumping because I knew I had to get through the HaveQuick checks. My head felt like it was in a pressure cooker.

On the radio I could hear, 'Spartan formation, check in'.

'Spartan Two,' I responded punchily.

'Three.'

'Four.'

'Loud and clear – HaveQuick check.'

I was fumbling away with the HaveQuick, trying to plug in the last codes quickly but cleanly, avoiding fat fingers and having to start all over again. I finished and pressed enter... that interminable pause... and then 'beep'. Thank heavens for that. Anything else now is a bonus. Just in time too.

We taxied past the ground engineers who held up boards with any last-minute threats, as well as reminders to check electronic warfare equipment and the radar homing and warning receiver (RHWR) are working. On a later tour in 2002 they held up the latest World Cup football scores.

Reaching the end of the taxiway we waited for final clearance. We were in position, slightly staggered so as to avoid picking up any FOD (foreign object damage) from the exhaust pipes of the jet in front. Our poor engines took a beating operating in the desert. Tiny stones were always being ingested into the huge engines, our 'sooties', the engineers who specialised on the engines, certainly had their work cut out.

We lined up and I watched the leader intently, waiting for his signal for spooling up his engines. Then seeing his head nod, to indicate that he is taking off his breaks, I eased my feet off the brakes and was pinned into my seat as the jet lurched forward. We reached our take-off speed and lifted into the Kuwait sky. As I cleaned up the aircraft, taking up the gear and flaps, the air-conditioning kicked in and came as a welcome, sweet blast of cold air. I was so hot and sweaty that my oxygen mask kept on slipping down over my nose. I had to keep my chin jutted out as if I was doing the world's worst impression of Jimmy Hill, just to keep it in position on my face. I settled behind number one in a holding pattern while we made sure everyone was up and OK.

All secure, I stuck about three-quarters-of-a-mile off the right wing of number one as we went through a final set of checks, known as fence checks, in preparation to push over the border. The first is simply switching off the lights. No point in advertising our arrival any more than we have to. One of the last things to do was make live the master arming switch (MASS) up on the top left console.

This meant we could now operate any of the jet's weapons and defensive systems, such as flares in case any missiles get a lock on the moment we cross into Iraq. In the UK the only time we would have the master arming switch to live is for take-off in case of emergency, when we need to jettison any additional weight, such as fuel tanks.

Down below, the heat of the late afternoon sun was creating a haze, consuming the desert and making it even more monochromatic. Only the occasional road, often arrow straight, punctuated the blank canvas.

There was no chatter, all very professional, what's known as a sterile cockpit when operational.

A lot of people ask what it is like at war. For ground troops I am sure it is a whole different ball game but as a fast-jet pilot I was still in my familiar office environment, just with a different view out of the window.

As we got closer to Baghdad there were more roads and more traffic. We'd been flying for about forty-five minutes and the sun was sinking into the ground. We were homing in on where the target should have been, in an area of sandbanks and berms.

'Thirty seconds to run,' I said into the intercom.

'Not positively identified,' replied Andy in a business-like manner.

He was working hard behind me, focusing closer on the area, enlarging his TIALD picture to get a clearer image. If the target was there at all it was likely to be camouflaged. Or it could have moved since we received our intelligence, or it was never there in the first place.

I flicked the Late Arm switch to live in readiness for committing the bomb and with my right thumb flipped open the cover on the top of my control column leaving the big red drop button exposed.

Knowing that a quick downward jerk of my thumb could lead to pain, destruction and death down below did not cross my mind. I was fully focused on the task in hand. The days for wondering whether you are doing the right thing are long gone. You sign up knowing you have to do this.

'Fifteen seconds.'

'Continue, not positively identified.'

'Five seconds... '

'Abort.'

It was all very clinical, with set phraseology. We kept it standard on every flight so that if you fly with someone different, you can still work well together as a crew. It also ensures that at critical moments there is no ambiguity, it's black or white.

I flicked the cover back over the button and made the Late Arm switch safe.

Mindful of my little incident in Wales I wasn't going to be pushing Andy to drop.

I radioed number one and we maintained our battle formation for the trip back home. We went through the comms procedure to re-connect with Kuwait air traffic control and landed back at Ali Al Salem.

I climbed out dripping with sweat into the warm night and was met at the bottom of the steps by Andy, who gave me a slap on the back. 'Good job, Mands, well done. I've flown loads of missions like this, some will work, some won't. You did really well.'

We walked across the apron together and joined the others in the debrief room.

I sipped hot sweet tea as the debrief began with the usual safety issues before moving on to what went right and what went wrong.

These debriefings were always very frank and at times brutal. You were very much expected to put up your hand to mistakes.

Using video footage from the Americans' unmanned drone, Predator, which flew far above us, they went through every detail of the mission in minute detail.

'You've turned in quite tight there Mandy, were your wings level at that point? You're not helping Andy there. You need to give him a more solid platform.'

Or, 'Number four you were two minutes late getting up on the HaveQuick, what happened?'

'Yep, sorry I had fat fingers there, I couldn't quite get the digits in properly.'

'OK, next time give yourself as much time as you can, try to remain calm.'

Your contemporaries could chip in too – in fact they were expected to – which always felt a bit close to the bone.

'Mandy, I lost sight of you for a few seconds there, what happened?' 'Yep, sorry, I got wide. I was distracted trying to sort out the radios.'

Technically, getting distracted shouldn't happen as you're supposed to be constantly chatting to your navigator. If one of you has to go 'heads down' to sort something in the cockpit, the other should be dovetailing and keeping his eyes out.

Obviously, in the real world this was easier said than done, especially when you've got a lot on your plate.

The saving grace of these 360 appraisals was what comes around goes around, and you were expected to do the same to them when it was their turn in the debrief hot seat. It was all about improving, personally, and as a team. This was a very honest, at times raw and exposing, but ultimately very effective way of doing it.

The upshot from our mission was the camera we were carrying couldn't spot the target either. It was roundly accepted we did the right thing not to drop the bomb. Wales might have been a cock-up at the time, but it was invaluable to have gone through that.

CHAPTER 16

SINGLED OUT

My initial misgivings about those pre-mission briefings wouldn't go away. It would depend who was taking them but if certain key characters in the squadron were running the briefs, I began to have issues.

One guy seemed to direct every single question at me, without fail.

Yes, you want to make sure your junior members are up to speed but it became ridiculous. He never asked any of the other new guys, he was constantly on my back.

I was taking on so much information I could barely focus, my brain was full. I was doing a lot of work in my room every evening just to try to stay on top of it. But it was getting to me that all the questions were fired in my direction. If it happens enough you begin to panic a little and then it looks like you don't know your stuff and then the questions keep coming. And... Oh God, I was beginning to hate this place.

As the only woman I didn't have the same camaraderie as the others and didn't have anyone to talk to about it.

I don't think they had any empathy for how hard it was being the only woman – there was one female ground crew – on a squadron of 250-odd people.

I was their first female pilot and they weren't used to it. I wasn't used to it.

They were mostly very experienced and senior guys, who just saw a woman who sticks out a mile, who's only been on the squadron a couple of months and now they've got to go to war with her.

It had all been fun up to that point. We'd been to Vegas and then the squadron had been on a high as we prepared to come to Kuwait. Now it all came crashing down. I felt sledgehammered by a sense of reality. Bloody hell, this is everything I've worked for and it's miserable.

I'd always been a strong character. Loud, confident, and always willing to take the lead. Some might even say overconfident. But for the first time in my life, however mild, I felt like I was being bullied.

This one personality, I found out later, was struggling being away from his young family himself and took out his frustrations on who he perceived as the weakest link. Me.

On top of that, I felt I was being marginalised. It got to the point where I could hear the guys chatting outside the hut during a break but when I went out to join them, they all seemed to go silent. It was always when this one individual was in their midst.

I could have been getting paranoid and they could have been just talking about football or something and stopped when I came out, thinking I wouldn't be interested. In my heart I knew that was not the case.

Either way, it added to my feeling of isolation and it stopped me from going outside with the guys and I kept myself to myself, which is extremely rare.

I was confused, too, about who – and what – I was trying to be. The old conundrum reared its head, larger than ever. Do I try to fit in with everyone else, be one of the boys, or do I stand out but leave myself open to accusations of being some sort of maverick?

Looking back, I was probably trying to be a bit more blokey, swearing far more than I normally would. Before we went to the Gulf, I was certainly drinking too much because it was very much part of the culture. I was just trying to fit into the mould of a junior fast-jet pilot, regardless of gender.

I'd worked alongside men throughout my career, some of my best friends were men, even my boyfriend was one! But out there the fundamental differences between male and female conversation really hit me. The men discussed things in a very straightforward, factual way and didn't ever talk about their feelings, whereas women crave those more personal and honest exchanges.

It was only certain key characters that made me feel this way. Pacman was very understanding towards junior pilots and helped us out where he could. GB and Jez were absolute stars and DWubs, who had been on the course behind me virtually all the way through training, was great too. I could go and ask them anything. But the nature of the tour was that people rotated in and out, so they weren't there all the time.

I didn't discuss the situation with this 'bully' or my general unhappiness with anyone out there.

There was no email in those days, just 'blueys', letters on thin blue forces airmail paper and we were allowed one twenty-minute phone call a week. Sometimes I tried to cram in speaking to my parents, Craig, my friends, but each would get five minutes. At the end of a slot the phone would just go beep... beep... beep. That's your time up.

I wrote a handful of letters home along the lines of, 'I hate this, my life is miserable, this is seriously making me wonder if I've made the right career choice'.

The gist of them was that I was lonely. It makes me cry reading them back even now.

I told Craig I'd never felt so low, that I'd made a monumental mistake and I was going to hand in my resignation. He was a rock and told me not to do anything hasty, to stay calm and don't give up because I'd worked for a long time for this.

I once rang my mum but she wasn't in, so I called Zoe, my best friend and burst into tears at the sound of her cheery voice at the other end as she wandered around the supermarket. 'Talk to me about something, anything, the price of fish,' I sobbed.

As it was, I had to find a way to get through the tour. The flying was stressful but having to deal with the bullying on top of this meant I had to dig deeper into my reserves of resilience than ever before. I resolved that even though I was miserable, I'd come this far I was not going to give it all up now, certainly not because of the actions of one man. I'd just got to dig in, focus and get through it. And then we would see.

We worked – in other words, flew – seven days straight with every eighth day off. When I wasn't flying, I went to the gym. I was determined to return home fitter and slimmer than I had ever been. It was also the outlet I needed to alleviate the stress.

There wasn't much else to do, other than sit around on the white plastic chairs under the camouflage net rigged up at the back of our hut. This was our chill-out zone, the place to kick back, chat, read or have a puff of the sweet fruit tobacco in the hubbly bubbly pipe.

Sometimes we'd get a pass to use the facilities at a hotel in the city. These were like gold dust, though, like Willy Wonka's golden ticket. The Sheraton was my favourite and it gave us the chance to go and laze by their pool and escape for a day. You could almost forget that you were out there on operations. We would order the alcohol-free cocktails and devour the best club sandwich that Kuwait had to offer. Or we'd go into Kuwait City and wander around the souks. Dressed appropriately in long trousers and long sleeves, I loved the smells and the atmosphere and the street food. It was a fascinating snapshot into the real Kuwait, not some airbase in the middle of the desert. I had beautiful tailored shirts made to measure, a cocktail dress and of course the purchase of the obligatory rugs.

One day, D-C chartered a yacht and took a few of us sailing. These rare days out finally gave me the opportunity to chat off base and voice some of my concerns about the bullying to others. I was wary though, as I was still the new girl and I did not want to be seen as whining.

As the entertainments officer – ironic given my state of mind – I would often take one of the pool cars to Camp Doha, on a peninsula jutting into Kuwait Bay halfway between Ali Al Salem and the city. This was a huge American army base, bristling with military hardware and equipped with a massive mall where we would stock up on burgers and beer (non-alcoholic) for squadron barbecues.

Nights out were rare, although one time we were invited to a shindig thrown in a huge mansion by a Kuwaiti army general. I volunteered to drive and loaded seven pilots into a big Mitsubishi 4x4.

The party was full of high-ranking Kuwaitis and they were shocked that as a woman I was driving. The host opened a huge fridge which was stacked with champagne and beer.

I said I couldn't drink as I was driving but he laughed, telling me that because there is no alcohol in Kuwait, there are no drink-driving laws.

He rooted around at the back of the fridge and found one manky box of tropical fruit juice, a third full and almost mouldy. I stuck to nibbles.

The next day, we tweaked our flight plan and flew over the marina, where our party hosts were lounging on a yacht, and dipped our wings to say thanks.

After that early bombing sortie all of our other missions were reconnaissance, either taking pictures of suspicious looking sites or keeping an eye on troop movements.

We would carry bombs and fly with a designated target should we get the go-ahead to prosecute an attack following a hostile threat, but none ever came.

Towards the end of the tour we were on a mission, where we had been focused intently on a particularly lengthy reconnaissance target, when suddenly the sky around us was filled with small puffs of black smoke. It took us a few seconds to realise that these were actual ammunition shells exploding about a thousand feet below us. We had been targeted by an AAA (Anti-Aircraft Artillery) site. We manoeuvred away from the threat, warned other crews in the area about the incident and continued with the rest of the flight. After the sortie we were called over by the Americans who wanted to show us some footage from their overhead Predator unmanned spy plane.

The eight of us on the mission piled into their hut and watched a black-and-white video of a man emerging from a bush, leaping in to man his S-60 anti-aircraft gun, point his weapon at us and let rip. It felt a little like an out-of-body experience and was almost quite comical watching this chap take pot shots at us flying at 500 knots, 20,000 feet above his head. It was also quite disconcerting. He only had to get lucky once and we could be in a whole world of trouble. Considering we had all the technology on our side, he hadn't been far off. The sad thing for me came right at the end of the footage, when the Iraqi soldier, who had been ordered to shoot down one of the evil infidels (us), jumped out of the gun and ran as fast as he could into the desert, trying to get as much separation between himself and the weapon. He knew that it was likely that he would have been targeted in the next few minutes. Luckily for him, on this occasion, we did not retaliate. The guys were all bantering but for some reason this made my stomach lurch. This was the reality of being at war.

Another reality was more mundane. In the Gulf it was important to drink lots of fluid to stay hydrated in the soaring temperatures. Not only did dehydration affect your performance, but if you had to eject and were dehydrated on the ground in hostile territory you were in a world of trouble. The guys could have a final tinkle next to the aircraft before climbing in but for me it was a ten-minute procedure to strip off my combat survival waistcoat, my life support jacket, my g-suit, my flying suit, long johns and pants. And put them all back on again.

Most flights weren't more than about ninety minutes so with some careful hydration management, I could last without needing a wee. I'd been involved in a few trials to find a solution for female pilots in the in-air ablutions department, but the best the RAF's boffins had come up with so far was a nappy. Which was awful. No matter how much I drank before the trial flight I didn't seem to be able to go. The she-wee, a sort of funnel that goes inside your pants and connects to a tube, hadn't yet been invented. The men had a roll-up plastic container with a dehydrated sponge inside which soaked up the wee. They had to unstrap to get at their willy, which meant putting in the ejector seat pins to make it safe. If the seat fired while they were unstrapped, they would be a goner.

Occasionally I'd hear my backseater pipe up, 'Just going to have a slash, Mands, can you make your seat safe.' If I was feeling mischievous, I would reply, 'Er, no, not this time actually. I'm going to make you suffer, seeing as I can't have one.'

Usually I was fine but one trip late in the tour with Andy in my backseat I felt the first signs of needing to go when taxiing out in the early evening. It's OK, it's a quick cross-border hop into southern Iraq to take pictures, nothing dramatic, I told myself. We'll be back in no time, I'll be fine.

An hour or so into the flight we got a radio message saying something was starting to kick off further north. Would we be available to do an in-flight refuel and head up there?

'Erm, the thing is, I'm now desperate for a wee,' I replied.

Andy burst out laughing. 'Pssshh,' he started whispering into the radio, trying to imitate a waterfall.

'Roger that, Spartan Two, we need you up there. Prepare to re-route.'

Bugger.

Andy plotted a route to intercept the tanker and we headed south to fly a holding pattern awaiting further instructions. By now my nether region was throbbing in pain and my bladder felt like a football.

'Know what I fancy now, Mands? A nice cool glass of refreshing water... pssshh.' Andy's banter was still going strong.

Then I started hyperventilating into my mask. 'Mands, you OK?'

'No, I'm in serious flipping pain.'

'OK, try to concentrate, let's just get home.'

Fortunately, the mission objectives changed and we were released from whatever it was they'd sent us up there for and turned back south towards Kuwait. I still had plenty of flying to do, fence checks to go through and a landing before I could have a wee and I was getting dizzy.

'Well done, Mands, keep it up, just focus on your flying, that'll take your mind off it.'

After nearly three hours I managed to get us back down on the ground at Ali Al Salem. The normal procedure was to stop outside the sun shelter while the groundies checked the outside of the aircraft, then roll forward a few feet for them to inspect the wheels. I slammed to a stop, opened the cockpit and signalled for a ladder. 'I'm shutting down now, please can you get me some transport quickly.'

I was hunched over and grimacing as I climbed down the ladder. I tripped halfway and landed in a heap at the bottom. 'Are you OK, Ma'am?' 'No, I need a toilet, quick,' I mumbled. A minibus appeared and I was bundled in. It sped off back to our lines as I began the unzipping process. It lurched to a stop outside the nearest toilet block and I speed-shuffled in. In the first cubicle I finished undressing and sat down on the hot steel seat, waiting for a torrent and that blessed feeling of relief. Nothing happened. I sat there for a full five minutes before my body, forced into shut-down for the past few hours, realised it was OK to start functioning again. Finally, I began to wee. Oh. My. Goodness.

But instead of skipping out of there a new woman, I was still clutching my stomach and doubled over in pain. Later that day I went to see the doctor and was diagnosed with a kidney infection because I had held it in so long. I was grounded and put on a week's course of antibiotics.

As it happened my tour was finishing in two days anyway. What a way to go out.

After twenty-two combat missions and a lot of heartache, I just couldn't wait to get home.

It had been eight weeks of soul searching and I'd had to look pretty deep at times to find it.

I landed back at Brize Norton in late May and went straight back to Winchester. Craig greeted me at the airport and when we got home, he was itching to show me how he had given our bedroom a new lick of paint. It was a dusky pink colour. He was so excited and very proud of his handiwork.

I was so pleased to be back I didn't have the heart to tell him I thought it was a bit sickly. In fact, I've never told him, until now.

It was a Friday night in the bar at RAF Marham and I fell into conversation with the guy who had made me so inherently miserable in Kuwait.

Craig was up for a visit, and combined with the Dutch courage of a few drinks, I decided to tackle the issue head on.

'Are you aware of how tough you made my life out in Kuwait?'

His face drained and his wife looked at me questioningly. I told him how he came across and how miserable it made me. I described how I had felt so demoralised that I had even considered handing in my notice. He said he was shocked; he had no idea.

The next working day he asked me to come into his office. I thought I was in trouble. He apologised again and said he was oblivious to the fact his behaviour was affecting me so badly. He had a new baby at home and was upset to be missing out on the first few months of her life. His wife was finding it hard with two children under two. He said he was so sorry that he was taking his frustrations out on me and he said he wished I'd spoken to him earlier about it.

I thought, well, fair play, that took balls as well. It's almost ironic, by clearing the air, I've always got on well with him since then.

I was glad I had finally handled the situation. It goes to show that sometimes facing your demons, however hard it may be, can pay off. Also, you never know what is going on in someone else's life. I probably should have spoken up earlier, but I just felt he was being so insensitive, it could have backfired and made him even angrier towards me. I finally felt I could breathe a little more easily. Another obstacle tackled on my journey to being fully accepted onto the squadron.

Since then I have always tried to be so much more up front with people, tackling the small issues before they escalate into something that they are not.

Back home at Marham, the flying schedule was still full-on, often four trips a week, sometimes six. It was a real mixture. There was some more air combat training, recce practice trips, instrument-rating tests and bombing competitions on the east coast ranges.

Sometimes we flew low level up the east coast or we'd climb to high level across the Wash and drop back into the weeds north of Hull and go into the north Yorkshire moors and up towards Newcastle.

The only thing we couldn't practice at Spadeadam was the use of chaff – millions of tiny aluminium fibres fired out of the jet to distract radar-guided missiles – so we did that on a range in the North Sea. At other times we would take off and climb up to high level to join the air corridors that would take us across country before dropping down to low level in Devon and Cornwall, doing the same on the way home.

Once one of our aircraft on another sortie had to divert to Reims in France. I was delegated with D-C to go and fly it back, so we got a commercial flight to Paris, hired a car and flew the jet home. All these little trips just helped build up experience operating out of your comfort zone.

While I was in Kuwait I had resolved to get my own place near Marham. I was tiring of mess life now, especially as most of the guys were married and in their own houses and even many of the singletons had moved out.

I scoured the area and eventually bought a great little terraced house in Cambridge, which was forty minutes from work. Craig was now a commercial pilot for GB Airways and if he was staying, it was near enough to get to Heathrow if he was called in while on standby.

Some semblance of normality was returning and I started to have a bit of a life outside the air force.

My domestic bliss didn't last long.

At the end of July we flew back out to Goose Bay in Canada for operational low-level training.

The difference this time, compared with our last trip here and our normal low-level flying at home was we now had to nudge ourselves down from 250ft to 100ft above the ground-OLF (operational low flying). It is essential to practise this as it enables you to fly beneath the scope of enemy radars if required. To push yourself down to under half that height and still at the same speed is extremely challenging. It is known as 'as low as your sphincter will let you'. Your bottom clenches so tight, and to start with you can't physically get yourself to fly any lower. The pilot workload is massive.

At Goose Bay there is an added element of danger, if the OLF isn't enough to get you revved up.

Most of the flying area is over huge forests, however, the catch is that some of it is new plantations. This can be, and has been, a killer if you are not clued up on it.

When you are 'OLF-ing' at 100ft you do it visually, not on your radar altimeter (RadAlt), which records your height directly above the ground

The trouble is it can be a bit unreliable at such low level, and when the margins are so fine, you can't afford any mistakes.

From above, these young forests look like normal huge fir trees, but in reality, they could be only about six feet tall. So what you thought was 100ft above the tops of the trees could actually only be about thirty feet up. This is definitely squeaky bum time. This factor has cost quite a number of lives.

Once we were comfortable flying near the deck, the training was ramped up another notch to factor in bombing runs, often working with special forces on the ground who talk you in to targets.

Then we moved on to flying in a four-ship trying to evade enemy bounce aircraft flown by instructors. It was some of the most capacity-sapping but exhilarating flying I've ever done.

Once, while working on the ops desk, I could hear the rotor of a large helicopter out of the open window. The phone rang and a voice said, 'Paddington's arrived, where do you want him?'

'I'm sorry?'

'We've got the big bear you shot, where do want us to put him?'

The special forces guys working as forward air controllers to talk us onto targets stayed in cabins in the woods. They had been warned that the local population of bears often found a great deal of interest in their activities, especially at night when the coast was clear and the larder was full of food.

One night a massive bear had walked into one of their cabins. With no other option, they shot it and called in a helicopter to take the carcass back to base. I looked out of the window and saw the unusual sight of a helicopter with a large underslung load, from which poked out four hairy legs and four huge paws.

'I don't know what to do with it,' I replied. 'Where do you normally put your dead bears?'

CHAPTER 17

CONDUCT UNBECOMING

I love Cornwall. I love going down there in the summer. The beaches, surfing, big skies. Carefree days.

I'm not such a fan in January. Not when you're at combat survival school, anyway. Nope. Not a fan at all.

Almost a year after my first tour in a hostile environment I was sent on the infamous Conduct After Capture course, learning what to do if you're ever shot down and have to eject over enemy territory.

It might have been handy for Iraq the first time, you'd think, but apparently there is a grace period before you have to take it.

The next ten days at St Mawgan would be more like a disgrace period.

I'd been there before, on a university air squadron summer camp, two weeks of fun, flying, frolicking and general hi-jinks. This was as far removed from an ice cream-gorging Cornish holiday as you can possibly imagine.

RAF St Mawgan, near Newquay, was the only RAF station south west of Oxford, and although the airfield element was sold to Cornwall County council for Newquay Airport, it has long been the home of the joint RAF and Navy survival training schools.

The station's motto was 'Vigila – be watchful'. Its unofficial motto, 'We teach the best to survive the worst'.

The Conduct After Capture course educates aircrew and other military personnel on procedures for being stranded behind enemy lines, from defence and survival to evasion, resistance and extraction.

It is run by hardened combat survival experts from the RAF and Royal Marines. They were all like Bear Grylls, Ranulph Fiennes and Ray Mears mixed with a bit of Phil Mitchell and Ronnie Kray.

I was there with Jez from our squadron alongside a mixture of people from other outfits and my previous courses. There were twenty of us on the course and, as was standard, I was the only woman.

The course kicked off in pleasant enough fashion, with a couple of basic sessions of field craft in the classroom. We were also issued with the kit we would have if we had to eject.

A helicopter crew – if they can get out in an emergency – can take an entire rucksack full of sleeping bag, cakes, supplies, essentially whatever booty they can cram in.

For fast jet pilots you have to rely purely on what is in the rigid box built into your ejection seat. Inside are flares, a hypothermic silver blanket, sea sickness tablets, waterproof matches, a small tin to cook in, high calorie sweets, snares, knife, fishing line, survival beacon and a life-raft. The seat cushion cover has straps on and converts into a little rucksack to carry it all in.

For our first field exercise we mustered early on a crisp, bone-chilling morning in our survival kit plus flying suit. As a concession to the winter weather, we were allowed to wear a bunny suit: a big, green, ribbed, itchy woollen all-in-one under our flying gear.

So, we had on long johns, bunny suit, flying suit, and our cold weather flying kit of green bomber jacket and green dungaree outfit. We also wore thick woolly socks and flying boots, plus a balaclava and flying gloves, which are made of soft white leather and therefore offered no protection from the cold whatsoever. The first thing you have to do in the field is get them dirty to blend in.

We were given two twenty four hour ration packs to add to our survival gear, which was inspected thoroughly to make sure we hadn't smuggled any extra goodies with us.

The ration packs contained a breakfast of beans and sausages, a lunch of chicken and vegetables or bean soup, and dinners of chicken curry and rice, and tuna pasta – in a silver bag that you heated in boiling water. There were desserts, too, with the delights of sticky toffee pudding and a chocolate brownie, plus a couple of sachets of coffee, two tea bags, some whitener and some fudge.

We climbed into the back of an olive-green military truck and were driven from St Mawgan towards Dartmoor over the border in Devon. After about an hour the truck pulled up in a lay-by and we piled out into the frost and followed our smoking breath into the woods.

This, we were told, was our new home.

The first job was to rig up a shelter. The instructors gave us a demo and then we were on our own. I've always loved building dens, so I was right into this.

The idea was to find an overturned tree, a low branch or a long pole and create a low A-frame at one end. Then we piled up sticks on either side to make it look like a tent before plugging the gaps and lining the floor with moss and leaves if you can find any. It's quite tricky in January when the ground is rigid. The final piece of the jigsaw is to hope like heck that it keeps you relatively warm and dry.

The key is making them low. If it's too high the rain will come in or, if they are cavernous, you will be freezing.

We were also taught how to make a sleeping bag from our parachute.

The parachute is made in a series of triangles, so you fold and fold until you've made a pocket, like a huge sandwich wrap, and then bind the ends up with some para cord and a twig. You should end up with about ten layers of parachute silk, which trap the air and create a decent sleeping bag.

That night the instructors showed us how to kill a squirrel, which seemed to be no more complicated than smacking its head against a tree, and then how to skin it and cook it. When you take the tail off, they look just like rats. Urrgh. Then we were given our own dead squirrels to play with. Here's your tea, kids!

A few charred bits of squirrel with the fur still on didn't quite fill me up so I went to bed with a grumbling tummy and tried to get cosy in my DIY cocoon. I'd made sure the ground was smooth so I was relatively comfortable with all my gear on, and barring a chilly nose just peaking out of my parachute womb, I had a relatively decent night's sleep.

I woke early and got straight up to get some blood and heat flowing around the body. I sparked up my hexi burner and got some water boiling for a brew, using a tea bag and a sachet of whitener from the ration pack.

There was no time for breakfast though, the staff took us straight out onto the moor for some basic navigation exercises. It was simple stuff like map reading, taking bearings, and getting a feel for moving over different types of ground to reach a destination. Footpaths and roads were banned, but it made you realise that the shortest route might not be the best if it was through a bog. Or you might want to avoid tussocky ground because it is too easy to turn an ankle.

We came back into camp around mid-morning and were told to gather around for a lesson in chicken dispatch. The instructors produced a live chicken and showed us how to kill it. One instructor used what appeared to be a touch of magic, by placing the chicken's head underneath its own wing and fooling it into thinking it was asleep. Surely this wouldn't work? But it did, the chicken relaxed and with a swift flick of the wrist he managed to snap the chicken's neck, deftly and cleanly, proudly facing us, body in one hand, head in the other. Now it was our turn. They asked for a volunteer, and never being backwards in stepping forwards I raised my hand. He had made it look so easy after all. I took hold of my chicken, all warm and flapping furiously, but it appeared to know exactly what his fate would be and was putting up one heck of a struggle, making my job as difficult as possible. I placed its head under the wing and waited for the magic to happen, but this old bird was too wily. I was told to just get on with it, so I did. I pulled the head as far away from the body as I could but it was on a spring... my arms were almost outstretched and nothing was giving. This was awful. Everyone started laughing nervously. 'Twist it,' said the instructor. I did and eventually the head separated away. I dropped both ends in surprise, at which point the body started to run around the forest floor... an actual headless chicken.

Making an underground fire was another good lesson. We were shown how to cut a sod of earth and then dig a hole, piling the earth back up around it so you have something resembling a little sandcastle with a vent, with the sod placed carefully back on top. Inside the gap we placed twigs and ideally dry moss – not that we could find much – for kindling and tried to light the fire, feeding it with larger sticks as it began to take.

That afternoon we were told to dismantle our shelters and make a parachute shelter instead, using the canopy and para cord only. I wore all my clothes again and wrapped myself up in the remaining bit of the parachute but sleep that night was harder to come by and I lay awake shivering for most it.

For several days it was all about how to survive in general, not about conduct after capture. It was all about protection, location, water, food – the survival priorities.

There were also sessions on how to catch rabbits with snares, and how to forage safely for mushrooms, paying careful attention to the ones you absolutely mustn't eat. This was interspersed with more navigation, backed up with some exercises at night.

We learnt how to move tactically, using the contours and features such as a gully, riverbed or the edge of a wood to hide. With a full moon it's amazing how clearly you can see people moving across open ground.

The staff demonstrated why getting silhouetted on a ridge line was a definite no-no and emphasised the importance of staying below the horizon.

One night a Sea King helicopter came and landed in a nearby field; we worked with the crew, practising extraction techniques and how best to approach a heli tactically in the field. Four at a time would approach and launch ourselves in only to be turfed straight back out again to our disappointment at the thought of a night-time heli ride.

Another evening, we thought the staff had disappeared, so we lit a campfire and were sitting around it having a right old ging-gang gooly.

Suddenly there was a crashing and banging and the instructors came roaring into the camp. 'What the bloody hell are you lot up to? This isn't a sodding girl guide's jamboree. Put that fire out. Enemy force inbound...'

Bloody Nora! I dived over to my shelter and grabbed my flying jacket.

'They're coming...' shouted another instructor. I legged it into the darkness alongside everyone else.

I was half giggling with a combination of fear and fun as I galloped through the trees. We weren't allowed to just run away, we had to go to ground in the vicinity, so after hot footing it for about 400 yards I dived onto the ground and wriggled my way into the bottom of a bush.

OUCH! Bloody holly! I scratched my hands and face as I crawled in, but I made myself as comfortable as I could and lay still, my chest heaving and my heart seemingly pounding as loud as Big Ben's chimes.

The wood fell quiet as the last of our mob got into their hiding places. I lay there, contemplating the silence and the fact I was alone, hiding in a bush, in a wood, at night, in Devon in January.

Now and then I adjusted my position in slow motion to avoid making a sound. An hour must have passed but I didn't dare attempt to look at my watch. There was no sign of this apparent incoming force that was supposedly imminent as we tore out of the camp.

I heard a voice, half whispering. 'They're not bloody coming, are they?' It was one of my course-mates from somewhere nearby. Then I heard someone else giggling.

We weren't about to test this theory by leaving our dens voluntarily in case we got jumped. Fortunately, not too much later, we heard shouting. 'Stand down, stand down, the exercise is over.' The buggers had just done it to keep us on our toes and stop us getting comfortable. We all emerged back in the camp, which had been destroyed by the instructors, so we rigged up para shelters for the night, but sleep had now gone the same way as food. It was in very short supply.

Once the ration packs had gone, the only things we had to eat were tasting the odd morsel of squirrel or a bit of rabbit during demonstrations or what we could forage ourselves. And there was not much around in January, even the rabbits had scarpered.

In the morning the staff returned to the camp looking very pleased with their fun and games from the night before. They explained the scenario had changed, so instead of just survival, we were now in a conflict zone. The key was not to be found. It became more about evasion.

After that evening's night exercise, they said they would be back at eight a.m. and they didn't want to find any trace of us. Again, we weren't allowed just to run away, we had to hide. Wary now of what might happen at any moment and getting pretty knackered from the sleepless nights, we bedded down early.

We got up at about five. There was no need for an alarm clock, we had all been waiting for the opportunity to get up anyway; I'm not even sure I had fallen asleep. Trying to cajole some action back into my stiff joints I destroyed my shelter and spread the sticks around to make it look like I'd never been there.

Then, with the axe from my ejection seat kit I scratched away at a shallow grave for almost three hours like we'd been shown the day before. The idea is to dig a body-sized hole (your body, preferably), leave a lip around the edge and then place branches across the gap. On top of those you add some moss and replace the sods of earth you carefully cut out at the start.

Then you wriggle in, covering your head with a similar wood-and-earth hatch.

In practice, committing yourself to climbing into a grave is psychologically quite challenging. You are now buried under ground. The thought of it is quite horrendous.

One guy decided it wasn't for him and opted to climb a tree, so he gave the graves a final dusting to blend in.

I draped the parachute over my face so I couldn't feel any creepy crawlies and to make sure no bits went into my eyes. I tried to keep my mind calm and not panic that I was buried alive. Those first few minutes ticked by at glacial pace. The wood fell silent as everyone else retreated into their own worlds.

Down at the micro level there were still tiny noises, scratching, cracking, earth dropping onto me. Every tiny noise was amplified in my head and I fought the urge to imagine marauding spiders or killer worms. I could move a little but rolling over was out as the grave wasn't deep enough.

I decided to just concentrate on my breathing to give me something to focus on. In... out... in... out...

Sometime later I heard shouting. 'No duff, the exercise is over, I repeat, no duff.'

That was the safety phrase. It must be all over. I pushed up the hatch and looked at my watch. It was ten a.m. and I must have been asleep for nearly two hours. They had apparently walked over my grave, but I didn't hear a thing. I'm surprised they didn't hear my snoring.

We only had twenty-four hours left in the field but from everything we had heard from previous courses, I knew things were about to change dramatically. Anxiety was creeping up my body, like the tide coming in.

As dusk fell and the temperature dropped, we gathered around the staff in our small clearing and were given a map of Dartmoor with the first of a series of checkpoints marked on it.

We were also given a set of codes. These were to be used at the correct subsequent checkpoints to identify yourself and the personnel manning them, like meeting up with friendly resistance people.

The Black Watch, the 3rd Battalion, Royal Regiment of Scotland, were out there somewhere as the hunter force. This sent shivers down my spine as I remembered hanging upside down on barbed wire and getting caught during basic survival training. The regular army guys were very keen to catch themselves some aircrew and were liable to be fairly nasty if they did.

We slapped on some camouflage cream to our faces and hands and readied our kit. I knew the next twenty four hours were going to be intense and I tried to focus on the small tasks in front of me rather than letting my mind wander to what was coming, but it was like trying to plug a hole in a dam. When it was time I paired up with Jez and we set off on a brilliant but icy night, with a big moon and no rain.

We were carrying just our small rucksacks stuffed with our spare clothes to avoid getting too sweaty. Our eyes quickly become tuned into the dark and we made good progress, careful to avoid getting silhouetted and trying to stay in the shadows.

When we came to a road we holed up and waited until it was completely clear, then scurried across at a diagonal – all techniques we had been taught in the last few days.

We were getting close to our first checkpoint as we clambered along a steep-sided valley above a small river, clinging to roots and branches to stop ourselves slithering down into the icy water. My feet were already wet and freezing from stepping into unseen puddles, but it could be lethal getting the rest of me soaking at this stage.

The problem we had was that the checkpoint was on the other side of the river and it looked too big to try to wade across. The only way to the other side was a humpback road bridge but we knew this was an obvious pinch point for the hunter force to watch. We'd studied the map and worked out the river narrowed three miles upstream. It was extra walking, but if it avoided getting caught it would be worth it. Early capture meant more time in stress positions ahead of the interrogation phase.

We scrambled towards the old stone bridge, to see if we could pass under it.

There did seem to be a shelf on either side we could edge across but as we inched under the bridge, we heard shouts and the sound of hurrying footsteps above our heads. Then shouting and the sharp crack of rifle fire... blanks. 'Get down, on your face, don't move, don't you effing move.' Blimey. Jez and I looked at each other wide-eyed, clinging to the brickwork as we tried not to slip into the swirling water. The echoey bridge made my breathing sound like it was coming out of a megaphone. We were right about trying to cross. That sounded like Archie, my old instructor from Valley days getting caught. Good luck, guys.

The scuff of boots and snatches of conversation lasted about fifteen minutes until the noises grew fainter.

I had been thinking while I was standing there that now might be a good time to chance it and nip across the bridge. Sensing they had moved off I whispered to Jez and he said he'd been thinking the same thing. The only worry was they had left behind some sentries but we reckoned we would be OK.

We emerged from under the bridge and painstakingly tip-toed up the earth bank to the road, like mountaineers moving slowly and deliberately at high altitude.

Reaching the road level, we paused for a few minutes behind the wall to listen out for any signs. It seemed quiet. I nodded to Jez. He gave me a thumbs up. He hauled himself over the low wall and waited for me to join him. After 'three' we pegged it as quietly as we could the thirty yards or so across the bridge and dived into the trees on the other side.

We crept up to where the checkpoint should be, by a stile on the edge of a steep wood and met a man dressed in civvy gear, with a peaked cap and green Barbour jacket. 'Bravo, Charlie, Echo,' I offered. He whispered 'Three, two, one,' and then gave us the co-ordinates for the next checkpoint.

We melted back into the trees and set off at a fast walk through the bottom of the wood. The next checkpoint was several kilometres away, near the top of a hill. This would require us to cross open country as we neared the target. Before we left cover, we stopped to have a swig of water and a look and listen. It seemed clear so we moved out onto the moor and followed a sparse row of Hawthorn trees into some bracken. The checkpoint should be somewhere up to our right on a diagonal climb from where we were. The scrub was about waist high so with a stooping crouch we could keep fairly well hidden as we pushed up through it. We couldn't avoid making a noise but our eyes were wide, dancing this way and that, and our ears straining for early alerts to danger like nervous deer in a herd. We kept close, taking it in turns to lead, using hand signals for direction.

We were making progress but we needed to check the map, so Jez indicated to join him. We burrowed our way into the bracken and covered our heads with some spare kit to switch on the flashlight without being seen. We had already taken the precaution of colouring the glass of the torch with a red marker pen. It created a filter and stopped you from losing your night vision that takes about twenty minutes to re-establish.

We were close. I switched off the torch and we lay there for a few moments for our night vision to return before slowly rising to peak out, like meerkats in the desert. The sky was mottled with cloud now and the moon was obscured, which was better for us. I set off in front, resuming the stoop, to edge up what should be the final few hundred yards. My eyes and ears were back on duty. CRACK! What's that? I froze, the toes of my right foot barely on the ground. I sank slowly but silently onto my haunches, my heel still in the air to avoid a noise. My right hand was in a fist and my arm cocked at ninety degrees, the signal for Jez to get down behind me. He was silent as we watched two dark figures bustling down through the bracken to our right about fifty yards away. I looked at Jez to check he'd seen them. He nodded. They must have come from the checkpoint. I pointed to the ground and indicated with two wriggling fingers we should crawl the last bit. No point in getting complacent now, even if we were unlikely to get bounced this close. On elbows and knees we squirmed through the stems. Up ahead I could see them thinning out and I nosed to the edge of a clearing. In the middle I could see a dark shape and drifting towards me on the night air the unmistakable whiff of a cigarette. I carried on crawling across short grass. 'Bravo, Charlie, Echo,' I whispered. We'd found our man.

Our night of stealth went well and we got to the final checkpoint in the bottom of a valley before dawn.

Knowing this was the end of the evasion phase, we put on all our spare clothes in readiness for what was to come.

Then we found a bush to hide in to sit out the rest of the exercise. By not getting caught we had avoided extra time being held in stress positions, so we were quite pleased with ourselves.

Making sure we were hydrated and had some sugar in the system were other tips we'd been passed on, so we gulped down the rest of our water.

Jez had a small amount of fudge left from his rations. The packet said it was out of date but he swallowed it anyway. We were lying side by side in the bottom of a thicket, the wind ruffling the leaves, but otherwise it all was quiet.

The minutes passed. Jez and I were lost in our own thoughts. But then I heard a gurgling sound coming from behind me.

'What's that?' I whispered. 'I don't feel great,' he said. 'Sorry Mands, I'm going to have to trump.'

Seconds later there was an explosion from deep within his layers of clothes. 'What's happened?'

'Oh Bugger. I think I've pooed myself... sod it, I'm going to leave it for them. That will be a treat when they strip us down!'

We lay still for a while, Jez contemplating his bowels, me wondering what will happen to us. I'd heard some stories and had been given a few snippets by people who had already been through it but there had also been an element of 'mum's the word'. Not having the full picture made it worse as the imagination filled in the gaps. I knew they wouldn't physically hurt us but I didn't know any other women who had been through Conduct After Capture and I was very anxious about how I would be treated. Would it be worse for me because I was a woman? Would there be any sexual connotations? I had a growing sense of dread, and now the adrenaline of the night had worn off I suddenly felt very alone and vulnerable. I also knew that I was wet, cold, tired and hungry and none of those were likely to improve over the next twenty-four hours. It was at times like this when a standard office job seemed a little more tempting.

Light crept over the moor. Then a voice shouting, surprisingly close by. 'The exercise is over, well done, big tick for you, you've avoided the agony your mates are in, now get out of your holes and show yourselves. And bloody well hurry up.'

We whispered 'good luck' to each other and roused our stiff limbs to disentangle from the undergrowth.

The second I wriggled out from my bush I was plunged into blackness as hood was rammed over my head. At the same time a powerful grip wrenched my arms around my back and tied up my hands. I was helpless now and at their whim and was forced down onto the freezing ground. Despite Jez's involuntary ablutions, I hadn't been to the toilet for a long while and was now desperate for a wee.

After a painstaking hour lying face down, I managed to raise a finger despite my hands being bound. Amazingly, someone spotted it and shouted, 'What do you want?' 'I need the toilet,' I mumbled through the hood. 'For God's sake.' I was hauled up and shoved into the undergrowth, still blindfolded. My hands were released and I fumbled with my clothes before crouching down. 'Jesus, you're pissing like a flipping horse,' I heard the voice say.

I was thrown back down on the ground for a while as they policed up everyone else. All common decency had gone at this point. There was a lot of shouting and swearing.

I heard the rumble of an engine. Hands grabbed me under both arms and hauled me up. I was told to walk but I was mainly pushed and shoved across grass and then more of an uneven, stony surface. My hands were untied and placed on the cold metal of what must have been a truck's tailgate. Someone grabbed my right foot and put it on a step. 'Climb up,' shouted a voice. I stepped up and more hands grabbed me and pulled me up. My hands were thrust behind my back again and bound with rope and I was shoved onto a bench, sandwiched between other bodies. I didn't dare to speak. There was more shouting and I could sense others were being loaded but soon the truck pulled off.

We were driven around winding, country lanes, bouncing up and down on the wooden bench and bumping into the bodies on each side. The only way we could steady ourselves was with feet braced wide on the floor. I knew Jez was close by, mainly by the smell emanating from his nether regions. Under my hood I was getting more and more disorientated. My sense of time was also being blurred.

After what felt like an hour but could have been less or more, the truck finally came to a stop and the engine went off. The silence was brooding, ominous and put me on edge. I tried to tune my senses into my new environment.

The noise of feet on gravel. The tailboard creaked and clanked. I could hear the scuffling of boots and then various grunts and groans from people around me. 'Up.' Hands gripped my upper arms and pulled me to my feet. I was shuffled forward. 'Turn around.' More hands grabbed my ankles and my right foot was pulled down and placed in a step at the back of the lorry. I could feel hands on my backside as I was pushed down from above and scrabbled to get my left foot into a foothold. 'Jump.' I pushed off and arms caught me as my boots crunched onto the gravel.

A shove in the back sent me flying forwards. The rough surface under my feet went hard and by the change in atmosphere and the light coming through my hood I could tell I was in a building. Another push from behind sent me stumbling and strong hands gripped my arms and forced them wide apart, slightly above my head, with my palms against a bare, brick wall. I felt my feet being kicked apart so I was spread-eagled, leaning against the wall.

The room was bright and echoey and I could feel the presence of others.

Fairly soon I felt a tug at my arms and I was dragged away from the wall. I was shoved forwards and took small, shuffling steps, unsure of my footing and what I might bump into. At the same time, I was trying to stay alert and build a mental picture of the layout. I was suddenly yanked left and almost fell as I was guided down a step. The ground surface felt rougher. A voice said, 'Strip. Everything.' My hands were undone and I began to peel off my layers, hands shaking over my zips and fumbling to get my boots off. I hesitated when I got to my bra and pants. The voice said, 'Leave those. Bend over.'

I'd heard the stories so I was prepared for it but even so I felt so utterly exposed, vulnerable and degraded. I felt hands run over me briefly – a woman's probably, by law – as they searched for hidden contraband.

Then I was told to stand up. 'Put this on.' My hands reached into space and I felt some kind of clothing. It was cold to the touch, damp too. I shivered as I pulled it on. It felt like a flying suit. Quite possibly my own. I was standing in bare feet on a rough concrete floor, which didn't help the shivering.

From an adjacent room I heard the outraged outpourings: 'You **** disgusting ****!' A smile spread across my face. They'd obviously just discovered the aftermath of the out-of-date fudge. Jez described afterwards how he'd taken a lot of pleasure from the moment he stripped – completely naked for the men – it was all about the small victories at time like this.

I was manhandled out and taken to what felt like a new room. Hands pressed on my shoulders and thrust me down until my backside met a chair.

We had been taught the technique for interrogations and I was running through them in my mind, trying to keep focused. You were allowed to give the Big Four – name, rank, serial number, date of birth. You were not supposed to say anything else, only 'I cannot answer that question.'

You're urged to be the grey man and just plod on, so you don't stand out. Being the only woman on the course was going to make that a bit tricky.

My hood was yanked off and I blinked as the light hit my eyes. I was facing a desk with a man sitting behind it. He was pale and looked quite normal with a regular short haircut and wearing nondescript dark clothes.

'Name?'

'Wells'

'What were you doing there?'

'I cannot answer that question.'

'Name?'

'Wells.'

'Rank?'

'Flight Lieutenant.'

'What was your mission?'

'I cannot answer that question.'

We went through this charade for twenty minutes or so. In my head I was thinking, 'This is OK, I can handle this.'

All of a sudden he said: 'You're not giving us anything, are you? Bugger off.'

The bag was pulled down onto my head from behind and I was dragged out of the chair and bundled off.

I heard a door opened in front of me and from inside I could hear the high-pitched screech of static, like a badly tuned radio.

I was pushed in and put in the same position as before, hands flat on the wall slightly above my head, feet and legs spread wide about a metre away from it. This room was colder than the first and the white noise massively grating but I tried to retreat into my head and block it out.

Time ticked slowly by. At first it didn't seem so bad but soon my calves were shaking. I was struggling to keep my position. My legs began buckling and I jerked them back to try to stay upright.

Arms grabbed me and I was pushed onto what felt like a tiled floor. I was told to sit cross-legged with my hands on my head and my back straight.

'Oh, thank God for that,' I thought. It was quite a relief to be out of that position and I started to relax.

Soon though, everything was beginning to strain. I slumped to ease a stabbing pain in my back but got a boot in the kidneys. I began to shake, mildly at first and then uncontrollably, violently. I was paranoid I was getting hypothermia, so I put my hand up.

'What?'

'I need to see a doctor. I'm going hypothermic,' I mumbled.

I was pulled up and marched down the corridor into

another room. I felt my blood pressure being taken and hands inspecting me. 'You're not hypothermic. Are you fit to carry on?' 'Yes.'

I was taken back and put on the floor, cross-legged again. I could feel the shakes coming back and I was willing it to be time for another interrogation, so at least I could move. They're not called stress positions for nothing. Pretty soon my wish was granted as I was pulled up and my hands tied behind my back.

With someone clutching my left arm I was steered to what must have been another new room. This one was quiet and warm and when my hood was taken off, I could see it was some kind of outbuilding, with hay bales stacked up.

'Gosh, isn't this awful? You must be so cold,' came a voice from the shadows. 'Yes, I am.'

Oops, shouldn't have said that.

'It's nice and warm in here, isn't it?' A man in dark green overalls emerged. 'I can't answer that question.' He laughed. 'That's not a question, I'm just trying to help. Do you want to stick some straw into your flying suit to keep warm?'

'I'm sorry, I can't answer that question.' I took some anyway and stuffed it into my suit, and then instantly regretted it because it was itchy.

'I bet you really want to get a message to your family to let them know you're OK don't you?' His voice was very soothing and he seemed kind and nurturing.

'I cannot answer that question.'

'But who would you contact if you did?'

'I can't answer that question.'

'Now, come on Mandy, we know why you were there, so you might as well just tell us.'

'I can't answer that question.'

'OK, have it your way.'

The blindfold was thrust back over my head and I was soon back in a stress position on the tiled floor. The white noise had stopped and I could hear the odd muffled sigh or a shuffle of feet. Staccato lines of Arabic came from the guards. Every so often the sound of a gun cocking. The familiar nagging and then searing pain from the stress positions began to build. I knew if I moved I would be hit. My nerves were as taut as the muscles in my back.

The next interrogation was in a completely white room with piercing strip lights. The man sitting behind the table had an earring and a moustache and seemed very angry. I was trying to keep my mind clear and get into the rhythm of this one, when... CLANG!

A violent, piercing metallic shot rang out near my right ear. I had no idea anyone else was there and jolted backwards in shock, like the recoil of a rifle. I very nearly wet myself. I was absolutely terrified. What the bloody hell was that? A voice from behind screamed: 'Stop lying to me.' CLANG!

It happened again. This time I saw a hand brandishing a metal pipe, which he whacked against the metal frame of my chair. I felt suddenly very tired. This didn't feel like a game anymore.

I had no idea how long I had been in captivity, but I knew I needed to go to the toilet again so when I was taken out of the interrogation I asked if I could go.

A short while later I was led out. My hood was taken off and I was pointed towards a small run-down toilet cubicle with bare brick walls. It was such a relief to have a few seconds on my own and when I was coming out, I met another lady washing her hands at a rickety basin.

'This is horrible isn't it?' she said. Without thinking I answered, 'Yes, it's disgusting.' 'Where's home?' I looked at her again. She was wearing jeans and an outdoor jacket, with long hair in a neat ponytail. Not the look of a prisoner of war on the run with little food or sleep in the last five days. I clammed up. I'd nearly fallen for one of the oldest tricks in the book. I was about to let my guard down and open up, purely because I wasn't in an official interrogation.

We had been warned that at some stage we would have to start giving a bit more than the Big Four. It was known as the slow release of information. We were also told we would know when that time had come.

For me it was when I was taken outside, forced onto my knees, my hood was lifted a little and I was told to open my mouth. A cold, metal cylinder, possibly the barrel of a pistol, was pushed between my lips. I heard a click as the weapon was cocked, ready to fire.

This was very real and very scary. I could no longer separate the exercise from reality.

'Are you willing to talk now?' yelled a voice smelling of coffee and cigarettes very close to my face. With the gun still in my mouth I mumbled a 'mmwhh' and nodded my head. I was dragged up by the arms and shoved back inside.

My hood was taken off again and I was in a different room again, this time with cream plastered walls and grey carpet on the floor. Two men in plain green army uniforms sat behind a desk.

'Where do you live?' asked one.

'Kent.' The other wrote this down.

'Where in Kent?'

'Tunbridge Wells.'

I had some friends from university there so I could at least picture the place.

'Are you married?'

'No.'

'What's your boyfriend called?'

'Craig.' What are you doing, you muppet? Why give his real name?

'Where does he work?'

'In a bank.'

'Which bank? What's his job? What hours does he work?'

'NatWest, he's a bank teller... er, nine to five.'

I was completely making it up now.

'Bull, my sister's a bank teller and she doesn't work those hours. Do you really expect me to believe a Tornado pilot is interested in a bank clerk?'

I found all the shouting and the 'I can't answer that question' fairly bearable – you didn't really have to think. Now my sleep-deprived brain was trying to crank back up to speed and offer scraps of detail without saying too much.

In theory you shouldn't release any private information. You don't want the bad guys to pay Granny Elsie a visit while you're in captivity and use her as leverage to get information out of you. In practice, the consensus is if you do start talking at least have a solid story to stick to.

I was so befuddled I was forgetting what it was I'd lied about and getting caught in my own web. The more information I gave the deeper they dug.

'Where were you born?'

'Who did you live with?'

Then the tone changed.

'Why would a woman go into this world?

'Who would want to put themselves through all this suffering?'

'Is it a reaction to your miserable childhood? Did your Dad leave when you were young?' Bingo.

He was hitting a nerve but I was trying hard not to show it.

'I'm not surprised. Who could love you? Look at you, you're a six-foot-tall woman doing a man's job. Who's going to want to be with you?' Bastard. I was fighting hard to keep back the tears. I clenched my jaws tightly together and stared at him. I was close to losing it, but I was buggered if I was going to let this scumbag win.

It went on until abruptly the questions stopped and I was bundled back into the other room.

In my last interrogation I was lying down but even that was painful because I wasn't allowed to move. My feet were at a funny angle and my legs went into spasm.

'We've got your colleague and he's told us everything. He says he was the pilot, so who are you?'

What has Jez been saying?

The mind games tie you in knots.

I was shaking from the stress position, cold, fatigue and sheer terror.

'What were you doing there?'

'We were on a recce mission.'

'No you weren't, the aircraft had bombs on it.'

Oh, did it?

The hardest part was that because it was just an exercise Jez and I didn't have a proper story worked out between us. All the information was contradictory which made it even harder work to stay on top of the story.

By now I'd convinced myself I was being interrogated for real, which is ridiculous in the cold light of day. I knew I was in Cornwall and that I was on a training course, but because I'd had very little sleep or food for a week and had no energy because I'd been yomping across Dartmoor all night in the freezing cold, I was losing my resilience and becoming brainwashed. It's very powerful and very clever.

I was just a shell, barely aware of my own name, sitting cross-legged on an earth floor with my hands on my head. Well done guys, you've won, you've broken me, I might have said if I had any awareness of the real world. I was vaguely aware of a voice coming from somewhere in the back of my mind. Slowly, it came more into my consciousness, like I was slowly emerging from a dream. There it was again. 'The exercise is over, no duff.' I stiffened but stayed completely still. 'No duff, it's over. I repeat, no duff. We're not playing the game anymore.'

I didn't believe anything anymore. 'I cannot answer that question.'

'Mandy, it's over. Relax, time to go home.'

I was too numb and tired to cry. I took my hands off my head and just sat staring into my lap. Someone asked me what time I thought it was? Morning or afternoon? I hadn't a clue.

I was helped up and escorted outside. I had to shield my eyes from the brightness. It felt like a morning. The breeze was sweet and I breathed it in. All the others were there but no-one spoke. I couldn't even bring myself to catch anyone's eyes but having a quick glance around all look sunken and tired and deathly pale.

We climbed back into the truck for a silent trip back to St Mawgan, punctuated by sighs, the stretching of aching limbs and the odd half smile of empathy, as if to say, we've made it.

Back at the base, after a scalding hot shower I crawled into my bed and retreated into my own world of sleep, punctuated by dark dreams and torment.

The following day, a Saturday, the staff had hired a local pub and closed it off to the public. We'd all been through a traumatic experience and you need to talk about it. Today was the day to get it all out of your system so when you leave here, that's it. There were a lot of tears and it was a powerfully cathartic experience as everyone shared their stories.

What was quite funny was seeing the people who were interrogating us. They were specialists at their job and ultra-professional, but I was thinking, 'You were so horrible to me I can't actually speak to you.'

When someone is probing into very personal areas people do get traumatised.

Some people have been so emotionally scarred by it they have had breakdowns. It's not the intention to break people but it is trying to give them a flavour of what could happen if they get captured behind enemy lines.

I've since spoken to John Peters who was shot down and tortured in Iraq and he said unfortunately the training doesn't even remotely come close. For example, when someone is sticking tissue paper down your back and simulating lighting it, you're going to tell them whatever they want.

The only difference between myself and the others, as far as I could tell, was being allowed to keep my bra and pants on and the fact there had to be a woman present when I stripped.

There was nothing sexual and apart from the odd dig in the ribs or smack on the leg, no-one was beaten, although one guy broke a tooth when he was accidentally hit by a pistol butt.

The course was supposed to be valid for ten years, but the general consensus was we'd rather leave the RAF than have to do that again.

CHAPTER 18

JUNIOR JUNTA

Ihad a gnawing, nagging, slightly sick feeling whenever I thought about it. We were going back to Kuwait and I was nervous. I'd had a pretty miserable experience there last time and I wasn't looking forward to it in the slightest. Craig and I had been living together in Cambridge and I was loving the fact we could spend so much time together. We would see Elliot and Chessie at the weekends and the thoughts of one day having my own children were starting to take hold in my mind. The thought of not having him by my side for the next two months filled me with dread.

On the plus side, it was eight months on and I felt far more established on the squadron with a lot more flying under my belt. I was no longer the junior pilot and there had been a few changes in personnel in my immediate sphere. There were some new guys on the squadron who I got on with a lot better. Guys like Spenny, Cozy, Tom and Holfs.

They were younger than me and behind me in the system and their arrival felt like a breath of fresh air. The 'junior junta' was a lot stronger than it had been. Up until then the navigators on the squadron were all quite senior but to have people in some ways looking up to me changed the dynamic a little bit. I was generally feeling so much more confident, not just in my flying capability but in my position within the squadron. I had moved on from just being accepted to being at the heart of squadron life.

Flying into Ali Al Salem felt like Groundhog Day. It was the beginning of February so not quite as broiling hot as before but warm enough.

Arriving at our lines, it was so familiar it was as if I had never left, apart from the fact someone had redecorated my room with porn again in my absence. I stripped it all off in time-honoured fashion and chucked it outside. 'Porn's up, guys!'

I made a brew and went outside to sit under the net, smiling to myself as I realised how comfortable I now was in that environment. On my first tour everything was daunting and I was operating at maximum capacity the whole time. But this time I almost felt at home. I felt confident and ready for it. The surroundings were familiar, I knew the working conditions wouldn't phase me, I was comfortable with the intensity of operations and I was used to the language. I also had the mental back-up to know that I had done it before. My shoulders felt lighter than they had in ages. It looked like this time I had remembered to pack my mojo.

The action was hotting up across the border. The Iraqis were developing decent radar installations and fibre-optic networks which could push their whole communications systems under ground, which would have been carnage for our intel guys.

Over in the States, George W. Bush had just taken over the presidency and there was a feeling he wanted to make his mark in Iraq.

We were there as part of Operation Resinate South, a continuation of our previous Operation Bolton, just with a new name.

Our first week consisted of high-altitude – about 22,000ft – day-time reconnaissance sorties, filming radar sites and AAA batteries in southern Iraq.

To give me something to focus on away from the flying, I set myself the challenge of losing weight during the tour.

It seemed like I wasn't the only one, and one evening sitting around under the net after work eight of us agreed to stick a tenner into the pot to see who could lose the most weight. We hung a big chart on the corridor wall to provide very public motivation. I went to the gym every day and was very careful what I ate. No more super-size helpings ladled out by the chefs or tucking into stodgy puddings every mealtime.

Ten days in we assembled in the briefing room after breakfast as usual to get the day's tasking.

This time we were told the details of the mission must not leave these four walls. They didn't want any intelligence leaks to families, friends, the press, anyone.

Ooh, how exciting, sounds like we've got a good one here.

The Americans wanted to bomb some radar sites on the outskirts of Baghdad. The sites that had been proving problematic were above the 33rd parallel, the line just south of Baghdad denoting the no-fly zone. The Iraqis didn't recognise the no-fly zone and had been taking pot-shots at us since 1998 but they seemed to have upped their game in recent months. It was to be a massive joint British-US operation, flown at high level and conducted at night. We had never flown this far north before and clearance had to come right from the top of government.

That familiar buzz of adrenaline mixed with nerves flicked around the briefing room. Backs stiffened, eyes and ears focused.

This sounded like a big deal, prom night and a cup final rolled into one.

The brief was punchy and to the point. When we broke up for the planning phase it was all business. No-one cracked a smile, there was no banter, no wasted chat, no endless cups of tea.

While I worked on the piloting aspects of the routing, I debated in my mind whether to load my personal weapon given the chances of being shot down would be much greater. If you had to eject into enemy territory having a loaded weapon on hand to protect yourself might be helpful. I decided to load it.

I was flying with Andy again in what's called a cooperative attack as a four-ship formation. Our job was as 'designator', highlighting the target with our lasers for my wingman DWubs to drop the bomb.

We launched at about ten p.m. into a sparkly velvet black sky and headed north.

We were towards the rear of this massive push of allied aircraft: nearly twenty-five bombers and almost eighty aircraft in all.

The first wave was the fighters, then came the Prowler aircraft, the American EA-6B which jammed the surface-to-air missile systems for long enough for the bombers to get in, do our stuff and get out.

I completed my fence checks and roared over the border into the empty southern Iraqi desert. There were no lights down below, and it wasn't until we neared the main road heading north we had any indication of life below us. Then Andy piped up from the backseat.

'You got your night-vision goggles up or down Mands?'

'Up at the moment.'

'You might want to keep them that way.'

Obviously, I clicked them down, like a toddler being told not to do something. Up ahead, targeting the first wave of aircraft on the way up to Baghdad, was a full-on Bonfire Night or 4th July firework display. It looked like they were expecting us.

All the surface-to-air missile cells had woken up and were firing randomly. Sparks flashed from the guns of vehicle-mounted anti-aircraft batteries hidden in the pitch-black desert, their tracer rounds streaking up into the sky like roman fountains.

I looked out to my right and saw the outline of DWubs' jet about a mile-and-a-half away, straining forward like a greyhound alongside us. On the radio everyone in the formation was very sharp and professional. I straightened in my seat, ready to play my part in a serious night's work.

There was lots of chat on HaveQuick from the forward aircraft about 'spikes' – tracers – going up or new threats spotted. Andy was working hard in the boot, watching the Radar Homing and Warning Receiver (RHWR) to make sure we were in the clear.

'SA3, left ten o'clock.'

'Painting.' That was DWubs' navigator saying he'd seen the same thing on his radar.

'Come right twenty degrees Mandy.'

I didn't feel particularly threatened as I could see they weren't targeting specific aircraft but you're always a bit nervous because they only have to get lucky once.

Even though we'd planned the route according to where our own intelligence told us the threats were, there was always something different to adapt to in reality.

A radar installation would require us to almost tip toe around the outside of its missile engagement zone, flying corners like the shape of a fifty pence piece to get past. We also had to be mindful of drifting into someone else's airspace without letting them know what we were up to.

Nearing Baghdad, it was time to forget about the light show, which was getting more intense as we closed on the capital and knuckle down to our task.

We found the target on our display and switched on the TIALD (thermal imaging airborne laser designator) pod to track it and supply the bomb's guidance system with the information it needed to complete the attack.

Andy was checking the laser code, making sure it corresponded with DWubs' weapon.

'PRF 6179, check.'

'Confirm, 6179.'

I made sure I was flying a precise course, positioning us on the best side of the target so the weapon got a better view of what it was trying to hit.

The key is to provide the navigator with a stable platform but you don't want to be too straight on the target for too long otherwise you're a sitting duck. It's a balancing act of not turning in too soon but giving yourself enough time to get stable.

'Thirty seconds to target.'

'Lase on.'

'Fifteen seconds.'

'Five.'

'Commit. Weapons away.'

That was DWubs committing the bomb off. Because we were flying at high level there was no need for any radical pulling up or rolling away from the target. I kept on my course until I got the new heading from Andy and he watched through his TIALD as the Paveway laser-guided bomb found its mark.

'Splash,' he said, to indicate the weapon had gone bang on the ground.

'Routing to next point, heading 170.' Andy delivered the new course in as flat a voice as if he were directing a taxi back in Cambridge.

There was no excited chatter, no whoopin' and a-hollerin'. This wasn't the movies. We'd only got to the top of the mountain. Now we had to get back down for it to be a success.

I pushed the stick right to tip us over on our side and set up a big arcing turn away to the south. We flew our jinking course back down towards the Kuwait border, avoiding the threats we knew about. Al Nasiriyah, Al Najaf and Basrah harboured some serious danger areas so we were certainly not out of the woods.

'SA6, right, three o'clock, head 165 degrees.'

'Roger.'

I only really relaxed when we crossed back over the border into Kuwait.

We landed back at Ali Al Salem just after midnight. I shut down the jet, climbed down the steps, and shook hands with Andy on the tarmac.

The engineers were buzzing around us. 'Well done, Ma'am. Sounds like a good one.'

Walking into the operations building I sensed everyone was pumped up. I could smell the testosterone in the air as we met the other crews and slapped each other on the backs.

Even though the mission had gone well, we went through the usual close-to-the-bone debrief. No-one was safe from having a few spears chucked their way to sharpen us up for next time. Fortunately, none came our way on this occasion.

It's always easier to accept the comments after a successful trip – the cloak of confidence deflects the spears or at least stops them digging in too much.

The energy jumped another notch when we got a call from the Americans saying they had some unbelievable footage we had to see. They sent over some tape from one of their Predator unmanned aerial vehicles (UAV) flying above the whole mission.

The infra-red video showed the square, white outline of the building we were targeting. We saw the white figure of a man come out of a building clutching a mug with steam wafting up from it. He had a cigarette and took a few sips before throwing the dregs onto the ground, opening the door and going back inside. Literally at that moment the bomb entered the building and exploded.

Unbelievably, what was left of the door opened and the man ran out, jumped into a nearby car and screeched off, in a straight line, through the compound fence and into the desert as the building collapsed behind him.

From our remote office at 22,000 feet it's easy to feel removed from the consequences of our actions but this brought it home. The banter suggested what everyone thought about it. Have some of that, me old mucker, was the general consensus. But I felt a slight sense of relief that the man had escaped. I couldn't put my finger on the emotion at the time, but I decided it was probably best to leave that thought to myself.

We sat outside our hut that night chatting through the mission again in the still sticky night air, decompressing over a few strawberry pipes and a smuggled gin and tonic miniature.

The first thing the following morning I sneaked a phone call back to my parents. 'If you see anything in the news, I'm safe.'

'No dear, nothing has been reported back here.'

It feels at the time as if what you are doing is massive and the whole world is watching but our biggest mission to date didn't even hit the press back home.

It did get picked up in some papers a couple of days later. US military described it as 'essentially a self-defence operation', while Bush was quoted as saying it was a 'routine mission to enforce the no-fly zone'.

Mindful of my experience last time in Kuwait I'd volunteered to do this one as a split tour to break it up in case I hated it as much as before.

So, after a month I flew back to Blighty and straight back into work at Marham for a week.

Still, it wasn't all bad. The Red Arrows were using the base for practice ahead of their busy summer season of air shows and one day I blagged a ride in the back seat of Red Nine behind a pilot called 'Cutty'. They went through the whole repertoire, red, white and blue smoke and all. Even as a Tornado pilot I was pretty revved up after that.

Back in Kuwait life followed an almost mundane pattern of high-level recce trips by day, like having a normal job with set hours, except the commute was in a van around a dusty yellow airfield to a jet parked under a huge domed sunshade next to a pile of rubble and an office that moved at 450 knots.

One day I was flying over the southern Iraqi desert when I felt the urge to pee. I'd done a big gym session earlier and drank a load of water when I finished. It was apparently now keen to come out. Mindful of what had happened before I tried to hold it in, I told my navigator Finnster I was considering doing it in my seat.

'I gave myself a kidney infection last time so I'm just going to hot leg,' I said. 'Can't see I've got any other choice.'

'Cool, Mands. You're so hydrated it's not like it's going to be disgusting is it? We'll just wash the seat cushion.'

I composed myself and then relaxed to prepare for the inevitable. Nothing happened.

'Finnster, mate, I can't go. I might have to try a power-wee into my water bottle.'

I glanced down at the water bottle beside my right leg. It was still half full. What happens if I produce so much it starts to overflow?

'Bugger. I'm going to have to drink my water first to make room in the bottle.'

I slurped down the rest of my water to add to my already full bladder and then contemplated my next move. I was going to have to release my straps, take off my life support jacket, my combat survival waistcoat and my flying suit just to get at all the zips on my various lower layers of kit and then get my knickers down enough to work the water bottle under my bottom. While still flying the aircraft. In a war zone. In Iraq.

Taking off the straps and putting the ejector seat pins back in made us extremely vulnerable. What if we got locked-on by a missile now? We were right down on the southern border and there weren't many threats about but look what had happened before.

'OK, Mands, go for it, I'll only call the major threats.'

'Don't speak to me, Finnster. I'm just going to try to get in the zone.'

'Roger that.'

Slumped down with my bum perched on the front edge of the seat I tried to squeeze out a jet of enough force to get it into the bottle.

'SA6, right, two o'clock.'

'Shut up, Finnster, I'm trying to concentrate.'

Ok, right, relax, nearly there... here it comes...

'SA8 left, nine o'clock,' whispered Finnster into my headset.

'Bloody hell, Finnster, leave it.'

'I'm sorry, Mands, I have to call them.'

'I know but you're making me lose focus. Trying again.'

I still couldn't go. 'Forget it, mission aborted. I'll have to cross my legs on the way home.' I edged back into my seat, zipped up my flying suit and strapped back in, which increased the burning sensation in my crotch. Obviously, I'd made it worse by downing the contents of my water bottle.

I pulled the ejector seat pins out and tried to focus on the flying for the last minutes of our trip. I was struggling to concentrate on what Finnster was saying as he called the threats but at least this time when I landed, I didn't have to go to hospital.

I flew seventeen combat missions in all on that tour though none as intense as the night up near Baghdad. It had been a fun time, still challenging, but the whole atmosphere had been different to my first tour.

The Junior Junta had found their groove and we'd earned our spurs.

And I lost ten kilos, which was nice.

We were replaced by 14 Squadron, and soon after I got back, I got a message from Rob saying, 'Seen your chart. Well done on losing all that weight but my golly you were a fat git when you got out there.'

CHAPTER 19

TWIN TOWERS

I t was time to take on a more responsible role in the squadron. This meant I needed to take on a secondary duty. I knew I wasn't an electronic warfare expert – all that wiggly amp stuff was a bit out of my comfort zone – so I chose the running around option. Combat Survival and Rescue Officer.

To qualify, I had to take a two-week course back down at that old favourite, St Mawgan. You might think out of the frying pan into the fire after my last experience down there, but this would be different. No interrogation, just the fun part of survival in the field, with a bit of what-to-do-if-you-crash-in-the-sea training.

I'd only been there five months before, so the staff greeted me warmly when I rocked up. It seemed there was a different level of respect for me having been through the rigours of the Conduct After Capture course.

The rest of the course of about a dozen was made up of pilots and navs from other units across all three services, including multi-engine guys and helicopter crews. The first week was spent in the classroom and field, building shelters again, learning field techniques, how to capture food and evasion tricks, but with an emphasis this time on how to teach them. I can now survive in a hole or under a bush for months.

More importantly, I can teach you to do it, too.

We also learned how to do a good river crossing. You don't want to lose any kit or get it wet, so the first thing is to strip off. I was allowed to wear a swimming costume to preserve my dignity and the men were allowed to keep their pants on because there was a woman on the course. The tactic then was to send someone across first to attach a rope or piece of para cord around a convenient tree to act as a safety guide for everyone else. Once you've got to the other side, you dry off with a pair of socks, get your kit on and off you go.

We also spent a lot of time in the pool being taught how to instruct life-raft techniques. The practical element involved being chucked into the sea off Fowey, the same as we had when we learnt about ditching during the early weeks at Valley.

No survival course would be complete without a good old game of hide and seek, otherwise known as four days on the run back on Dartmoor to practice escape and evasion skills. We were blindfolded, loaded into a van and dropped off at a certain point with just our ejection seat gear. I was grouped with two helicopter pilots who had their nice rucksacks stuffed with goodies including a chocolate cake for one of their birthdays. They laughed at me constantly for my meagre supplies which consisted of two ration packs.

We were always on the move evading capture from army regulars. There wasn't much time to catch food and set snares, so other than a few berries, we didn't eat much for four days, although they did share the cake.

On the last morning we were hiding in a barn when we heard the welcome noise of a fast jet overhead. This was playing the part of an aircraft searching for downed airmen. The On Scene Commander. We listened in on the radio. 'Call sign Bronze zero two. Over.'

'That's my boyfriend,' I blurted out.

It just happened Craig was based out of RNAS Yeovilton flying Hawks and had been assigned to be our 'eyes above'.

I was desperate to radio back saying, 'Hi sweetheart, I feel rubbish,' but you've got to stick to the protocol, even after four days on Dartmoor.

If I thought I had lucked in with my first Red Flag trip, I hit the jackpot in August when I found myself back in Vegas. It was unheard of for a squadron to get two Red Flags in quick succession. It felt like we had won the lottery.

This time, with about 1,000 hours of flying under my belt – and 400 on the Tornado – I would be taking part in the air, not the planning room.

Like before, I got a real thrill entering Nellis Air Force Base, this time as a pilot about to mix it with the Americans and lots of other squadrons in the massive coalition exercise above the Nevada desert. The philosophy is that you train harder than you will ever have to fight for real.

My navigator was one of my favourite people, Jeffers. We did an hour's familiarisation trip on our first day and then seven live missions as part of Red Flag in ten days.

The flying was superb – lots of low-level stuff, live bombing against real SAM sites sending out radar emissions and ducking and diving in the vast crystal-clear summer sky.

As with all trips it was about precision timing, starting with making sure you didn't miss your slot to take off as they tried to get 100 aircraft airborne in twenty minutes.

That meant having your personal administration together right from the start and maintaining laser-like focus for the whole trip.

To test our mettle, the staff would throw in more and more complex scenarios or change the mission halfway through. The scenario might be that an aircraft has gone down and your formation might be tasked with setting up a combat air patrol on station overhead and talking to the search-and-rescue teams coming in.

We'd strut our stuff burning holes in the sky during the day and be home in time for tea and medals with all our friends in the evening.

The whole thing was very cool. I was in heaven. It felt like the world – my own small part of it anyway – was in a very good place. I didn't want it to end.

But I was also looking forward to my first trip in the jet back across the Atlantic.

I set off from Nellis on 9th September 2001 in a four-ship formation with GB, Block, Nick, Ady, DWubs and Michel and flew for four hours to Bangor, Maine, refuelling from a Tristar on the way.

The next day we set off from Bangor headed east for Lajes air base on Terceira island in the Azores, roughly in the middle of the Atlantic due west of southern Portugal. The 2,300-mile flight would take about six hours, which meant we would have to refuel in mid-air again on the way.

The pressure to refuel crossing the Atlantic is massive. If you mess it up, you have to turn back which leaves you red-faced and the RAF quite cross. That's why they don't let inexperienced crews bring the jets back, although there becomes a point when you have to learn.

The refuelling is planned meticulously and divided into brackets. You have to get all four aircraft through in the specified time in that bracket, otherwise the last one might be running low on fuel.

It takes about ten minutes to fill up a Tornado so allowing time to swap positions and a couple of basket misses means each bracket is about an hour, and to get to Lajes would require three brackets.

We left the US coast and settled into the flight, two Tornados either side of the tanker. I was flying as number two, so I was the inside aircraft on the right-hand side with Jeffers in my back seat. My autopilot didn't seem to be working so I was hand flying which is quite tiring.

To relieve the boredom of flying in a straight line there was plenty of radio banter and miming at each other out of the windows.

GB and his nav Ady were on my right wing, filming the whole thing with a video camera. DWubs and Block, an Aussie exchange nav, and Nick and Frenchman Michel were on the left of the Tristar.

We even had a game of Who Wants to be a Millionaire, with one of the Tristar crew as quizmaster.

'Number two, do you want to phone a friend?'

'Roger that, I'll call number four.'

The first bracket was coming up but the weather ahead was deteriorating so we were called into close formation. This is quite taxing because you have to stay fixed to a reference point on the other aircraft. If you drift, the person on your wing will drift and before you know it you've lost the tanker.

DWubs was first up and he dropped back and then edged forward into position behind the tanker amid a barrage of banter on the radio.

'Here he comes, getting close, the probe's out, it's wafting about like a windsock on a Wurlitzer... oooh, he's hit the rim, any damage? No damage.'

You are painfully aware that if you damage the nozzle, probe, or basket you've probably buggered it up for everyone and the whole mission will have to turn around because of your inability.

What with the concentration of flying, the competitiveness of playing 'Who wants to be a millionaire?', the bad weather and the pressure of refuelling my heart was hammering.

When it was my turn I dipped from my position and crept towards the basket trailing out of the back of the tanker.

All I could think was, 'Please don't mess up, please don't mess up.'

I nudged forward and the commentary sparked up again from all the other cockpits. 'And it's Big Bird, making her mid-Atlantic debut, let's see what she's got. Better not balls it up, we've all got homes to go to... The probe's out but she doesn't seem to be able to get it in... we've not heard that before...'

This was so much more stressful than being shot at in Iraq.

'... oooh, there it goes but she takes the spike, what will the judges make of this?'

Ramming your probe through the spokes of the basket can cause them to break off. If they fly into your engine you've got real trouble.

'No, looks like she's OK, the fuel's going in. That's a seven out of ten for Big Bird, a decent effort and one I'm sure she'll build on.'

I was more pleased and relieved that I had done it than the day I was accepted into the air force.

Once we had all been refuelled it was time for some lunch. I pulled out my ration pack, which had been handed to me in Bangor, only to discover lunch was a sort of Pot Noodle. Which obviously needs hot water. Where the bloody hell was I going to get hot water from up here? I seemed to be the only one with this. The others found that hilarious as they tucked into their sandwiches. Jeffers graciously offered to share his but I stuck with the apple and cereal bar instead.

To make me feel even better the Tristar crew were cooking themselves a nice curry and showing me all the ingredients as they went in. 'Ooh, look at this nice chicken, and here are some juicy tomatoes, this curry is going to be delicious... how are you doing out there with your Cup-a-Soup you can't heat up?' Brilliant.

Someone suggested I wee into it, which was obviously revolting, but it was also more complicated than it sounds. First, I would have to get all my layers off, but more importantly I couldn't wee because I had deliberately dehydrated myself by not drinking anything since the night before.

So dehydrated, tired and with nothing to eat I tried to think about other things in between refuelling. Flying over thousands of miles of featureless sea is slightly unnerving. When the banter has died down and everyone's gone quiet it's easy to feel a bit vulnerable and a long way from safety. Spotting the Azores as a tiny speck on the radar gave me something tangible to cling onto.

Dusk fell and the small green spot on the screen grew larger until we could see the lights of Lajes airfield twinkling in the distance, like a port in a storm.

We landed in the dark and after shutting down the jets the Tristar guys invited us over for a cup of tea. I clambered into the back, still a bit unsteady on my pins after sitting on my unpadded seat cushion for six hours. There were two big catering urns on one of the benches, so I went to pour some tea from one and it came out clear. Must be just water. I tried the other. Tea coloured this time, but still cold. 'I think you'll find this is special tea,' said one of the tanker crew, Nick, a friend from officer training. They had made up one pot of G&T and one pot of Pimms for our arrival. Welcome to Lajes.

We took off the next day in relaxed mood for the final 1,500-mile hop back up to Blighty. The cloud was thick at altitude, so we fell in around the Tristar in close formation, our wings seemingly touching.

I was settling into the flight, musing about various things I was going to do when I got home, the jet flying on autopilot after it had been fixed overnight.

Then the radio crackled and the Tristar pilot said they were picking up some weird radio traffic from back across the Atlantic. Something seemed a bit odd and they wanted to check out what was going on using the high-frequency (HF) radio, which is used for long-range reception because the shorter wave lengths bounce off the ionosphere and can therefore travel 'over the horizon' instead of longer waves which travel in a straight line.

Although Tornados do carry an HF radio, we were not cleared to use them as in early trials they had interfered with the fly-by-wire system, causing it to malfunction.

So that they could tune to the HF safely and listen in to the strange goings on across the pond, the Tristar crew asked us all to drop back to a looser formation. This involved the two outer jets taking a twenty-degree outward heading change for twenty seconds before straightening up, before the two inner jets made a ten-degree change for ten seconds before getting back on track. Now we were in a wide formation, all separated by altitude increments of 500ft for good measure.

But while we were safe from the possibility of bits falling off our jets, this gave us other problems. By dropping back in this thick cloud, we could be in danger of losing the Tristar and with it our vital fuel supply.

Our nice relaxing jaunt home had just got edgy. We were in the dark and chatting amongst ourselves on the radio about what could possibly be going on.

Eventually the Tristar radioed us to start closing back in again which involved reversing the procedure one by one.

When we were all back on station by the mother ship, he gave us the bad news. American airspace had been shut and all inbound aircraft redirected. I felt a cold blast of anxiety deep inside my flying suit.

What the hell is going on? What could be that big and important that they have closed America? The immediate issue for us was all aircraft heading inbound into the US from the eastern Atlantic would be heading back our way.

We were out of normal UHF radio range, so the Tristar guys warned us to keep our eyes peeled on the radar and out of the cockpit. In the military you are taught to 'control the controllables', we might not understand the bigger picture but you manage what is within your power to do so.

Approaching the UK, we tuned into the emergency guard frequencies and picked up some radio chatter from a US aircraft carrier on exercise off the south coast.

'To the small aircraft approaching us, please declare yourself or we will shoot you down. You are on a direct course. I repeat, if you come within five nautical miles, we WILL shoot you down.'

I'm thinking, 'Oh my gosh, we're about to witness an American carrier shoot down a small puddle jumper aircraft because they are not monitoring the right frequency, in the UK, on a glorious September afternoon'.

As we were the nearest airborne assets, we were ready to intercept. We asked ATC to give us radar vectors to the aircraft, we started to descend, but right at the last minute we managed to reach the aircraft on the radio. 'Er, sorry, we're a bit lost.' They immediately diverted their course. We relayed it to the Americans and the situation was defused but hearing the escalation was really chilling, given we had no idea what was going on.

We carried on to RAF Marham and landed without any issues. Walking into the squadron building was like walking onto the set of a zombie movie. No-one spoke, everyone just sat staring at the TV.

'What on earth is going on guys?' Following their gaze I took in the scene unfolding on the small screen. An aircraft appeared to have flown into one of the Twin Towers in New York. Surely it was some sort of horrendous accident? Then we watched the towers collapse and the full horror of 9/11 begin to emerge. It was the most shocking thing I had ever seen. I almost felt like I had been part of it, having left the States yesterday and then listening to this chilling build-up on the radio flying in from the Azores.

We didn't make it any further than the engineers' room that morning. Our debrief amounted to 'Anyone got any points to bring up?' 'No.' We sat staring at the TV.

We even forgot to sign-in the jets.

CHAPTER 20

LESSONS IN LEADERSHIP

owards the end of September, I was working with the SAS in Wales. The special forces guys were acting as the forward air controllers (FAC) on the ground, talking us onto targets. I had a German exchange navigator, Major Blockhaus, in my back seat and our job was to interpret the SAS's 'Nine line', a set of nine lines of information relating to the target they want taking out; including coordinates, the whereabouts of enemy forces, their weapons and friendly forces in the area. The FAC talks you in from the big picture into smaller and smaller detail.

'Can you see large barn by big tree?'

'Visual barn.'

'Left of barn, is T-shaped copse.'

'Visual copse.'

'Western edge of copse is lone tree.'

'Visual lone tree.'

'Target is stone bridge left of lone tree.'

'Visual bridge.'

'Cleared hot.'

It was really important to practice this chat and be totally comfortable working with the eyes on the ground. It's a technique that was used all the time in Afghanistan. One morning we'd just simulated bombing an old barn at the edge of a wood and were leaving the target when we suffered complete radio failure. Nothing. The comms just went completely dead.

I could still speak to Major Blockhaus on the internal radio but not to anyone in the outside world. About 20 tonnes of speeding bullet and no way of telling anyone where we were, like a runaway speedboat careering around a busy shipping lane in thick fog.

The weather was pretty terrible and we needed to get back to Marham but we couldn't go back across the country with no radio. The nearest base to land at was RAF Valley but we couldn't tell them we were coming either. We had to go into a procedural loss of comms, where you hit a pre-select button on your transponder to let various air traffic controllers know you've got no radio. We poked our way up towards Valley but it's such a busy airfield you can't just head in and land. With a good look around I positioned us on a long final approach. We managed to join the circuit, like filtering onto a thundering motorway and inched down for a simulated approach to check out the runway.

We were looking for a white caravan, manned by someone from air traffic control, who would run up a signal to let us know where to land. As you fly past on your simulated approach, they check your undercarriage is down and let off a green flare to say you are cleared for landing next time around.

We made it down and popped into Valley for a coffee and a chat while our radio was fixed. On the wall I spotted my old course photo and it immediately transported me back to cycling round, perfecting battle turns. It felt like a world away from the front line flying I'd just returned from.

My two-year anniversary as a qualified Tornado pilot was approaching and I was deep in preparation to become pairs-lead qualified.

This would mean I could officially lead a two-ship into battle. Up to now I'd led plenty of missions but with a senior navigator in the backseat. Now I was gearing up to take on an enhanced workload as formation leader with junior navigators under me.

Pairs-lead work-up was an ongoing process, intermingled with a lot of FAC work, recce trips, some four-ship training with the Hawks of 100 Squadron and air-to-air refuelling practice.

The reconnaissance flying was pretty mundane. I didn't know there were so many different categories of electricity pylons and sub-stations. We were expected to flash over the top of selected towers at 250 feet and 450 knots and spot what category pylon it was and report back. 'It's a category 16 self-supported steel lattice structure with three vertical antennas and seven dishes oriented east-west.' In the debrief we'd look back over the video to see if what we'd reported was correct. Let's just say this did not exactly play to my strengths.

On other trips we'd be given a line to fly along between two sets of coordinates. Again, we had to report what we'd spotted as we flew over. One line involved flying over the Tank Museum in Bovington, Dorset. I was pretty happy with my recon skills on this one and trotted out a whole list of stuff, like a contestant recalling the items on the conveyor belt in the old TV show the Generation Game which I loved watching as a kid. Fondue set, cuddly toy...

'So, you didn't spot the tank in the service station down the road?'

'No, sorry, must have missed that one.'

To finish my pairs-lead qualification we flew up to RAF Leuchars across the bay from St. Andrews in Scotland to make up the numbers on the Qualified Weapons Instructors (QWI) course.

The course was for the top-dog QWIs across the RAF and beyond and was like a mini Red Flag with aircraft from all over Europe joining in for a big combined exercise. All the QWIs took it turns to be mission commander but by the last day everyone had been through.

All eyes looked at me. 'Mandy, fancy giving it a go?'

No flipping way. Not in a million years.

'Sure, why not?' I spluttered, trying to sound confident, even though it felt like I was about to drown. I grabbed Jeffers for a detailed talk on what was required and he helped me formulate a plan of attack.

Still slightly quaking in my boots but with my best leadership voice, I took a deep breath and stood up in front of a room of more than thirty pilots and navs in the hangar for the mass briefing. I'd seen Suraya do this brilliantly at Red Flag, so I modelled myself on her and jumped in.

My job here was to describe the scenario we had devised, flying south through the corridor between Glasgow and Edinburgh, arcing east through the Borders before bombing multiple targets on the Spadeadam range in Cumbria.

The plan had to incorporate the various roles of aircraft involved in the exercise, starting with a German Tornado squadron fitted with ALARM, an anti-radiation missile for suppressing enemy air defences (SEAD) and knocking out radar stations associated with surface-to-air missiles. Then there were Tornado F3s in a fighter role, taking on the enemy intercept force flown by instructors, before the bombers – us, Jaguars and Harriers swooped in. Once I had painted the picture and assigned various tasks, the aircrew went off to fine-tune their own plans.

Timings were acute, so if you were dropping your first bomb at 1137 you needed to work backwards to plot your path through the downed air defence systems within a specific timeframe, usually minutes. Refuelling had to be taken into account and contingencies made for attacks from enemy aircraft.

After a couple of hours everyone came back to the hangar and went through their plan. My job was to check there was no conflicting routes and that all the timings would work. It's very intricate and takes up plenty of capacity before you've even flown, much like planning a week's childcare without leaving one of your kids stranded somewhere.

In many ways flying the trip was the easy part as I just had to concentrate on getting our two-ship on target on time, but it was easily the most sapping mission I had ever done in the UK because of the pressure of the bigger picture, the feeling that it all rested on my shoulders.

Still, I managed to keep all the balls in the air, scored a direct hit with my own bombing run and everyone came back safely. Jeffers signed me off as two-ship qualified and I promptly led another joint-ops mission to take over Ma Bells pub in St Andrews. I had finally slayed the imposter on my shoulder.

Around this time a new navigator arrived on the squadron, by the name of Helen D. I was thrilled to finally have some female company. We even made history by flying the first all-female crew together. Apart from an article I wrote for the Marham magazine entitled, 'Two birds do it together in a Tornado,' the event passed without any significant fanfare.

It was my twenty-ninth birthday and I was back in Kuwait flying a training sortie with Andy. It was supposed to be a quick forty minute reintroduction but as we headed back to Ali Al Salem, we had complete hydraulic failure. We managed to get the landing gear down but I had no steerage on the front wheel. This meant I wouldn't be able to control the aircraft on the ground. There was only one option – use an arrestor wire strung across the runway to bring us to a very abrupt halt, like jets landing on the deck of an aircraft carrier. I had never done one for real, only in the simulator, and had to have a hurried thumb through the cards in my leg pocket to remind myself of the correct order of procedure. Right, OK, yep, got that, er... what could possibly go wrong? First, we had to fly out over the sea to dump fuel to make ourselves as light as possible.

Flying back over Kuwait Bay, with the glow of the lights from Kuwait City shining to my left, I set up the approach and began descending down the path, half nervously, half curious to see what would happen. As we neared the runway, they raised the wire and I released the hook out of the back of my aircraft at the prescribed time.

I nudged the jet down... lower, lower, easy does it... and braced for impact, waiting for the hook to grab the wire. Will it, won't it? Ooof. I fired forward into my straps, my head nodded and my chin dug into my chest as the wire clutched us to the ground and the aircraft came to a fairly abrupt halt. Still, down in one piece. Happy birthday.

Our operational routine followed the same pattern as before. Morning briefing followed by planning, lunch, snooze, gym or cup of iced tea and a chinwag relaxing under the net, before gearing up for the night's mission about mid-afternoon.

There was plenty to watch out for on the main Baghdad-Basrah highway but down in the southern desert near the Saudi border it was like flying in space. Just blackness down below, save for sporadic lights twinkling like stars.

Our nightly trips had been pretty uneventful for a while and life was as run-of-the-mill as it could be, given what we were doing for a living. But while I was still laser-focused on the flying, I could allow my mind to open a new tab and drift off into it now and then, like driving down the motorway thinking of something else other than how actually to drive a car. I was going home the next day, I was looking good with a great suntan. I was thinking about a new dress I was going to buy to surprise Craig.

And that was when the angry man with the missile picked me out for target practice.

'BREAK RIGHT, MANDY…'

The urgent shout hauls my head out of the daydream like a cartoon character yanked by a hook, and my hand automatically snaps the stick over, like a snoozing schoolgirl suddenly waking up and scribbling furiously to cover up her nap.

I briefly ponder why my right ear is now pointing at the ground when moments before I was straight and level and mulling which restaurant to hit first when I get home.

'Missile launch, five o'clock…' says the strained voice of my nav into my headset.

Like the split-second delay before the onset of pain, the enormity of the situation is now flooding my brain. WOOAH! This is very, bloody… urgghh… real. The g-force is pinning me into my seat, squashing my face and making my g-suit bite into my legs as my left hand forces the throttles forward and I pull back the stick with my right.

'Where is it, Jacko? Can you see it?' I squeeze out, despite the effort of fighting the g and steering us the hell out of town.

And then, BOOM! The flash, crackle and white-hot pop of the flares and then the missile exploding behind us dazzle my eyes, like a strobe light in a disco, except much less fun.

Every nerve in my body is buzzing, like I've injected industrial strength caffeine into my heart and my brain is pulsing with the thought of what's just happened. Someone down there has actually tried to kill me. Hell fire, they came close, too. Way too close. But you can't dwell on that now, Mands. You've got to get a grip. You're the formation leader.

These guys are relying on you, not just to get home safely, but to carry out Her Majesty's business, like you've trained to do.

I muster my calmest pilot's voice to radio the Commander in Chief, flying in the AWACS command and control aircraft over the Persian Gulf.

'Warrior, this is Spartan One. We've been locked-on by a SAM. We've evaded it. Are you happy for us to engage targets?'

'Roger that, Spartan One. Stand by.'

I get on the radio to the boss who was out to my right but, frankly, could be anywhere now and dish out jobs to the rest of the team, who were behind us but now presumably are somewhere in front as we ducked and dived through the dark desert sky. We can almost hear the buzz from the AWACS aircraft as they furiously work out a plan of action.

The radio crackles to life again.

'Spartan One, you are free to engage targets.'

Jacko's done a brilliant job keeping us alive by tracking the missile and his first job now is to get us back in touch with the others. I know there's no enemy air force up here, but I'll feel much better when we're back in formation.

The radio falls silent as the guys work out where we are, where the tanker is, where the target is, where home is and how we're going to wage war while flying on fumes.

One by one they report back, serious voices on, clipped, professional, business like.

My head tries to suck in all the information as my eyes scan the green glow of the numbers on the head-up display in front of me.

It's clear it's going to be super-tight to try to go straight to the target, make an attack and get home safely. There's a chance, but as I've learnt by now, taking a chance is not a good policy.

Right, decision made. We're off to play hunt the tanker.

It must be here somewhere. It's a great big American thing with a ridiculous name like 'Extender' or 'Stratotanker' and is about five times the size of us, but it's dark, we've been wrapped up by a sandstorm and it's blowing old boots. The jet is bouncing up and down and visibility is nil minus a bit more. I'm flying on instruments and Jacko is straining at his screens behind me.

The tanker should be flying a racetrack pattern, like a big oval around a fixed point. We can see him on the screen, but can we get our eyes on? Can we heck.

The fuel is becoming an issue, too, and I'm getting those first pangs of concern, like when you gamble on pushing on to the next motorway services and then wish you hadn't. Eventually through the soup we spot its hulking shape but there's a queue and aircraft from all over are stacked up behind it.

I radio across to let them know we are here. An American drawl from the deep south rolls into my ear.

'Spartan One, fuel check?'

'Bingo, plus fifty.'

The evading action from the missile lock has cost us more fuel than the others.

'Roger that, standby... cleared to tank.'

Thank you, gentlemen, ladies first.

Trouble is, the Americans use a different system, where they fly a drogue at the end of a long boom onto your probe. I'm not actually qualified on this. I haven't had any practice in daylight, let alone in the dark in a raging sandstorm. Normally a pilot instructor would teach this to me from my back seat in a twin-stick training aircraft.

Still, best not to worry too much about that now. We've got two or three minutes of fuel left, tops, to get this done or we'll have to bug out and go home. Tanking is stressful at the best of times and I'm acutely aware that everyone else in the queue is watching and listening. Will she? Won't she?

I nudge the throttles with my left hand and we inch forward. The probe extends out above the right side of my cockpit. You're taught to keep the basket in your peripheral vision rather than focus on it and let your nav talk you in. Jacko has eyes on. 'Right a bit, right, stop, stable, forward, three metres, two metres, right a tiny bit, left, stop.' The American drogue operator takes over and flies the refuelling drogue onto our probe.

I wait for that satisfying clunk as the probe clicks onto the nozzle.

But can I connect? That'll be no, then.

I drop back and give my head a little clearing shake and widen my eyes, as if that will make me see better. 'Come on, Wellsey.' Forward we go again, a nudge on the throttles, right a bit, left a bit. I can hear a big clock ticking in my head. Why won't you go in, you chump?

This is horrible. My cheeks feel hot under my mask, a sure sign I'm embarrassed. My forehead is beading with sweat.

'We need to try again, just one more prod Mandy,' urges Jacko.

Hundreds of eyes seem to be burning at me, the other pilots no doubt muttering some nonsense about women drivers or something equally hilarious. Still, it doesn't help my fragile frame of mind.

But this isn't personal, it isn't me trying to prove to everyone else that I can hack all this as a woman. This isn't me trying to show what a great pilot I am or, in this case, am not. It's not about Mandy from Manchester. I'm the leader of this mission, I am Spartan One, with my boss in the jet behind me. I have an executive decision to make. However, overruling an experienced navigator is not something you do lightly. My stomach is churning but I can't dither.

Right, we're going to have to turn back.

I radio the call and drop away from the tanker to let number two have a go. Number four takes his place and sticks with me.

I ask Jacko to plot us a course back home to Ali Al Salem airbase. Silence.

Something's up. I speak again. Nothing. Then a mumbled 'Roger.'

The atmosphere has turned frostier than a Mr Freeze factory.

Now that the pressure is off – albeit we've got even less fuel and we've got to get home – I begin to feel guilty.

Even though I'm on my third tour of Iraq I'm still a relatively junior pilot and I've just overruled an experienced navigator. I should feel confident, a mistress of my universe. But I feel like a failure. That little devil voice on my shoulder is giving me a hard time. What a numpty. Can't even refuel a Tornado. The first bit of real action you've had in eight weeks, the thing you've been training to do for years and you cock it up. My guardian angel on the other shoulder fights back. You made a good decision under intense pressure. You've given the rest of your team a chance of completing the mission. That's what it's all about.

We land in massing cloud and gusty wind and taxi towards our designated shelter on the outskirts of the rough, dusty airfield. I rip off my mask and gulp a few deep breaths of hot, dry air. I sit still in the cockpit for a few moments to gather my thoughts.

Too soon my space is invaded as the ground crew open the canopy and I grudgingly unfold myself. I barely acknowledge them. Despite being surrounded by people, I feel utterly alone. Jacko is already out and waiting at the bottom of the stairs.

I avoid eye contact but we fall in step walking across the tarmac towards a waiting minibus. This is awful. I have to say something. I force a 'Sorry.' He puts his arm around me and says something about not being stupid and how he shouldn't have put me under that pressure. It transpires later that in his previous job, he had been on the development and testing team for brand new weapons and was desperate to be the first to fire an Enhanced Paveway laser-guided bomb in the Iraqi theatre. He was aware that he had been motivated by emotion, and good decisions are never made when we are fuelled by passion rather than facts. His words help but I still feel terrible.

The van pulls up outside our lines and I follow Jacko inside, pausing under the huge fan in the middle of the briefing room, as if the cooler air will wash away my woes. I am still raw and keep saying how frustrating it was trying to tank, but Jacko has moved on and thrusts a cup of tea into my hand. He gives me a pep talk, saying I shouldn't be hard on myself, I'd never done it before and I made the right decision.

We walk over to the ops room and sit around listening to the radio chatter as number two and three switch from a secure comms frequency and cross back over the border. Sounds like a successful mission. I'm pleased but I feel like a sixth former who has missed the big party on Saturday night. It was now about two a.m. and I can feel the adrenaline of the mission wearing off and tiredness kicking in, which doesn't help. An hour or so later, Stinger, the boss, Fred and Block burst through the door like cowboys walking into a saloon.

'Morning all, get the kettle on...'

They are buzzing, and oozing energy and testosterone, with chests puffed out like footballers after a good win.

'What happened to you lot?'

I glance around at the other three. We are all a bit flat and can't offer much banter in return.

As mission leader it is my job to lead the debrief. My stomach is churning as I ponder how it will pan out.

The guys settle down in their seats and I stand up in front of the projector. All eyes are fixed on me. I try not to lock on to anyone's gaze. What are they thinking? As my first words come out I am aware I am not quite at full gusto. My voice is faltering, I'm sure I will be highlighted as the weakest link.

We run through safety issues and then get onto the mission. When we get to that part, I tell my side of the story. There are a few follow up questions, a few, 'Could you have tried, or why didn't you do this...?' but quite quickly the discussion moves on to the bombing part. Spartan Two and Three located their target and we watch the video from their aircraft, which confirms the direct hit.

The debrief is winding down when one of the ops team calls me out. Someone from command wants to speak to the formation leader on the phone in the other room. The chatter stops and my face flushes as I walk out. Picking up the phone I brace myself as a man's voice, with an accent like cut-glass, pipes up.

'Congratulations, that was a successful mission, you achieved a direct hit. It's been confirmed by Predator, I just wanted to pass that on to your team. Well done.' I thank him for his words and the phone clicks off. I catch myself just holding the receiver and looking at it, which tickles me.

I can feel my shoulders lifting back up, like a bouncy castle slowly being refilled with air. That's when it really hits me about being part of a team. We were successful. It doesn't matter that I wasn't part of the final stage. It is about achieving as a team and using the skillsets of the people around you.

I poke my head back in the debrief room but it is empty.

As I step outside, I gaze at the yellow hint of the creeping dawn and pause to take in the sound of crickets in the desert. It is warm and smells of dust, sweat and aviation gas. I wander past rows of identical billets back to our area.

That time alone is what I needed to reflect on what had been a close call that night. I'm so often asked if I feel fearful when I'm flying, but that is never the emotion you experience. When you are in the air, operating under intense pressure, you focus on getting the job done, completing the mission. The training that you've been through prepares you for that, allowing the flying and your reactions to become second nature. It becomes automatic and that frees up the capacity to focus on more creative aspects, thinking outside the box to come up with better solutions to more complex issues.

The leadership that I witnessed that night was outstanding, and I'm not talking about my own. My boss was my number two and I had been trusted to lead the mission when the mission was a standard, everyday flight. The second that the missile was launched against us, the complexity changed completely. It must have been very tempting as the boss of the squadron to leap in and take control, but that is not the way it works in the RAF. When you have been put in charge, you continue to lead that mission, however difficult or demanding the conditions become. It pushes you. It encourages junior team members to make decisions under pressure and be happy to be held accountable for those decisions. It develops the next generation of leaders from the earliest stages of their careers. It creates empowerment. As leaders you can never tell people that they are empowered, all you can do is to create the environment and give people the skills and tools to enable them to grow. You feel valued for the part that you play and from that you breed loyalty. Loyalty not only to the team, the leadership, but to the organisation as a whole.

When I reached our hut, the guys are all sitting around outside, passing around the pipe. I pull up a chair and the boss pushes it in my direction. I suck in the sweet tobacco. Mmm, apple, nice. Not being a cigarette smoker, I get a mild giddy kick off it. Someone offers me a small sip of ready-mix G&T from a miniature bottle they'd been sent from home.

My mojo is stirring again. I relax back into the chair as we continue chatting about the mission. It was the biggest thing we've been involved in and we are still amped, although I am feeling increasingly spaced out. I stare up at the brightening sky, the vast stage for the night's drama. It feels good to be alive.

I drag myself to bed about five a.m., but the second my head hits the pillow the call to prayer from the local minaret begins its wail. Oh no, please, not now. I really need some sleep. Later today I am heading home and soon after I'll be wandering the aisles of Waitrose in Winchester as if nothing had happened.

CHAPTER 21

BYE, BYE BIG BIRD

Craig and I had been trying for a baby but nothing seemed to be happening, so I cracked on with the flying and focused on something that I could control.

I had also been put in charge of organising the festivities for the squadron's ninetieth birthday coming up in early September. It was a huge occasion and we planned to invite all former members for a weekend of celebrations.

Of our various money-spinners to raise funds, our best by far was a mini air show, pulling in favours from friends all over the RAF to bring in aircraft. We advertised in the aviation press and offered enthusiasts the chance to come and take loads of photos.

The Friday of the event was to be an all-ranks and partners hog roast and barn dance in the main hangar. On the Saturday we organised another airshow with lunch and then, in the evening, a full-on uniform and medals black tie dinner for 450 people.

We'd arranged for an old BE2 single-engine two-seater biplane, the first aircraft flown by the squadron in 1912, to be disassembled from the RAF Museum at Hendon and rebuilt in the hangar, with tables placed around it. There would be marquees with further seating out the back and video screens to pipe through the speeches. Virtually every high-ranking officer alive who had been on II(AC) Squadron would be coming.

The Sunday would feature a jazz luncheon for those still with enough energy to celebrate. It was going to be huge.

I had been back from the Gulf for just under two months when I found out I was pregnant. We were ecstatic. But it also meant I had been flying for about three weeks without knowing I was pregnant.

I didn't want to tell family and friends yet because it was still early days but I had to tell the boss, who instantly grounded me. I was worried how I would explain away my not flying to the squadron. 'Just tell them I've given you time off to organise the party,' he said.

Hoping it would eventually happen, Craig and I had a plan in place and I quickly contacted the posting officer to look into sorting out a ground job. A few days later he came back with a possible position at Strike Command at RAF High Wycombe. It would be at least an hour-and-a-half drive each way every day from Winchester, but it was a sacrifice I was willing to take to start a family.

The final preparations for the celebration were so manic it was quite a good job I wasn't flying but on the eve of the event I was feeling really ill with bad stomach cramps. Something wasn't right.

I went to the hospital on the Friday morning and was told they could not find the baby's heartbeat. I was shattered, numb and hollow. I broke the news to Craig who was equally devastated. I was too distraught to attend the festivities that day but compartmentalised my life enough to go to the dinner on the Saturday.

It felt like an out-of-body experience as I went through the motions while trying to suppress my inner feelings. It was a good job I had planned everything to the last detail. I held it all together for the whole weekend but on Sunday evening, after the last guests left, the floodgates burst and I spent the rest of the night in bed in tears. Among the myriad feelings of loss I couldn't help thinking that three weeks of being hit in the stomach by a g-suit couldn't have been good.

Aside from the devastation, I now had a practical problem. Now that I was no longer pregnant, there was no need for a perfectly serviceable fast-jet pilot to take up a desk job. The trouble was, in my head I was off to a new job. I came clean to the boss and explained that clearly, we would be trying again for a baby so why didn't I just take the job now anyway. He took some persuading but eventually agreed to let me leave.

I was back on the flying rota for three more trips but instead of easing down like the last few days of term, I was working to full capacity to the end.

On my penultimate trip with D-C we suffered a massive fire in our left-hand engine whilst transiting back to base. I went into the emergency drills procedure and shut down the engine, so we were just flying on one engine. We had to jettison the fuel tanks over the Wainfleet range and landed back in very poor weather on a precision-approach radar, which involved ten minutes of complete high-workload instrument flying.

For my swansong on the squadron I was down to fly with Ringo. We sat down in the briefing hoping for an easy day. It turned out the sortie was a four-on-one scenario, with us leading the four-ship against a lone bandit. 'Do we really have to lead today? Can't I just enjoy it?'

'No.'

The scenario was a low-level attack, bombing four targets on the range with the enemy set to intercept us several times during the trip. Because of the amount of evasion, we would be doing, we'd have to refuel in the air on the way back. Great, another mind-bender.

After three hours of brain-spinning, stomach-busting flying we landed back at Marham. I was handed a glass of champagne as the cockpit lid opened.

I sat in the seat and sipped the cool bubbles as I thought of all the great times and wondered what was next. I may even have given the jet a little pat.

Walking back across the tarmac I was jumped on by the others on the flight. I knew what was coming and told them I needed to take off my g-suit and LSJ which were expensive. Then I was ceremonially dumped into the stagnant water butt next to the hangar.

Bye bye, Big Bird. Thanks for coming.

I didn't know it at the time but that was my last trip as a Tornado pilot. 19th September 2002.

I had amassed 720 flying hours in the Tornado and 1320 hours in the RAF up to this point.

I had a lump in my throat for the rest of the day and was not quite my usual buoyant self. We had a couple of drinks in the bar but all the guys left in good time as they were flying the next day. I was suddenly an outsider but I knew deep down it was the right decision.

I didn't fly again until January 2004.

CHAPTER 22

FLYING A DESK

My heart sank further with every step I took up the gravel path towards the door. Crunch...What the hell have you done? Crunch...You could still be screaming around in your Tornado...crunch... a Top Gun too-cool-for-school fast-jet jock... crunch... but instead, you've come to work in this fusty old backwater... crunch... you utter muppet... crunch... what were you thinking? Crunch. Crunch.

What I was thinking was that I wanted to start a family and therefore I just couldn't live the life of a frontline pilot anymore. The miscarriage had proved that didn't work. But currently I wasn't pregnant and this felt like a condemned woman walking towards the noose.

I was in my blues rather than my green growbag for a day's work for the first time in years, back to trying to thread on tights every morning without snagging two pairs before I got it right. The uniform felt like a strait jacket.

Strike Command was the RAF's headquarters, the amalgamation of the former Bomber, Fighter and Transport Commands, and full of high-ranking officers. I'd have to be super smart and on my best behaviour every day.

It was housed in an old redbrick building in the village of Walter's Ash near High Wycombe in Buckinghamshire. I'd held here for a couple of months after Valley.

It was a soul-destroying two-hour drive to get here from Winchester and I'd have to face the same again to get back home. Every day. Help me, someone, please.

I pushed open the main door looked at the signs which directed me up to the third floor. I smiled weakly, sighed and trudged, heavy-hearted up those carpeted stairs, each one lifting me further towards purgatory. I found the office, took a deep breath, knocked and slowly pushed open the door.

Inside the room, three guys looked up from behind computers at desks. 'Hi, I'm Mandy,' I offered. Fortunately, one of them leaped up and broke into a beaming grin as he introduced himself as Sqn Ldr Darren Legg. His gracious welcome instantly relaxed me and after some chit chat, he showed me to my new home. I couldn't even stand up under the sloping eaves above my desk.

The others were squadron leaders, too, all Tornado pilots or navigators, doing a ground tour in preparation for senior command. It was a massive box-ticking exercise for these guys but one they had to go through before they could go back to their squadrons as wing commanders.

The department was responsible for all the administration to do with the Tornado in the RAF, from personnel and budgets, to software, engineering and armaments. It also fell on us to assemble a board of inquiry with all the relevant experts should there be a crash or serious incident involving a Tornado.

My main boss was the ex-chief of 617 Squadron and a brilliant guy. Down the corridor was the Jaguar office and there was plenty of banter between the two. Fortunately, there were no Harrier types around, which was always a bonus!

My role was 'gapped' and therefore normally empty, existing only on the paperwork for someone like myself who was grounded from Tornado flying. In reality, it didn't actually exist. I was their skivvy and initially I was given the filing system to sort out ready to computerise it. Oh my gosh. Shoot me now.

There was very little for me to do and I became a world expert at solitaire on the computer and a dab hand at the Telegraph crossword and I was commuting four hours a day for the privilege. The only saving grace was that I'd found out my great friend Sam Holmes, a supplier that I'd met during officer training was working in another part of the building and we had lunch together in the Officers' mess every day.

Occasionally, I'd accompany Leggo to a meeting at British Aerospace at Warton in Lancashire to discuss new equipment going on the Tornado. A lot of it was technical engineering speak and most of the time I didn't have a clue what was going on. In the end I had to put up my hand and say that I might have flown the Tornado but I've no idea what you're talking about, with all your engineering abbreviations. Can you please speak English so I can join in.

My one significant task in the early months was to write the Urgent Operational Requirement (UOR) document for Storm Shadow, the new £790,000-a-pop air-launched cruise missile which we needed to fast track to the frontline in preparation for the invasion of Iraq in March 2003. The weapon had a 450kg conventional warhead and a range of 560 miles and was fire-and-forget, so once its target had been programmed in and it was launched from the aircraft, that was it. Its package of destruction was coming, ready or not.

The UOR set out to the higher authorities why the RAF needed this new weapon. I hadn't got a clue how to even start writing one, it was like holding up a pen in the wind and going, 'Hmmm.' Leggo told me to find an old UOR and change the words a bit.

With my less-than-onerous workload it was also a good time to take the Junior Officer Command course, a two-week jaunt at Shrivenham in Wiltshire. It took place in a really imposing new building, a huge glass flagship for RAF training.

The course took a more academic view of war, terrorism and the development of asymmetric warfare, an unconventional conflict between forces of vastly differing strength and tactics. There were a lot of discussion sessions and leadership scenarios. My professional head was absorbed by it, particularly as I was beginning to eye the next rung of the career ladder.

I hadn't been at High Wycombe long when I was invited to hand out the Duke of Edinburgh's gold awards at St James' Palace in London. It was a great honour and I suppose recognition of my having earned the award all those years before.

It was a full pomp and ceremony affair and I arrived in my smartest No.1 uniform with Craig, my Mum and Stanley (my step-father) as guests. There was a sea of famous faces all giving out awards such as TV outdoorsman Ray Mears, the then England football manager Sven-Goran Eriksson and the actor John Hurt.

We were milling about after a lavish lunch when Prince Phillip and a very high-ranking Naval officer walked up. They shook my hand and then the Navy chap turned to Craig and said, 'It's Craig Hickson isn't it? You served on one of my ships...' The three of them had a right old chat, while I was standing there like a spare part. 'Ahem, it's my day...'

Pretty soon after joining Strike Command I was over the moon when found out I was pregnant again and in July 2003 I gave birth to a baby boy, Jack. Getting my head around the moods, rhythms, whims and logic of a new-born baby was infinitely harder than mastering battle turns. Craig and I sold both of our houses and managed to move into the house of our dreams in central Winchester. My home life had all come together, I just wondered where my career could go from here.

Much to the hilarity of my colleagues, I hadn't been back at work long when I found out I was pregnant again. At least this time I wouldn't have to wear the disgusting big blue tent dress the RAF issued for pregnancy clothes. They had now introduced baggy blue trousers with an expanding waistband which were far more fetching. Everything's relative.

One evening that summer I was invited to a very fancy cocktail party on the station. Craig came as my partner and we were dressed up in civilian rig. I was introduced to the most senior officer on the base, the Chief of the Air Staff. Turning to Craig, he said, 'And what do you do here?' Craig replied he was accompanying me, as I was the one who worked here. He turned his head and did a double take. 'Oh, of course,' he spluttered. 'So, what's your job?' 'I was a Tornado pilot.' 'Really...?' He looked at Craig again, wide-eyed, then back at me. He was clearly incredulous that I was a female Tornado pilot. I couldn't believe that in 2004 we were still going through this charade.

With a few changes in personnel – Leggo and Lardy had moved on – my role had changed slightly. I was now responsible for not only Tornado GR4 and F3 but also the Battle of Britain Memorial Flight (BBMF).

That meant I now had a few meetings at RAF Coningsby, home of the ceremonial World War II flight of a Lancaster, six Spitfires and two Hurricanes, the iconic aircraft which defended our skies against the Luftwaffe and turned the tide of the war. Looking around these old symbols of freedom was very evocative, imagining what the pilots and aircrew must have gone through. It was a different world to the sterile, remote, relatively high-tech cockpit of my fast-jet career.

On one trip I met a chap called Roger W, a retired squadron leader who was in charge of all the flight reference cards for the BBMF. By way of conversation I asked where he was based and he said Boscombe Down, my old stomping ground. 'That would suit me perfectly. Much nearer home,' I said casually.

'As it happens, we have a Tornado job coming up,' said Roger. My heart pulsed. Updating the flight reference cards wouldn't be the most riveting of jobs but it was half an hour from home and I was about to have two children under two.

I contacted the boss of what was known as Handling Squadron, Wg Cdr Dick J, and said I was keen on the vacant job. He agreed to hold it open for me, but only until April, which meant I would have four months at home with my new baby. I mulled it over for a couple of nights and then accepted. It was the right thing for the family. Now I just needed clearance from above.

I picked up the phone and told my posting officer I had found a job for my next tour when I came back from maternity leave. Could I take it?

His words to me were, 'You can, but if you do, you'll never be promoted. That will be death knell of your career.'

I felt like I'd been kicked in the stomach. 'I'm sorry?' I spluttered.

'Feel free to take it but unless I post you back immediately to the frontline or a flying instructor job you won't ever be promoted and you won't progress in the Royal Air Force. It's your call.'

He wasn't being deliberately unpleasant, just laying out the facts, but that didn't make it any easier to take. I was angry as I put down the phone. It was a really difficult conversation and was as if the axe was coming down on my career. I felt pulled in two completely different directions. My mind was swirling like a snowstorm. Was it more important that I was a mum that I kept a stable life going at home with a steady job, but gave up my career? Or did I go back to a single-minded flying job, with all the upheaval and complications that would bring?

They were talking about posting me to Valley as an instructor, which in another world I would have been really keen on but there was no way I could go back to Valley effectively as a single mum with two little boys under two, even with full-time help. Craig was based out of Heathrow, and he wanted to stay in Winchester to be near his older children. Trying to conduct some sort of long-distance family relationship was never going to work. I knew some people who had managed it – with huge help from their families and live-in nannies – but I'd also seen couples split because of it, Craig included. We had some very frank discussions late into the night, with tears and heartache all around.

If you're on a flying squadron, you're on a flying squadron, you're committed. There are night flights and all sorts of unconventional hours. You can't just say, 'Oh, sorry, I can't do this bit today.'

My 12-year short service commission was up in 2006 so I knew this would be my last tour. The posting officer had also spelled out that I would only be considered for a permanent commission (sixteen years' service) if I was in a flying job. I had always hoped to be promoted at least once, not necessarily to station commander but at least to squadron leader. All my appraisals had said I was highly promotable. The competition was very fierce, but despite three spells in the Gulf and a staff tour under my belt, the RAF was immovable. No flying role, no progression. That's it. Tough.

My world was spinning and I felt deep sadness to the core but I had no choice. With shaking hands, I picked up the phone and told the posting officer in a quavering voice I would take the Boscombe Down job.

'Fine, right, well your start date will be 4th April.'

On 4th December I gave birth to my second son, Jamie. With only seventeen months between the two of them, life was going to be full on to say the least. Fortunately, Jamie was a ray of sunshine, the happiest most contented boy I could ever have been blessed with. I had four months to get to know my second bundle of joy before going back to work.

The clock was ticking.

CHAPTER 23

AN HONEST WOMAN

The guys at Handling Squadron were pure gentlemen and couldn't have been any nicer to me. They were all retired pilots or navigators and loved to regale each other with compelling stories of derring-do and high jinks over lengthy RAF careers. They'd flown everything from Lightnings and Phantoms to Tornados. It was like sitting and listening to your grandpa telling war stories.

We were based in the lower part of the Boscombe Down site, in buildings known as Z blocks, two-storey affairs hastily thrown up on a concrete base in the late 1940s in anticipation of the Cold War threat. I appeared to be the only person under sixty, apart from Rob the IT guy and one of only several women, with the others working as secretaries.

I shared an office on the second floor with Steve Cox, a retired Tornado navigator. Talk about not judging a book by its cover. When I first walked in there was a little gentleman in the corner with white hair, a slightly expanding waistline, wearing a nice sweater. We got on like a house on fire and became best friends for the next five years. We talked about absolutely everything, sharing laughter and tears (from me) in equal measure. He was one of the most intelligent, genuine and funny people I'd ever met. He was even happy for me to bring our lovely black Labrador Barney into work where he'd sit under Steve's desk, warming his feet.

Handling Squadron was a tri-service operation looking after all the flight reference cards, aircrew manuals and documents for all aircraft flying in the British military, from fixed wing and multi-engine aircraft to helicopters and fast jets.

There were about thirty people from all three services, all experts in their field. My role was as the staff officer in charge of Tornado GR4 and F3, Hawk and Tucano. I regularly flew up to Warton and was in close contact with the operational squadrons at Marham and Lossiemouth. What I hadn't foreseen was a little perk which turned the posting from a job of convenience to a lifestyle choice.

From somewhere, for reasons either a closely guarded secret or lost in the mists of time, there was a budget for us to go flying. If any of the specialists didn't take up the allocation on their particular aircraft, the money was fair game to be used by the rest of us. Not only did this include getting qualified to fly PA28s and Cessnas out of Thruxton airfield on the A303 but also the Tutor, which I'd fly to meetings with Steve as my nav. Then there were Falcons down at Bournemouth airport: twin-engine business jets equipped with radar jamming equipment to work with Hawks practising ship attacks. With one eye on my post-RAF career and the inevitable commercial pilot route, I bagged as many Falcon hours as I could to get some multi-engine experience, along with the Piper Aztec. I also flew the Alpha jet, similar to a Hawk, and some Hawks again, down at RNAS Culdrose. I even scored a full course of lessons in the Squirrel helicopter.

In one three-month period I logged forty hours of flying. On II(AC) Squadron the maximum I was allowed to fly was eighteen hours a month, later cut to fourteen. Suddenly, what had promised to be a boring desk job, was proving to be a revelation. I was back wearing my growbag to work and was as happy as a pig in the good stuff. If I ever met any of my peers I was careful to keep this side of the job under wraps and played up to their commiserations for my dull-as-a-dull-thing ground tour.

On Saturday 11th March 2006 life took a dark turn when I received a call to say that Paul, Craig's younger brother had died tragically whilst supporting the United Nations following the earthquake disaster in Pakistan. I had to tell Craig, who was captaining a flight to Marrakesh that night. He called me from the flight deck after all the crew had left the aircraft. It was the worst day of our lives. Paul was only forty-two. We were all devastated, especially Craig and after attempting to hold everything together, I finally asked for some time off work with stress.

Paul had been living in Australia, where we had visited him on many occasions, so Craig had to head over numerous times to sort out his affairs. A particularly low point came when both Jack and Jamie had chickenpox and Craig was away in Australia. Jack was running an incredibly high temperature so was sleeping in my bed. He started to cry, so, in the dark, I filled up the Calpol into the syringe from my bedside table, leaned over and placed it into his open mouth. He coughed, said it was horrible and I repeated the procedure. Minutes later, I heard the gurgling of an alien infestation in my son's stomach, he sat bolt upright and projectile vomited everywhere. Confused, I turned on the light, only to realise I had given my son calamine lotion, which is poisonous if ingested. Not my finest parenting moment. You realise in times like this just how important your family and friends are who support you through dreadful times.

Back at Handling Sqn, Dick was the glue that held it together and he was a great boss. He was very happy to let you run your own ship and as long as the work got done, he didn't get on your back at all. Secret perk aside, the RAF was keen for pilots to stay current, so I also signed up to the Air Experience Flight, which meant a couple of times a week I would fly as an instructor with school children from various Combined Cadet Forces or from the Air Training Corps, my own route into flying.

After a few false starts, or attempts to get Craig down the aisle, I finally persuaded him to make an honest woman of me. In 2008 we tied the knot in an intimate ceremony with close family. Jamie, by now an active three-year-old, amused us all by performing gymnastics down the aisle as we said our vows. We grabbed a two-day honeymoon in Amsterdam, which didn't start well when Craig picked up the wrong suitcase as we headed to the airport. Thank goodness he had changed out of his Naval uniform or it would have looked like the cast from YMCA arriving in the Netherlands!

As life was settling into some sort of routine I applied again for a permanent commission and was again rejected. Dick suggested I just apply for an extension of service rather than an actual permanent commission. He said he would back me up, saying I was vital for the role and how he wouldn't be able to refill it if he lost me because of defence cuts and so on. Bingo. I was granted another two years, taking me up to 2009. I did it again two years later and earned another extension to beyond my thirty-eighth birthday, ironically the age I would have left if I'd be given a permanent sixteen-year commission.

With the end of my RAF career in sight, albeit in the distance for now, I threw myself into studying for my commercial pilot's licence, known as an ATPL (Airline Transport Pilot Licence). I wasn't that desperate to fly passenger jets for a living and unless we flew for the same airline and got a sympathetic roster, I couldn't see how Craig and I could both do that job.

It was just the thing that nearly all military pilots did after leaving the service, so I thought I better had too. It cost about £20,000 so I wasn't doing it lightly, but I knew I wasn't totally sold on the idea either. Even so, for eighteen months, I was up at five a.m., I'd go to work in the day, be a mum for a few hours around bedtime and then study until midnight. I had to take fourteen ground school exams, from instrumentation, navigation and meteorology to air law, communications, operational procedures and principles of flight. To get through all that lot I also did two two-week crammers at Oxford Air Training school to ram it all home.

I passed all of them first time and then took two weeks' leave and enrolled on the Instrument Rating Course flying twin-engine Aztecs down in Bournemouth. It was a forty-five hour course with thirty hours in a simulator flying proper commercial flights from, say, Manchester to Belfast, plus fifteen airborne hours in a Beechcraft Duchess aircraft.

A big difference to the military was that this was now costing me about £7,000 for the pleasure and if I failed a trip, I had to fork out of my own pocket for another. The exam alone cost £1,200. It was a real shock to the system and I couldn't get my head around it. That was the price of a holiday, for heaven's sake.

For my prep ride before the actual exam we were going to fly from Bournemouth to Alderney, one of the Channel Islands off the north west coast of France's Cherbourg peninsula.

It had been a pretty windy week in November and as usual I had been juggling work with the children, so my internal stress was pretty high. As we took off the instructor fitted the blind into the window. He can see out, but you can't. I flew south for an hour or so, navigating purely on instruments before setting up to join the holding pattern above Alderney, again all done by radar and looking at the angle of various needles on your cockpit display.

By now I'd settled into the flight and had put all my external distractions to the back of my mind as I focused on building a mental map of my position. Everything was looking good and I was happy with my approach when suddenly, all my instruments froze. Oh my gosh, is it me, or is the aeroplane?

Bugger. I tapped the dial a little bit. Nothing happened. What was I going to do?

Bloody Norah...help... I was racking my brain for the right solution while trying to keep flying and look calm. But I could feel my face starting to blush and panic rising inside me, not to mention the pound signs flashing in front of my eyes.

There was only one thing for it. I said to the instructor, 'Look, at the risk of failing, I think something has happened to my instruments.' He looked down. 'Jeez, they have.' He tapped the case of the dials. Nothing. Then a bit harder with his knuckles. The glass shattered and shards flew into my lap. There was a split-second delay as our brains processed what had just happened and then we both cracked up with hysterical laughter. I was hooting like a foghorn while trying to keep my hands steady on the controls. It was like a champagne cork popping and all the tension that had filled the cockpit drained away.

'Sorry, that's never happened before,' he said after gathering himself. 'So, what would you do now?'

I was just about to come up with some sort of cobbled answer when the instruments miraculously came back online. Result. 'I'll just crack on then, shall I?'

The exam proper was scheduled for a Friday and I was due back in to work on the Monday so I needed to pass it first time. The first thing I did when I got up early on the Friday was look up the weather forecast. It was horrendous with high winds and torrential rain. It was no day for flying but I thought I would go in anyway, to show willing. I was down to fly the test with the top examiner.

I introduced myself and he said, 'Right, you're going to do an approach to Alderney. I'll leave you to prepare your flight plan.'

Oh my gosh. He could have picked Jersey or Guernsey or Southampton or Exeter or anywhere. But Alderney, I'd just been there, so happy days.

I could see the wind was out of limits, but I went along with the game and called him in and briefed him, talking him through the full plan.

'Right, so what time are we going to walk out to the aircraft?'

'Well, that is the brief Sir, but the weather is out of limits and the forecast says it's only getting worse in which case we won't be able to fly the sortie I'm afraid.'

'Excellent, that's exactly the right call. Well done. So what do you want to do now?' he said.

'I'm not sure, Sir. I've only got two weeks' leave and today is my last day... Are you available next week?'

'I'm not,' he said, leaving a long pause. 'But I tell you what, because you made the effort to come in today, I'll do you a favour. I've got a medical on Monday, but I can postpone that. Come in first thing and we'll squeeze it in.'

On Monday the wind was lighter and from a different direction. He said, 'You did an excellent plan to Alderney, why don't we use that one?'

I passed my exam and gained my full ATPL in 2010. I also did a Crew Resource Management course consisting of plenty of human factors training – techniques designed to ensure safe and efficient teamwork, which is crucial in aviation.

By then I had reconciled myself with the fact I would soon be leaving the RAF and I felt professionally ready to move on. I knew it would be a wrench, but where leaving II(AC) squadron had been the end of the RAF as a lifestyle, leaving Handling Squadron would just be like getting a new nine-to-five job and I needed a new challenge.

In the old days of business, you got given a gold watch for long service when you left, but the RAF is the only career I can think of in which you have to give back your aircrew watch. I was gutted. I loved that watch. It was a Seiko with the main hands and several smaller dials on the face and handing it back into the stores at Boscombe Down felt like the final nail in my RAF coffin.

I also had to hand over all my uniform, my NBC kit, rucksacks, combat gear, even the little Dalton computer – or Dalton confuser as it was known – the plastic device we were issued at ground school for working out speed, time and distance calculations. Most of it was stashed at the back of my loft, if I even still had it. Once I'd given back all the stuff I could find, signed my discharge form and handed in my ID, that was it. I got into my car, switched on the radio, listening to Steve Wright on Radio 2 and drove out of the gates into the civilian world. No fanfare, no ceremony. Done. After sixteen and a half years. I felt lost and adrift, like a sheep separated from it flock.

A few weeks later I was invited back for a dining out night, a lavish black tie or full uniform-and-medals dinner. As tradition dictates, a speech was made in my honour and then I was offered the chance to reply. I had written a poem which was really well received by all the characters that I focused on. Finally, this was a fitting tribute and a great finale to my RAF career.

DREAM IT,
BELIEVE IT,
DO IT

I t's amazing how busy you can be with nothing to do. In between taking the kids to school, walking the dog, going to the gym, meeting friends, doing errands and generally pottering about, I was pondering my next move.

I was still flying with the Air Experience Flight back at Boscombe Down and one day, after my ninth flight with an assortment of students in varying degrees of enthusiasm, I had a sore bum and I was clock-watching.

I had gone through the same upbeat patter, the same jokes and I was bored by the sound of my own voice. Some students were great, keen as anything, sparky and full of questions. Some students were not and it looked like my last cadet of the day would be fitting into the latter category. As the groundcrew escorted her out she reminded me of an uncooperative dog being dragged out for a walk in the rain. She shuffled along in her parachute, with head down and shoulders drooping and my heart sank. Come on dig deep, half an hour more and you can go home, I urged myself.

'Hello, what's your name?' I offered in my bounciest voice, overcompensating for my lack of energy.

'Emily,' she grunted from somewhere under her helmet.

'Ever flown before?'

'No.'

'Looking forward to it.'

'S'pose.'

Great. Miss Monotone. This will be fun. Not. We walked out to the aircraft, a Tutor with side-by-side seats and a big canopy, perfect for training. I helped her climb in before taking my seat beside her in the cockpit. Looking across I could see her eyes were caked with make-up. I wondered whether the g-force would shut her eyes, what with the weight of mascara plastered all over the lids.

Taxiing out I tried again. 'Excited?' Grunt. Silence.

I took off and we pushed up through the white, puffy clouds into a bright, sunny day aloft. 'OK, the big thing for us is to keep our eyes out of the cockpit the whole time. If you see an airplane, you need to shout up in good military fashion. Imagine we're the centre of the clock face and say something like 'right, two o'clock, high'. Tell you what, if you're not feeling very talkative you can just point. We'll have a competition to see who can spot the most. Ok. Happy?'

'Ygghh.'

I showed her the basic controls, left, right, up and down. Then it was her turn. 'You have control.' I just about detected an, 'I have control, ma-am.'

Lots of students in the early stages are very agricultural, yanking the controls all over the place but Emily was smooth and relaxed. So relaxed, in fact, I thought she had slipped into a coma. This makes a pleasant change, I mused.

I took control again and demonstrated a medium-level turn with thirty degrees angle of bank. I explained that she needed to keep an eye on the first big marking on the attitude indicator – that was thirty degrees. Then I explained how she should do a scan pattern, looking out to check the air was clear, bringing her gaze back in to check the attitude, another good look left and then roll into a turn. When we hit thirty degrees on the instrument, I said, 'lock your right hand with the control column in it against your leg. Have a look out of the front for a snapshot of what thirty degrees looks like. That's your attitude,' and it's nothing to do with your general demeanour. I left this last bit out.

Emily took over and nailed it. Most students will go up or down by at least 200 feet as they go around. She had the aircraft on rails.

'Excellent, Emily. I don't think I've ever seen a student do that so well.' She raised her eyebrows a little bit. 'Tell you what, let's see if you can do a sixty-degree turn. This is called a high angle of bank turn.'

I didn't tend to do this with students on their first trip because most end up all over the place. The high angle means the wings are losing a lot of lift, so you have to add full power on the throttle and pull back on the stick to hold it level through the turn. I began to explain but Emily cut me short. 'I know, I've read about this. You don't have to tell me.'

Righto, smart arse. Let's see it, then.

This could be fascinating, I thought. If you don't do all of those things the nose comes through horizon and you end up in a spiral descent... possibly to death. Crack on, Emily!

I handed her control. She looked out, glanced inboard, back out, rolled over, pushed the throttle forward with her left hand, pulled the stick hard back with her right and flew the exact parameters all the way round. Flipping heck, she's better at this than me.

We started to fly around the clouds, pulling g-force, having fun and when I looked across, I saw her mouth twitching.

I asked her if she fancied trying some aerobatics. I normally gauged this by asking if they liked roller coasters. If not, chucking the aircraft around the sky probably wouldn't be their bag. 'Yeah.' I explained how a loop would work, and how we would need to brace ourselves against g-force by tensing our legs and tummies. 'Imagine doing a poo. That's sort of what it feels like,' I said. I explained how we would check all around us and then lower the nose, accelerating to 140 knots. Another check to see if we're clear above and then pull back hard, keeping the wings level as we come up through the horizon and climb over the top, remembering to yell out 'yeehah' just for fun when we go upside down. I told her that when we pulled out of the bottom of the loop, we might feel the airplane shaking, but that was OK because it just meant we were flying though our own slipstream which showed we had completed a perfect loop.

I demonstrated by pulling a smooth loop with no shaking at the bottom and then handed over the controls. Emily pulled gently back on the stick and up we went. At the top I shouted out 'yeehah' as we went inverted but Emily was silent. I felt a bit embarrassed. Emily did not. She brought us back around to complete the circle and sure enough, at the bottom the whole airframe shook for a few brief seconds. Emily looked across at me with a big, beaming grin, as if to say, 'Mine was better than yours.' She was probably right, but the grin betrayed the fact I was cracking her.

At the end of her session we landed and taxied to a stop. She was still a bit morose. 'Well, Emily, did you enjoy that?'

'Yeah.' She began to climb out. I hate it when they don't say thanks. I stopped her and said, 'Emily, I don't often say this, but in twenty-two years of flying I've never met anyone with such natural ability.'

'I bet you say that to everyone,' she mumbled.

'Er, no, actually. I've never said it before. And what's more, you're potentially the best pilot I've ever flown with.'

For the first time her head and eyes came up to meet mine. 'You're joking?'

'I'm not.'

It was like a dam had burst. All of a sudden, in a soft girl's voice the full story came flooding out.

'Oh my goodness, it's just that this is all I've ever wanted to do. This is the best thing that's ever happened to me. I've only ever wanted to be a pilot. I was so scared about coming here and failing. I thought, 'What happens if I try really hard and I fail? What will I do then?'

'On the bus coming here everyone was laughing and joking and I was getting quieter and quieter. I decided I wouldn't try. Then if I failed it wasn't that I was no good, it's because I didn't try. I could always blame it on that.'

I told her she couldn't go through life like that. 'How many opportunities are you going to miss if you're not open to grabbing them with both hands?'

I asked how she was getting on at school. 'Terrible, ma'am. I can't see the point.'

'Well, if you do want to become a pilot, either commercially or in the military, you're going to have to see the point. The only way you're going to become a pilot is by working hard to achieve that goal. These things don't come easily and I'm the first one to know that. Please, start engaging with it. Good luck, Emily.'

Over a year later I was walking down the corridor ready to take out another group of cadets when I saw a girl in full make-up. It was Emily.

'Hello, ma'am, I bet you don't remember me.'

'Hi Emily, of course I do. How are you getting on?'

Her face lit up.

'I've got all my GCSEs and I'm doing A levels now. Would it be possible to fly with you again, ma'am?' Absolutely. She was just as good second time around, if not better.

This was it. My lightbulb moment. I suddenly realised this is what life is all about. I started off being told I couldn't achieve the things I wanted to, but I went on to prosper. I believed in myself because other people believed in me. My parents, the boss at UBAS, the list is endless. Often, we just need that catalyst. We can do so much for other people by simply passing on that gift of belief by encouraging them to be the very best version of themselves that they can be.

I'd reached a turning point. I realised I didn't want to follow the gravy train and become a commercial pilot. The fortune teller in Byron Bay was right. I wanted to encourage the next generation – and anyone else for that matter – to achieve their goals and pursue ideals they felt passionate about, irrespective of gender or diversity.

I now speak about my experiences and hope some of it inspires other people to achieve more. It's why I've adopted this as my mantra, we can have dreams, we can believe them, but until we put them into action, we are going nowhere. You've got to "Dream it, believe it, do it!"

GLOSSARY
OF TERMS

AAA
Anti-Aircraft Artillery

AAR
Air-to-air refuelling is the process of transferring aviation fuel from one military aircraft (the tanker) to another (the receiver) during flight.

AFTS
Advanced Flying Training School at RAF Valley

ACM
Air combat manoeuvres

ALARM
Air Launched Anti-Radiation Missile

ATC
Air traffic controller/ Air Training Corps

BANDIT
An aircraft identified as enemy

BOGEY
A radar or visual air contact whose identity is unknown

BFTS
Basic Flying Training School at RAF Linton on Ouse

BIM
Basic Induction Module (first 4 weeks of officer training)

BINGO
Pre-determined fuel state for monitoring fuel consumption

BULLDOG
British two-seat side-by-side training aerobatic aircraft

CHAFF
Radar countermeasure in which aircraft spreads a cloud of small, thin pieces of aluminium, metallized glass fibre or plastic, which either appears as a cluster of primary targets on radar screens or swamps the screen with multiple returns

CHICKEN
minimum fuel state for a recovery to base

C IN C
Commander in Chief

DOGFIGHT
Aerial battle between fighter aircraft conducted at close range

FAC
Forward air controller

FLARES
Infrared countermeasure used to counter an infrared heat-seeking surface-to-air missile. Flares are composed of a pyrotechnic composition based on magnesium or another hot-burning metal, with burning temperature equal to or hotter than engine exhaust. The aim is to make the infrared-guided missile seek out the heat signature from the flare rather than the aircraft's engines.

FLIR
Forward looking Infra-red

FIREFLY
Two-seat aerobatic training aircraft, built by Slingsby Aviation

FLT LT
Flight Lieutenant

FOD
Foreign object damage

FLT
Field Leadership Training (stage 2 of officer training)

'G'
Unit of acceleration. One 'g' equals the force of gravity

G-SUIT
Flight suit worn pilots who are subject to high levels of g force (g). It is designed to prevent a black-out caused by the blood pooling in the lower part of the body when under acceleration.

GPS
Global Positioning System

HARRIER
Anglo-American vertical/short take-off and landing ground attack aircraft

HAS
Hardened aircraft shelter

HAWK
British single-engine, jet-powered advanced trainer aircraft

HERCULES
Four-engine turboprop military transport aircraft

HUD
Head up display

JAGUAR
Twin-engine, single seat Anglo-French ground attack aircraft

JEFTS
Joint Elementary Flying Training School

JUNTA
military slang for junior aircrew

LOFT BOMBING
A method of bombing in which the aircraft approaches the target at a very low altitude, makes a definite pullup at a given point, releases the bomb at a predetermined point during the pullup, and tosses the bomb onto the target.

LSJ
Life support jacket

NBC
Nuclear Biological Chemical Warfare

NIMROD
Multi-engine maritime patrol and attack aircraft

NTOCU
National Tornado Operational Conversion Unit

NVGS
Night vision goggles

OLF
Operational low flying

OPS
Operations

PAR
Precision approach radar

PAVEWAY IV
Dual mode GPS and laser-guided 500lb bomb

PICKLE
Weapon release

PT
Physical Training

QFI
Qualified Flying Instructor

QWI
Qualified Weapons Instructor

RADALT
Radar altimeter

RAFC
Royal Air Force College
Cranwell

RHWR
Radar homing warning
receiver

SAM
Surface to air missile

SA-6 GAINFUL
Russian tracked medium-
range surface-to-air missile
system

SAS
Special Air Service

SEAD
Suppression of enemy air
defences

SIDEWINDER
Aim 9L heatseeking short
range air-to-air missile

SQUINTO
Squadron Intelligence Officer

SQN LDR
Squadron Leader

TFR
Terrain Following Radar

TIALD
Thermal Imaging Airborne
Laser Designator

TORNADO GR4
Twin-engine, variable-sweep
wing aircraft designed to excel
at low-level penetration of
enemy defences

TORNADO F3
Air defence/fighter variant of
Tornado

TRANSPONDER
Electronic device that produces
a response when it receives a
radio-frequency interrogation.

TUCANO
Two-seat turboprop basic
trainer aircraft

UBAS
University of Birmingham Air
Squadron

UAV
Unmanned aerial vehicle

UHF
Ultra High Frequency radio

VHF
Very High Frequency radio

VC10
Four engined British AAR
tanker and transport aircraft